HOW TO
RESTORE & REPAIR
PRACTICALLY EVERYTHING

HOW TO
RESTORE & REPAIR
PRACTICALLY EVERYTHING

BY LORRAINE JOHNSON

MICHAEL JOSEPH •LONDON

Dedicated to my brothers, Bob and Chris

Special thanks to all the consultant restorers and to Hampstead Decorative Arts, London NW3, who loaned the painted objects featured opposite page 31.

This revised edition
first published in Great Britain
by Michael Joseph Ltd
44 Bedford Square
London WC1B 3EF
1984

Originally published by
Michael Joseph Ltd in 1977;
second impression 1978

Johnson Editions
30 Ingham Road
London NW6 1DE, England

ISBN 07181 24898

Printed in Singapore for Imago Productions (FE) Pte Ltd

Introduction

This book is designed and written for amateurs in the field of restoration, and although it assumes some manual dexterity, it is not intended for the expert. It is also a handbook on caring for antiques and a guide to the kind of repairs that are both feasible without specialist equipment and wise without specialist knowledge.

Although the book is entitled HOW TO RESTORE AND REPAIR PRACTICALLY EVERYTHING, and deals with both of these topics, as well as conservation, it is essential to clarify the difference between the terms. Restoration means attempting to make an article as good as new, and may include the manufacture or purchase of new parts or fittings, the retouching of paintwork, etc. Repairs, on the other hand, generally involve mending what is already there, such as glueing joints, but without retouching the surrounding wood or refinishing the joint afterwards.

Conservation is very different – it means salvaging what is left and preserving it for the future, without attempting to make the article look as it did originally. This term is often applied to textiles, when, as often as not, a total reweaving is simply impractical. Instead a strengthening operation is usually advised.

The above distinction gives rise to another serious question facing the amateur restorer – should an item always be restored? To attempt an answer, the restorer should bear in mind that restorative processes should never be carried out to cover a fault or flaw, or to affect a date which gives the lie to the truth. However, dirt and deterioration are another matter, and there are very few things which cannot be improved by careful cleaning. As a rule of thumb, the potential restorer can do anything to arrest the ravages of time, employing any means, provided that the treatment is sensitive to what has happened to the piece in its lifetime – more antiques are devalued by inept restoration than by any other misfortune, so when working with anything of value, remember that they have already survived for many years and that they are only in your care for a relatively short time, so give them the best possible home by caring for them properly and sensitively.

Each of the following fourteen chapters begins with a brief historical précis of the material involved, then discusses cleaning, and proceeds through restoration to repairing and/or conservation techniques. However, before doing anything to any item, look carefully to make sure it is not signed or marked in any way. If so, it may be too valuable for amateur attentions and may require expert care. (As you gain experience, you will be able to tackle better and better pieces, but at first, stick to less valuable items.) In addition, before commencing, it is also a good idea to date the piece, by consulting books on decorative styles and/or by visiting the nearest museum with a collection of similar pieces.

You may discover after a little investigation that the piece is valuable, although it is unsigned. In this case, consult a museum expert or qualified restorer before attempting even so much as a gentle cleaning.

Once you are satisfied that the article cannot be devalued by your attentions, organize your workspace, bearing in mind that although many of the steps described on the following pages involve small amounts of time, the process is sometimes spread over several days, and it is essential that your work is left undisturbed. Also remember that some of the chemicals involved are potentially harmful, and the appropriate care should be exercised, especially if there are children or pets around. Finally, take your time – restoration can involve the devotions of a lifetime, and regardless of the monetary value of an object, it deserves your very best efforts.

I would like to thank the following people who contributed invaluably to this book. Firstly, all the consultant restorers who gave so freely of their time and expertise; secondly, the editorial team who perfected the text: Penny Clarke, Georgina Harding and Gabrielle Townsend; the photographer, Stanli Opperman who took the inspiring and informative colour photographs, Ray Gautier who did the layout, Clare Finlaison who did the paste-up, Richard Hayes who handled production and the four illustrators who somehow managed to do the necessary 800 drawings: Aziz Khan, Janos Marffy, Pavel Kostal and Graham Rosewarne.

CONTENTS

Tools and supplies

A handyman's guide from 1902 offers the opinion that without tools, the hand would be powerless. It was some 500,000 years ago that the first implements were used, probably scraps of stone or bone picked up off the ground in a moment of frustration. These days our tools are highly specialized and costly, but a well-made tool will always make a job easier and more enjoyable.

On the following pages, tools are divided into groups according to their use—you will find tools for hammering, gripping, sawing, etc., with similar tools illustrated in close proximity.

Tools should be kept clean and sharp, in a suitable container such as a tool box, or hung on the wall near the workspace. Probably the most important items, after the few essential tools listed below, are clean cotton rags and containers with lids—it seems that you never have enough of either. Get in the habit of saving all clean scraps from pure cotton clothing, sheets, etc., and keep them handy. Also hoard glass jars, tins and other containers with lids, but do bear in mind that some chemicals, such as spirit-based ones, tend to dissolve plastic, while some react with acids. Finally, keep all tools and supplies properly labelled.

Ammonia
Beeswax
Benzine
Cardboard, white
Chalk, powdered or stick
Chamois
Cotton wool or absorbent cotton
Denatured alcohol (methylated spirits)
Double boiler
Empty glass jars, tin cans and atomizer spray bottles
Glue, general purpose or PVA
Japan paints
Jewellers' rouge or pumice powder
Kerosene (paraffin)
Linseed oil
Masking tape, acid-free
Matches, wooden
Pencils, hard and well sharpened
Powdered pigments, especially raw umber
Purified water
Rags, soft cotton
Shellac
String
Thermometer, cooking
Turpentine
Turpentine substitute
Tweezers
Varnish
Vinegar
Wire mesh strainer, small

BASIC TOOL KIT

Abrasive paper, sanding block, and assorted abrasive papers
Combination pliers (6in/15cm) square-nosed type, with side cutters
Knife with replaceable blades, which also takes saw blades
Metal ruler (12 – 18in/30 – 46cm) for use when cutting along straight edge
Screwdriver (6in/15cm) and bradawl for starting holes
T (or try)-square (6in/15cm) to ensure right angles

The following tools are nice to have, but are not essential for beginners:
Bench vice
File, combination, for use on wood or metal
Hand drill, bit brace and countersink bit
Panel saw or tenon saw
Power drill and attachments (sanding and buffing wheels, masonry bits, etc.)
Combination oilstone for sharpening the blade
Wood chisels (¾in/2cm) bevel-edged firmer (¾in/2cm) and mallet (4½in/11cm)

ABRASIVE PAPERS

Store abrasive papers in a warm, dry place and never attempt to use them on damp wood. Always use at least two grades when trying to get a really smooth finish; coarse paper, worn smooth, will not give the same effect as a finer paper. While working "snap" abrasive paper to unclog it. Incidentally, there is no such thing as "sandpaper" and although these papers feel gritty, sand has been replaced by more effective smoothing agents.

The five types of abrasive paper used for smoothing woods are as follows: Glass paper, with grains made from crushed glass (once reputedly derived from crushed port bottles). It is available with a base of cloth or paper and is commonly used for hand smoothing. Garnet paper, with grains made of crushed garnet stone, so it costs a bit more but it is very durable and recommended for smoothing by hand. Aluminium oxide paper, used when really heavy cutting action is desired—its synthetic grains are very tough. Silicone carbide paper, also known as "wet-and-dry" paper because it can be used damp (not wet) for fine smoothing of paintwork or dry like other abrasive papers. When damp it leaves a black-grey "gravy" which has to be washed off, but when lubricated with water, it lasts a long time. It can be used on both metal and wood and is also available on a cloth base. Flint paper, rarely used any more, although it is inexpensive, it is not recommended because its grains are softer than glass or garnet, and it has a short life.

Both garnet and aluminium oxide papers come in "open coat" and "close coat"—with "open coat" there is more space between the grains, making it less likely to clog and therefore better for smoothing softwoods; while in "close coat" the grains are more closely spaced and are best for hardwoods.

Steel wool can be used for smoothing wood and the finer grades are recommended after smoothing with fine abrasive paper to give a final perfect finish. As with abrasive papers, always work with the grain. Wear a handkerchief tied "bandit-style" to protect your throat and lungs when sanding.

GLUES AND GLUEING

Glueing must be the simplest repair to do! Strangely it is often neglected which is unfortunate, because a little glue applied after slight damage can prevent more extensive problems. The section below deals with glue suitable for porous materials like wood, paper, textiles, some plastics and rubber. A wooden matchstick is often perfect for applying non-water-soluble glues. Always save even the smallest splinters and chips and glue these in place after the main piece has set. For glueing glass and pottery, see the detailed chapters concerned.

There are six basic types of glue in common use today.

Traditional glues such as animal and fish glues, casein glue and scotch glues are gradually being superseded as they are neither heat- nor waterproof. Although they are not generally recommended some craftsmen prefer them—such as gilders, who use rabbit glue.

General purpose glues, cellulose- or acetate-based, and usually sold in tubes are water-resistant, free from staining and excellent for fixing plastics, metals, and most inlays to wood. Do not work with these near an open fire—they are inflammable—and avoid inhaling the fumes.

Epoxy resins are modern, synthetic-based glues. They are strong and versatile, perfect for home use, and usually come in two part kits—a glue and a hardener. Most take about six hours to set but a warm room will speed the setting. Follow directions on the package as the mixtures vary slightly. Caution: synthetic resin glues become rubbery if kept unused. They should not be used for glueing wood as they are harder than the wood itself and allow no natural movement and thus may cause splitting.

Polyvinyl acetate (PVA) glue is a thick, white, cold-setting, inexpensive resin-based glue and can be used extensively, although it is not waterproof. It will keep for several months (though not in a cold place) but may stain the lighter woods and tends to creep a bit. PVA is a good general purpose glue and is often sold in a squeeze bottle with a handy pointed nozzle. It is water-soluble.

Contact adhesives, which are usually rubber-based, are only recommended when clamping is difficult but a strong bond is desired. The glue is applied to both surfaces and, when tacky, they are brought together. The two pieces are immovable upon contact, so adjusting is impossible. They are very useful when bonding other materials to wood.

Latex glues are derived from the milky fluid of the rubber tree, although synthetic latex is now manufactured. They can be applied either to one surface or both and are thinned with water. Their odour is slightly objectionable. Latex glues are perfect when working with textiles, although some fabric dyes seem soluble, so test an inconspicuous spot before application.

Caring for tools

Tools should be stored in a dryish atmosphere and away from children. After using tools with a metal part, it is a good idea to spread a film of light machine oil over the metal surface to prevent rusting. For this purpose, keep an oiled pad in a sealed container near the work area. Tools with wooden handles should be kept smoothed and well sanded to avoid splinters.

BRUSHES

Many different kinds of brushes are used in restoration and it is worth choosing them with care. A paintbrush has three parts: handle (1), ferrule (2) and filling (3). The filling, or bristles, can be made from boar (used in the best quality brushes); horsehair (used to bulk out better filling); oxhair, squirrel and sable (used for thin artists' paintbrushes); fibre (from the stem of the palm tree); or, increasingly, synthetic fibres (from filaments such as nylon). If possible, always invest in a good quality brush — it will hold more paint and apply it better than a cheaper brush and is less likely to shed its bristles. Test brushes before purchasing by making sure the bristles fan evenly and that they are firmly set into the ferrule. Keep them in good condition by cleaning and storing as directed in Steps 1 – 6.

Three useful paintbrushes for the restorer are: a flat paintbrush (A), a stencilling brush (B), and a lining brush (C). Another useful brush for many jobs is a wire brush (D).

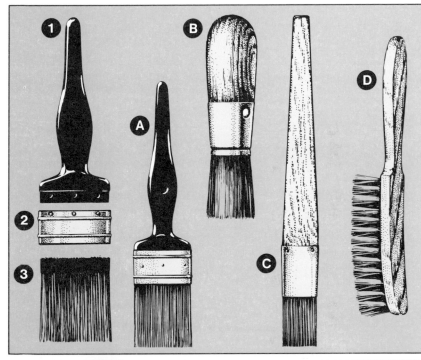

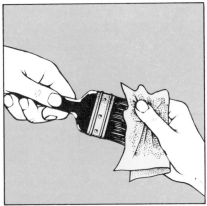

CLEANING BRUSHES

1. It is imperative to clean brushes when you have finished using them, or to soak them if leaving the project for a few hours. (Should you forget to soak the brush, the paint will harden on the bristles; only a very strong paint remover will restore the brush to usefulness and it will never be the same again.) Always remove excess paint from the bristles first by wiping them over old newspaper.

2. In order to soak the brush, prepare it by drilling a hole in the upper handle, as shown, then inserting a dowel which will suspend the brush in water up to the first ½in/13mm of the ferrule. (Use a container deep enough to keep the brush from resting on the bristles.) Some experts recommend storing brushes in white spirit, but this seems to dry out the bristles unnecessarily.

3. When you need to use the brush again, remove excess water from the bristles by squeezing them in soft absorbent cloth or paper towels.

Cleaning brushes cont.

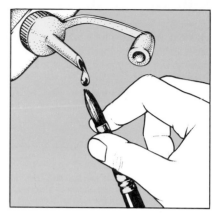

4. To remove oil-based paint from a brush, fill a glass or metal container two-thirds full of turpentine substitute. Agitate the brush in the liquid, pressing it against the side of the container to force out the paint. When the liquid can absorb no more paint, repeat until most of the paint is removed. To remove water-based paints, use the same technique in a jar of warm water.

5. Inspect the bristles near the ferrule to see if the paint is removed, then wash the bristles in warm, soapy water. Rinse and repeat Step 4 if necessary before washing and rinsing again.

Shake or blot out the moisture and leave to dry naturally, away from any heat source which will only dry out the natural oils in the bristles. Store the brush by wrapping it in brown paper, secured with a rubber band as shown, laying it flat if possible. Keep brushes used for water and oil-based paints separate, and reserve a 2-3in/5-8cm brush specifically for varnish and shellac.

6. To keep small artists' paintbrushes in good condition, clean as above in Steps 4 and 5. Then point the brush by placing a drop of light machine oil or linseed oil on the bristles and slowly rotating the bristles between the thumb and index finger.

Carving tools

Chisels and gouges have narrow cutting edges and are each designed with a particular task in mind, so purchase the various types as they are required. The metal part is usually fitted to a bulbous handle made from boxwood or impact-resistant plastic.

Chisels are designed for cutting with or across the grain, while gouges are used for less drastic action on wood.

The main types of carving tools are: firmer chisel (A), available with blades in a variety of widths, often driven with a wooden or soft-face mallet although a hammer may be used with plastic-handled chisels; bevelled-edge firmer chisel (B) with a slightly less rigid blade, used for lighter woodworking tasks such as undercutting dovetail housing joints, not designed for use with a mallet but tolerates light tapping; paring chisel (C) with longer blade, used to trim long grooves; firmer gouges (D) with curved blades of two types—one with the cutting bevel on the outside, used to make concave shapes, the other ground on the inside, used to make straight cuts that are curved in cross-section—both used with a mallet; paring gouge (E) for hand paring (without a mallet), ideal for cutting curved shapes of all kinds; and cold chisel (F) used to cut metal (for example for chain links, sheet metal and bolt or rivet heads), struck with a heavy hammer.

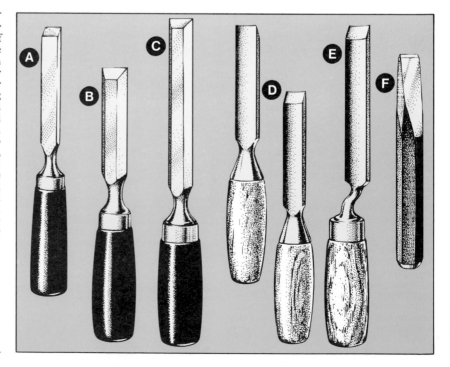

Cutting tools

Probably the most useful and versatile cutting tools are the knives with replaceable blades. There are four types of these, all with disposable blades which come ready-sharpened. The blades are terrifically sharp and should be stored and used with great care. The four types are: general purpose knife with replaceable blades (A), sometimes with blades that may be retracted and stored inside the handle; knife with snap-off blade (B), also retractable; and surgeon's knife or scalpel (C), with blades removed manually.

Various useful kinds of scissors are: aviation snips or compound action snips (D) which will make straight or curved cuts in metal—they have specially firm jaws and comfortable plastic hand grips; pinking scissors (E) with a zig-zag cutting edge which makes the cut edge of fabric less likely to fray; embroidery scissors (F) with elongated blades ending in a fine point, useful for work on carpets and textiles; and cuticle scissors (G) with a curved blade, used in découpage.

A glass cutter (H) has a hardened steel wheel mounted in a holder, and is used to score a line across a sheet of glass. Small pieces can be "nibbled" off back to the scored line using the notches on the side. (It helps to remove any grease from the glass with turpentine substitute and oil the cutting wheel before starting.)

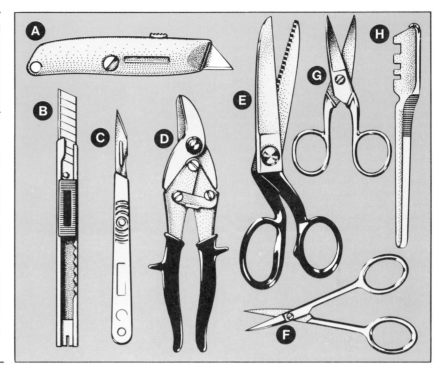

Drilling tools

When using any drill, try to keep the pressure constant. If the drill wobbles, the drillbit may snap. When drilling metal select the appropriate bit and oil it lightly before starting; it may also help to make a small hole in the metal with a punch or awl. When using a power drill, take care to disconnect it from the power source before making any adjustments, and be sure to examine the cable regularly for signs of damage or wear. Also, avoid wearing loose clothing or accessories that could get caught in the moving parts.

A hand-drill (A) has a chuck shell at one end which turns anticlockwise to open the jaws that hold the bit. When the drillbit is centred, rotate it to establish it in position, then use the drill at the desired speed. Various hand-drill bits are available for special tasks: twist bit (B) for metal and wood; dowel bit (C) for the side and end grain of wood; countersink bit (D) to recess a hole to accept a countersunk screw head; glass bit (E) for use at slow speed to drill holes in glass, mirror and porcelain; masonry bit (F) for drilling holes in brick, stone and ceramic tiles. A push drill (G) can be used to make small holes in wood or plastic, using special drill points. A power drill (H) is probably the most versatile tool available; accessories include circular saws, sanding discs, grinders, rasps, even paint sprayers. Small hand tools such as augers and gimlets (I) can also be used to drill holes in wood; augers drill fairly large holes, gimlets shallow ones, often to take a screw. Bore the hole by twisting the tools in one direction only. Bradawls or awls (J) are used to start holes in timber for nails and screws and to make holes in leather. The bradawl is twisted right and left; the awl is inserted with pressure.

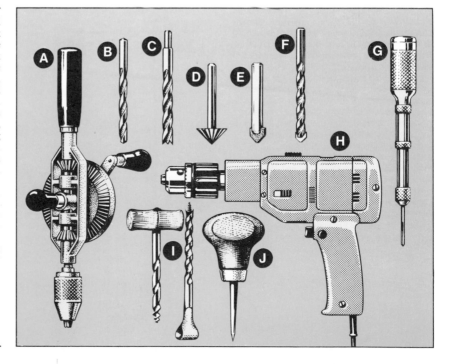

Gripping tools

Professionals will opt for a bench vice or a clamp-on vice (A), but these require a sturdy and steadfast table or workbench. Amateur restorers can make do with a variety of gripping tools, purchased as required. These include: "G" or "C" cramp (B) for clamping wood or metal work, used with a block of wood between the cramp and wood to prevent marking; spring cramp (C), a manual device to provide light pressure to an object while glueing; mitre cramp (D) to hold mitred joins together while glue sets; needle-nosed pliers (E) to grip small objects in confined places, available in a variety of shapes and proportions, all with serrated jaws; slip-joint pliers (F), with a pivot joint which provides two widths of jaw opening; carpenters' pincers (G), with curved jaws which meet at a bevelled cutting edge, designed to extract nails and tacks from wood; and upholsterers' pliers (H), used to stretch webbing across the chair frame by gripping the folded end of the webbing while the lower jaw touches the frame.

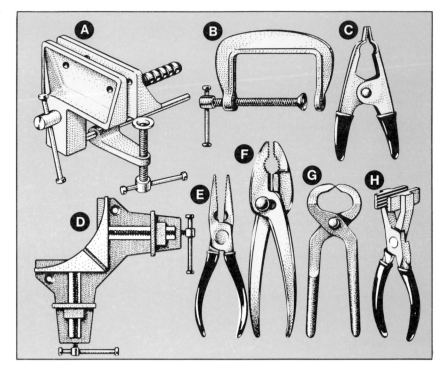

Hammers

The most useful hammer is the claw hammer (A), which may be used for removing bent nails as well as for driving nails home. (When pulling nails out, always protect the surface with a small block of wood placed under the front end of the hammer.) Others are: lightweight pin hammer or ball pin hammer (B), used for driving pins or tacks; upholsterers' hammer (C), with a small rounded face for driving tacks in a confined space, and magnetized so that it holds the tack in place as it drives it home; soft faced hammer (D), used for driving or shaping materials such as soft metals which would otherwise be damaged — these usually have a socketed head into which soft bases are screwed; similar are soft faced mallets (E) with rubber or rawhide heads; and lastly, heavy carvers' mallet (F), designed to drive various chisels and gouges.

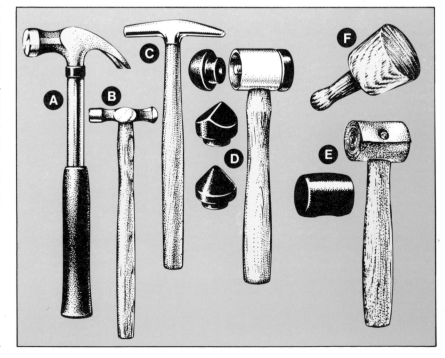

Fitting a new handle to a hammer head

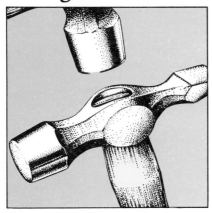

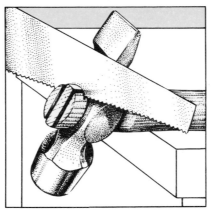

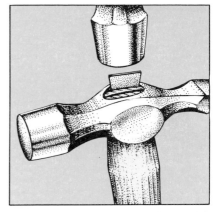

1. Choose a new handle with an even, straight grain to the wood. Begin by cutting two evenly spaced slots across the head of the new shaft, two-thirds the depth of the hole. Drive the hammer head onto the shaft using the side of another hammer.

2. Cut the shaft flush with the top of the hammer head.

3. If steel wedges were used, drive them in with another hammer until they are level with the top of the shaft. If there are no steel wedges, make some from bits of hardwood. Finally grind or file the wedges flush and varnish the exposed wood.

Measuring tools

When making measurements, avoid using the common wooden yardstick, which is too inaccurate. Instead use an engineer's steel rule (A), ideally one scribed with both metric and imperial measurements; a folding or zig-zag rule (B); a push-pull steel tape (C); and (for fabric only) a tape measure or a new digital rule (D) which is run over a surface and indicates the length in its display. To achieve accurate right angles, use a T or try square (E) or steel square. (The metal rule is highly recommended as it will not only measure, but also serve as a straight edge to guide a knife along when cutting veneers, plastic, leather etc.)

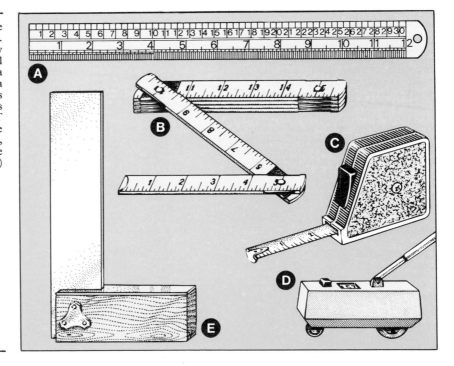

Sawing tools

There are three main kinds of saw: large handsaws, stiff-backed saws for cutting joints, and special purpose saws. With all types, the greater the number of teeth or points per inch, the finer the cut. If a saw blade is rusty, clean it by rubbing it with steel wool dipped in turpentine substitute. If sticking occurs, rub the blade with a wax candle, but if the problem persists, the blade may need sharpening, resetting or replacing.

Large handsaws (A) include: panel-cut saw for cutting with and across the grain, cross-cut saw for cutting across the grain and rip saw for cutting with the grain. All handsaws should cut freely under their own weight and your forward pressure. Stiff-back saws include the back saw, or tenon saw, (B) for cutting joints. Various specialist saws are: coping saw (C) for cutting curves in plastic or wood; fretsaw (D) for tighter curves in wood or plastic; hacksaws (E and F) for cutting metal; and pad saw (G) for cutting holes in a panel. Knives with replaceable blades can also be fitted with saw blades although these are only designed for sawing lightweight materials.

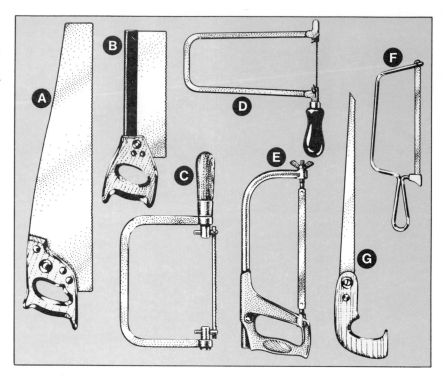

Scraping and filling tools

Scrapers are indispensable to the restorer and are not interchangeable, although they, and some filling knives, look somewhat alike. Various scrapers are: paint scraper (A), with a stiff blade for removing softened paint; filling knife (B), with a wider, flexible blade; putty knife (C), used to shape and smooth putty — available with three shapes of blade depending on the preference of the user; palette knife (D), used to scrape pigments and mix media; skarsten (E), for smoothing timber or removing paint; and combination shave hook (F) — the most useful of the shave hooks with its curved and straight blades, ideal for scraping awkwardly shaped surfaces.

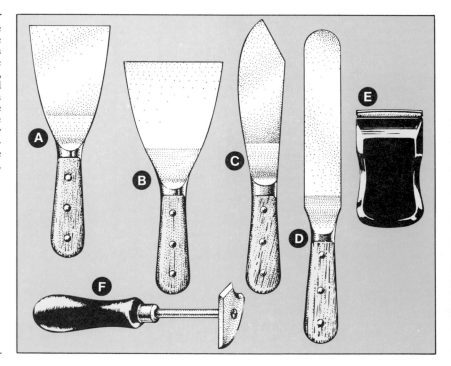

Screwdrivers

Screwdrivers come with wooden, plastic or rubber handles and with a variety of tips, each designed to fit a particular type of screw — the commonest being the standard flared tip and the cross-shaped Phillips tip. It is most important that the screwdriver blade exactly fits the notch in the screw head; it should be neither too long, or it will damage the surrounding work, nor too short, or it will not grip the screw correctly. On the whole, screwdrivers with fluted handles are easier to grip than those with smooth wooden ones, and ones with a ratchet mechanism are easiest to use. Various screwdrivers are: cabinet screwdriver (A), the woodworker's traditional tool; spiral ratchet screwdriver (B), which drives screws more easily by exerting pressure; ratchet screwdriver (C), which drives screws without altering the grip; offset screwdriver (D), for driving screws into inaccessible areas; and jewellers' screwdriver (E), for very small screws.

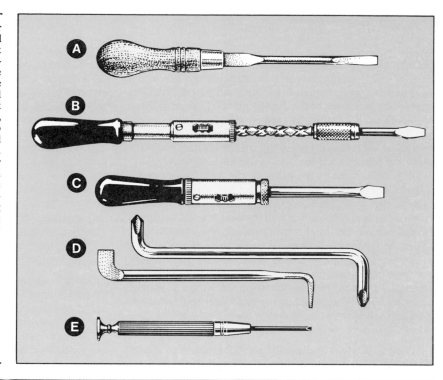

Sharpening tools

Oilstones, sometimes referred to as whetstones, are rectangular blocks of manmade stone used to grind tool blades to a sharp edge. They are available with coarse, medium and fine grits, the most useful is the combination stone with a medium grit on one side, and fine grit on the other. Always oil the stone before use with a small drop of light machine oil and try to use the entire surface, to prevent uneven wear.

1. If the stone becomes clogged with oil, dust or metal particles, scrub the surface with a stiff bristle brush soaked in paraffin or kerosene.

2. To regrind the stone, sprinkle carborundum powder on a sheet of glass, and, keeping the surface of the stone moistened with water, rub it over the surface of the glass until it is perfectly flat once again.

3. To sharpen the blade of a new plane or chisel, a second angle of 30° must be honed on the edge using the oilstone. (It already has a ground edge of 25° but a sharper honed edge must be formed.) Put a drop of oil on the stone and rub the blade at the required angle up and down the stone in an "X" pattern, maintaining constant pressure. When a burr or rough edge is built up along the flat side, turn it over and rub the burr off with a single stroke. Test for sharpness by drawing the blade down a vertically held piece of paper—it should make a smooth cut.

FURNITURE STYLES

Broadly speaking, furniture styles, like most other forms of art, have followed overall trends, with different countries developing their own variations. In most settled communities, one of the first items of furniture was a box or chest for storage. Then, most likely, somebody sat on it, or put something on it rather than in it, or even put the baby to bed in it. Thus, gradually, other types of furniture evolved to meet man's changing needs, resulting from his ever more sophisticated activities. For centuries, however, anything beyond the most basic item was a status symbol. As late as the sixteenth century, even the grandest houses were sparsely furnished, and it is only in the last hundred years or so, with the advent of mass-production, that our homes in the West have become as full of possessions as they are now. Until then only the well-to-do could afford the fashionable "urban" furniture; this was copied, with variations, usually in a humbler wood, for the lesser gentry; cottagers made their own few modest items or bought from local joiners, who paid little attention to current trends. Provincial furniture might be made in a style which had beeen fashionable decades earlier, or in established regional traditions, or even according to personal idiosyncrasies.

Leaving aside the stylish and beautiful furniture of ancient civilizations, furniture traditions in the West began in medieval Europe. Wooden chests, benches, stools, chairs with arms, beds, trestle-type tables and cupboards survive in many forms from this period, from primitive constructions of plain planks and nails to more sophisticated panelled examples decorated with carving, painting or wood inlay. The aristocracy, churches and monasteries were the major users of furniture at this time. Carving and inlaid work became more and more magnificent for those who could afford it, and by the early seventeenth century highly skilled craftsmen were producing showpieces such as the cabinets made at Antwerp, which have painted panels, tortoiseshell and ebony veneers, and those of Augsburg and Nuremberg with their finely executed marquetry.

In the sixteenth century, the principal items in English manor house were boxes and chests, extendable tables known as draw tables, small folding tables, open-shelved court or buffet cupboards (ancestors of the dresser and sideboard), close cupboards or presses, benches, many small stools and four-poster beds. Servants had small truckle (or trundle) beds. All these were of oak. Chairs, which were generally reserved for the head of the household, developed from a panelled, box-like structure with back and arms, through lighter forms retaining the straight legs of the original frame but dispensing with the panels, to "joyned" chairs with turned baluster legs. The common X-frame chairs were beech. Upholstery, if it was used, might be of plain velvet or worked wool.

Carpenters in the Middle Ages had often merely nailed together a few planks to make basic furniture; but the spreading craft of joinery brought in the frame-and-panel type of construction. As a result furniture became lighter and more portable and the problems of warping and splitting were to an extent overcome, since the panels were not nailed but simply rested in the grooved frame. Linenfold carving was much used on chests, chairs and on panelling for walls; Renaissance motifs, such as profile heads in roundels, were often used as decoration. By the end of the sixteenth century the massive, bulbous "cup and cover" and

similar heavy motifs became common for carved supports such as table legs and bedposts, and gadrooning — chunky, ribbed ornament — adorned the edges of many surfaces. Over the following years the styles remained rather solid and were often somewhat plainer than before, particularly during the Commonwealth. With the restoration of the monarchy in 1660 a certain frivolity became apparent and much more ornament was used on furniture, due to Continental influences. Twist-turning — giving the popular "barley-sugar" effect — was used on chair legs and backs, table legs and elsewhere, and carved scroll shapes were also popular. The day-bed — ancestor of the chaise longue and sofa — was introduced at this time, with cane often used for seats. The chest of drawers made its appearance in about 1650 and gained in popularity towards the end of the century. Ball or bun feet were usual.

At this time oak was still the most commonly used wood in Britain; in other European countries walnut was more extensively used for solid carved furniture. But more ornamental finishes were catching the eye of wealthy patrons everywhere. Inlays, veneering and marquetry techniques became increasingly advanced throughout Europe, and the finer woods were much sought after. Oriental lacquer first reached Europe in the early part of the seventeenth century, and by the 1680s had many imitators. The lacquered or japanned chest-on-stand was a showpiece, ideally surmounted by blue-and-white porcelain vases. The Low Countries particularly excelled in floral marquetry. In late seventeenth-century France André-Charles Boulle developed his intricate technique of marquetry using brass, tortoiseshell and pewter; the rich, ornate appearance of his vast cupboards and cabinets was highly admired. The Italians perfected *pietre dure,* an elaborate inlaying method using marble and semi-precious stones such as agates, lapis lazuli and chalcedony; but by then end of the century an artificial material called *scagliola* had been developed to imitate marble, using different pigments, in place of these materials.

In the late 1680s numerous Huguenot craftsmen fled to England from religious persecution in France; while William and Mary brought Dutch influences and workers; thus more and more European styles and techniques filtered into England. By this time walnut was increasingly used for elegant furniture, and deal was the base for a variety of decorative veneers. One of the favourite techniques brought in by the Dutch craftsmen was marquetry, and the later years of the century produced, in particular, some fine, large cabinets in various styles. The later Queen Anne period is renowned for charming, neat walnut chests

Veneer samples opposite illustrate the tonalities and grain patterns in various woods (in numerical order): Afara (1), Afrormosia (2), Afzelia (3), Agba or Nigerian Cedar (4), Ash (5), Aspen (6), Avodire or African Satinwood (7), Ayan or Nigerian Satinwood (8), Beech (9), Canadian Birch or Yellow Birch (10), Bird's Eye Maple (11), Bubinga or African Rosewood (12), Cedar of Lebanon (13), Cherry (14), Elm (15), Eucalyptus or White Mountain Ash (16), Iroko or African Teak (17), Lacewood or European Plane (18), Larch (19), Laurel or Indian Walnut (20), Lime, Linden or Basswood (21), Mahogany (22), Makore or Cherry Mahogany (23), Mansonia or African Black Walnut (24) and Oak (25).

of drawers and bureaux with bracket feet, tall-backed chairs with cabriole legs and shell motifs, and upholstered wing chairs. Walnut pieces were often copied in oak or beech in the provinces; but country areas also had their own simpler styles. These included Windsor chairs, which commonly had elm seats, with other woods used for the remainder and ladder-back and spindle-back chairs with rush seats, generally made in the north of England.

For nearly the whole of the eighteenth century, France set the international styles — royal patronage ensured top-quality crafts-manship and imaginative and artistic innovations. The rather rigid formality under Louis XIV gradually gave way to a freer, lighter mood. The symmetry of the earlier style was at first retained, but lines became gently curved, and the cabriole leg became fashionable on chairs and tables. Towards the middle of the century, in the reign of Louis XV, was produced the most flamboyant, fanciful and perhaps best known of French styles: rococo. Flowing lines, asymmetrical shapes, shells and C-scrolls typify the furniture of this time, along with fine floral marquetry, and swirling ormolu mounts. Lacquer — either oriental or imi-tation — was also used, with chinoiserie motifs. Comfortably upholstered chairs made their début and added to the relaxed, informal air of the times. Many kinds of little tables and cabinets were also fashionable, but the piece of furniture most associated with eighteenth-century France is the commode — a highly decorative chest, raised on legs, with cupboards and/or drawers and a marble top. After a transitional period embracing old and new elements, the rococo finally gave way to the neo-classical in about 1770. Lines lost their curves and became more severe, legs straightened and tapered, and there was a fashion for furniture with ingenious mechanical devices and moving parts — little drawers opened by hidden springs, smoothly rolling cylindrical tops for bureaux, and so on. The mood was more fastidious, but still showy. Ornamentation became a little more restrained and geometrical, and included the use of Sèvres medallions and plainer, smaller ormolu mounts.

However, the upheavals caused by the Revolution put a stop to such frivolities. A certain austerity marked the furniture around the turn of the century, though the traditions of fine craftsmanship naturally lingered. A heavier and more angular look was now fashionable, and an "Etruscan" style was followed by an "Egyptian", with appropriate motifs.

In England from the 1730s mahogany was used for the better pieces. The many large country houses built during the century needed quantities of good-quality furniture, and this period saw

Veneer samples opposite illustrate the tonalities and grain patterns found in various woods (in numerical order): Australian Silky Oak or Prickly Ash (26), Pollard Oak or Brown Oak (27), Obeche or African Whitewood (28), Olive Ash (29), Opepe or Yellow Wood (30), Padauk (31), Paldao or Pacific Walnut (32), Pearwood (33), Peroba Rosa (34), Scots Pine or Swedish Pine (35), Tulipwood (36), Purpleheart (37), Indian Rosewood (38), San Domingan Rosewood (39), Sapele (40), East Indian Satinwood (41), Sycamore or Maple (42), Golden Teak (43), Tola (44), African Walnut (45), Australian Walnut (46), Black American Walnut (47), European Walnut (48), Zebrawood (49) and Pommelle (50).

the rise of the cabinet-maker. From the mid-century Thomas Chippendale and others published pattern-books showing designs for furniture in various styles. Among these, the French influence is seen in the rococo style with its C-scrolls, naturalistic elements and asymmetrical shapes, and more generally in the curved lines and less severe look which typified the Louis XV style. Also featured are the "Gothic" style, with architectural motifs such as arches and turrets, and the "Chinese" style, with simulated bamboo, fretwork and pagoda shapes. Chippendale himself is particularly remembered for his generously proportioned carved chairs and the monumental desks and bookcases still seen in many collections today. He also worked with Robert Adam in the neo-classical style which followed in the 1760s, and which continued, with variations, until the end of the century. Lighter woods such as satinwood were favoured, along with mahogany, and marquetry remained much used. Painted decoration also used.

Inspired by the ornament of ancient Rome and the newly discovered finds at Pompeii and Herculaneum, Adam fostered this lighter but somewhat more formal style for use throughout the décor of the house: a wall frieze of honeysuckle or swags of husks or bellflowers, interspersed with rams' heads, medallions or sphinx-like figures, might be repeated or complemented on sideboard, urn, pier-glass, table and chair, with carpets echoing the ceiling decoration. While Adam designed for the greatest houses (he was not concerned with anything less), it was the designs of George Hepplewhite, published in 1788, which helped to fill the gap between the elite and the growing merchant class. He included quantities of designs for many types of furniture based on the neo-classical style. Outstanding among them are drawings for chairs with oval, heart-shaped and shield-shaped backs, enclosing delicate openwork wheatsheaves, classical urns, rosettes and Prince of Wales feathers. Although he included designs for many other articles of furniture, it is for his chairs that Hepplewhite is best remembered. The next great name at the end of the eighteenth century is that of Thomas Sheraton, a designer renowned for straight lines, square chairbacks and painted decoration who adapted the neo-classical style. He was influenced both by the Louis XVI style current in France and by what followed it, and led the way into what became known as the Regency style.

Suddenly, rather than simply using classical ornamentation, designers began to take the actual shapes of classical furniture as their models. Chairs, couches and stools were particularly suitable for this treatment. Also popular were round tables with a single central leg in various styles supported on three or four feet. Doors of sideboards and small cupboards had grilled or latticed brass with pleated silk behind. Ornament included lion's paw feet and brass mounts in the shape of lion's heads or sphinxes. Rosewood became fashionable, as well as mahogany, satinwood and gilt and painted wood.

A more ostentatious style became the vogue towards the middle of the century. Large, heavy and somewhat fussily orna-mented pieces were made in imitation of some earlier styles of both French and English furniture. Substantial, sprung upholstery with deep buttons became popular from the 1830s, as did military chests and desks, davenports and japanned papier mâché. Balloon-back chairs were also introduced at this time and, with many variations, became highly popular as dining chairs. Several types of small chairs upholstered in velvet or Berlin woolwork appeared from the 1840s, and whatnots—smallish, narrow stands with a number of shelves for displaying china, etc—came more generally into use, with many variations in shape and size. Beds were usually still of the four-poster variety, although brass bedsteads became more general from the 1850s, and by the 1880s were common. Bentwood became popular during the 1850s. The Austrian, Michael Thonet (1786-1871) was the best-known exponent of this medium, which blended well with the other popular style: japonaiserie.

Mass-production was now well under way. Standards inevitably dropped, and such descriptions as "exaggerated", "finicky" and "debased" have been used of furniture of this period. There is, however, an honest, no-nonsense solidity about other pieces of nineteenth-century furniture, particularly where good-quality mahogany is concerned.

A return to craftsman-made pieces and cleaner, straighter lines was heralded by William Morris and others from the 1860s; and the Arts and Crafts movement, founded in the 1880s, propagated the trend towards the integration of art and design and their application to everyday life.

British expatriate craftsmen in America naturally took with them the traditions and styles they knew. They also kept in touch with the current trends through observing what was imported into America from England, and continued to follow them, while making their own stylistic adaptations. There was inevitably some time-lag. The Queen Anne style remained highly popular for many years, the "highboy" (tall chest of drawers), for example, being made in this style, or with elements of it, until at least the 1770s. Available woods included oak, walnut, pine, maple and various fruitwoods; mahogany was used generally from the second half of the eighteenth century, though earlier mahogany pieces exist. Philadelphia, Newport and Boston were the main areas of furniture production, followed by Baltimore, and some of the smaller towns in Massachusetts.

Various innovations were made, such as the "butterfly" table (in which the hinged supports to the extending flaps have a graceful, winged shape) in the early eighteenth century. Windsor chairs were especially popular, with variations such as the Hitchcock chair with painted or stencilled decoration on the top rail, which itself might vary in shape.

In the second half of the eighteenth century the main style was American Chippendale, based on the mainstream of the English style. One of the specifically American features was the block front to a cabinet or chest of drawers, in which the front has the central part very slightly set back. Furniture of the Federal period followed the European swing to neo-classicism, again with adaptations, and assorted mixtures of designs from different sources, often giving a vigorous and fresh look.

Revivals of previous styles, particularly the more flamboyant, occurred in America as in Europe in the nineteenth century. New machines and other technical innovations made possible much experimentation and initiated mass-production. In the 1870s a new style was launched by Charles Lock Eastlake, whose name is given in America to a particular style of "art" furniture—rectangular, with straight lines and elaborate ornamentation, perhaps with inlays or painted panels, fluted columns and small, turned wooden spindles. There was also a vogue for Japanese decoration. The firm of Herter was one of a number producing "art" furniture into the twentieth century. The work of the designer Gustave Stickley, who promoted the ideas of the Arts and Crafts movement, is still well known for clean, straight lines and good hand craftsmanship. Later, the architect Frank Lloyd Wright designed functional furniture specifically for mass-production. These men and other contemporary designers fostered a fairly widespread and continuing appreciation of their particular styles.

Throughout the West, the twentieth century has seen a multitude of new materials, for good timber has become increasingly rare and expensive. In style, too, there have been changes. A general, international trend away from the heavy, elaborate taste of the nineteenth century, along with the demand for good design and low cost, grew through the Arts and Crafts movement toward various light, functional styles using tubular steel, fibreglass, aluminium, various plastics, rubber, leather, plywood and bent laminated wood as well as more newly available woods such as teak. All the decorative motifs of earlier periods have disappeared—although a certain amount of reproduction furniture has continued to be made—and most modern furniture of good quality is admired for its serviceability and uncluttered lines. Most craftsmen cabinet-makers today use the intrinsic beauty or interest of their materials and finishes to achieve their desired decorative effect.

Types of wood

Wood falls into two main categories: hardwoods, from broadleaved trees such as oak, mahogany, ash, walnut, elm, maple, cherry and teak; and softwoods, from trees with needle-like leaves, such as pine, spruce, redwood and cedar. The more expensive hardwoods are generally stronger, tend to move less when worked, and join and finish better. They are attractive for their variety of tone and closely-figured grain; and the more exotic ones, satinwood and ebony, for example, are used chiefly for veneer. Softwoods are generally lighter, and were often painted, stained or veneered in the past, though it is fashionable now to strip and bleach old pieces.

Before it can used, timber must be seasoned to stabilize it, and keep shrinkage and warpage to a minimum. However it remains sensitive to moisture, and may expand and warp in damp conditions or shrink and split if the air is very dry—for this reason, have a humidifier if antiques are in a centrally heated room.

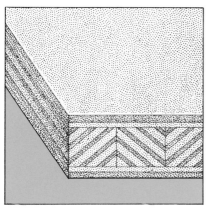

TYPES OF MAN-MADE BOARDS
Blockboard is made from thin strips of softwood laid edge to edge, sandwiched between veneers and pressed into sheets.

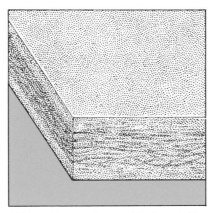

Chipboard is made from machined wood chips bonded together with a synthetic resin under heat and pressure. It is cheaper than blockboard and can be used in most do-it-yourself projects. It is available in thicknesses of ⅛in, ½in or ¾in/3mm, 13mm or 18mm.

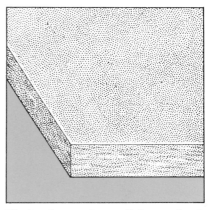

Fibreboard, sometimes called masonite, is formed from wood pulp or fibre and a bonding agent. It is used most often for wall insulation and bulletin boards. It is available in thicknesses from ⅛in to ¼in/3mm to 7mm.

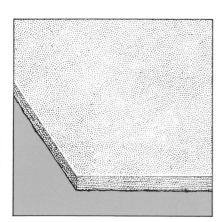

Hardboard is softwood pulp pressed into sheets 1/12th–½in/2.4-13mm thick, usually with one smooth face and one rough, textured face.

Laminboard (laminated board) is used in the manufacture of modern veneered furniture. It is similar to blockboard but the core is made of several ¼in/7mm strips glued together. The veneers commonly used are birch, poplar and gaboon. Its advantage over blockboard is that the pattern of the core is less likely to show through to the surface of the veneer.

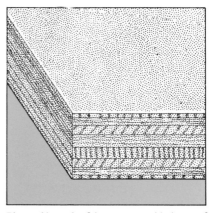

Plywood is made of three or more thin layers of wood, usually birch, alder, ash, gaboon or Douglas fir,with the grain of each piece at right angles to the layers above and below it. When glued together under pressure, this reduces most shrinkage and splitting. The more layers glued together, the stronger the ply is. It is available in thicknesses of ¼in to ¾in/7mm to 2cm. Faced plywood has one surface veneered with a more expensive hardwood like oak and is used where this surface will show. The types normally available are 3-ply and 5-ply.

Treatment of burns

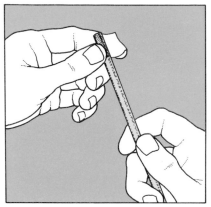

1. Deep burns need careful treatment. Sand the burnt area with garnet paper glued around the end of a piece of ⅛in/3mm dowelling, or roll a small piece of sandpaper to a point.

2. Twist this on the blackened wood without sanding the surrounding area, otherwise you will "sand out" the patina and have an ugly mark when the piece is repolished.

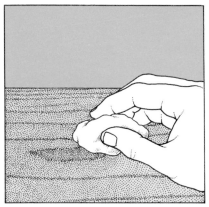

3. Once the charred wood is removed put a drop of bleach on the area to lighten the exposed darker wood using a cotton swab. Fill with stick shellac (see Step 4, opposite), smooth out with a cotton rag and polish if the burnt area is deep or large.

4. If the indentation is very deep after sanding, it may need filling with tinted beeswax. Use 2oz-4oz/60g-125g beeswax and a vegetable or wood dye which blends with the polished wood, but make sure it is acid-based so that it mixes easily with the beeswax. To make the filler, melt the beeswax slowly in a double boiler, adding small quantities of the dye. Do not over-tint – it is easy to darken, but impossible to lighten. It may be necessary to mix two dyes to match the original finish. Pour into an empty, clean tin and leave to set.

5. When the wax is hard, pry out of the can with a putty knife. Roll a bit between your fingers to soften it. Warm the blade of a palette knife over a flame, place the wax on it and let it drip into the damaged area until it is overfull (to allow for shrinkage.)

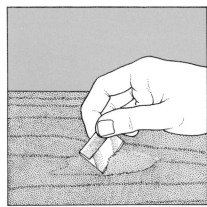

6. When the wax has set, carefully shave off the excess with a blunt razor blade. If the burn is on a very glossy French polish finish, build up the hole with layers of French polish (see Step 3, Page 44) until it is level with the surrounding surface. Polish until all the edges are well blended.

Surface repairs

1. Dents, like any other repair, should be mended as soon as possible. First, try this simple method: fill the hollow with hot water as this may swell the compressed fibres sufficiently to refill the depression.

2. If this fails, put a damp cotton cloth over the dent and heat it with an electric iron until steam rises. Try to apply the heat *only* to the dented area: use the tip of the iron for small dents, the whole iron for large ones. Let the wood dry completely before re-polishing or re-waxing the area. If the wood fibres have been crushed so that neither method works, the dent must be filled with shellac (see Step 4).

3. Knot holes are usually only troublesome on unseasoned new wood, but they sometimes appear after stripping a piece down to the base wood. To "seal off" knots that ooze resin, dissolve 5oz/141g shellac and 1oz/28g sandarac in 1pt/568ml denatured alcohol (methylated spirits). Strain through a wire mesh strainer and apply with an old brush to the knot and surrounding area. Alternatively use a proprietary brand of knot sealing compound.

4. Small scratches and gouges can be filled with wood-turner's cement, also called stick shellac, stick filler and furnisher's wax. It looks like a thick crayon and is simply "pencilled" along the line of the scratch. For deeper scratches melt some of the crayon with a match, dropping it on to a warm palette knife. Spread this onto the area, and remove the excess by polishing with a cotton rag. Alternatively make your own filler from beeswax and dye (see opposite). But remember that small scratches and blemishes are accepted as a pleasing part of antique furniture.

5. Chips, small holes, cracks, splits and enlarged pores all need filling. Use a proprietary wood filler like plastic wood, or make one up by mixing fine sawdust with woodworking glue until it is stiff. Apply the filling with a filling knife so that it projects a little above the surface. It will contract when dry. Sand the area afterwards if necessary to get a smooth finish. If either mixture appears too light, add some powdered pigment from the sienna to umber range, taking particular care in matching the surrounding wood on pieces that will be finished with a clear varnish.

6. For surfaces that are going to be painted use a filler made from one part whiting to three parts plaster of Paris. Tint with powdered pigment if you wish. Add water to form a paste and apply with a putty or palette knife.

Surface repairs cont.

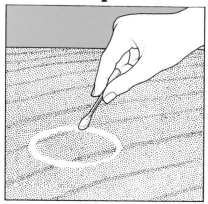

7. White spots or rings are formed by water or the bases of hot dishes. Rub the spot lightly with a piece of soft cotton moistened with spirits of camphor, or with a solution of one part turpentine or one part ammonia mixed with one part linseed oil. Brass polish is also effective.

8. Black spots are usually caused by water penetrating through a French polished surface and into the wood itself. There is not much that can be done, beyond removing the finish with denatured alcohol (methylated spirits) and steel wool (see Steps 1-3, Page 39) or lightening the spots using wood bleach applied on a small brush and then refinishing. (See page 39 for more detailed bleaching instructions).

9. Dull, dirty finishes can be revived with the following mixture, which will also improve a scratched French polished surface: one part linseed oil, one part turpentine, one part vinegar, one quarter part denatured alcohol (methylated spirits). The alcohol slightly softens the finish while the oil acts as a means of redistributing the polish into the scratches. Keep the mixture in a screw-top glass jar and shake well before using.

Treatment of woodworm and dry rot

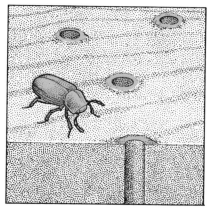

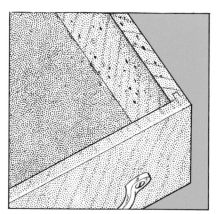

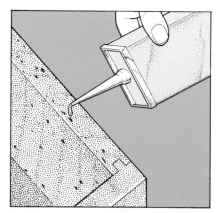

1. The grub or larva of this wood-boring beetle is usually introduced by bringing an infested wood or wicker item into the house. The insects emerge in July or August and fly to infest other pieces, so always check new buys for any sign of pin-head holes.

2. Attacks of woodworm often start in the cheaper softwood at the back or bottom of a piece. If a piece shows holes with fresh-looking wood inside, or sharp edges, or if wood-dust appears under it, it must be treated. Valuable or upholstered pieces will probably need treating by experts, but other items can be done by amateurs.

3. Before treating a piece, isolate it in a garage or workroom to stop the infestation spreading. Then treat the affected area with a commercial woodworm solution, kerosene or paraffin followed by wood naphtha or liquid ammonia. Put the liquid in a can with a small pointed nozzle (a clean oilcan is ideal). Squirt the liquid into *each* hole so that it penetrates to the larvae; work from the back or the inside of the piece to avoid damaging the exterior. After 24 hours wipe off any excess. Check often to ensure the infestation has not spread.

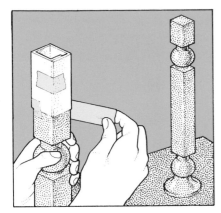

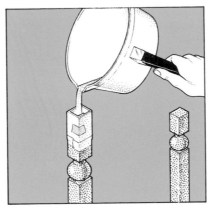

4. Badly infected parts may need cutting out and replacing (a job for experts), but this may be drastic action, and inappropriate for valuable pieces. In such cases feet and legs can be strengthened after treatment for woodworm. Turn the piece upside down and build a wall of cardboard around the woodwormed base, holding it in place with masking tape.

5. Make a hot solution of proprietary anti-fungal size and pour into the well formed by the cardboard. If the size is hot and thin enough it should penetrate all the worm holes. After 24 hours remove card and size will have solidified the affected wood.

DRY ROT

6. Dry rot is unlikely to affect furniture kept in well-ventilated rooms because the fungus needs warm, moist conditions to thrive. Infected wood is powdery to the touch and has a musty smell. If you are unlucky enough to acquire a piece of infected furniture, stop the rot spreading by spraying surrounding areas with a commercial fungicide.

Treatment of stains

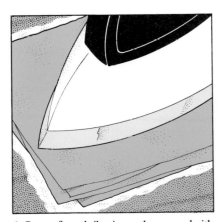

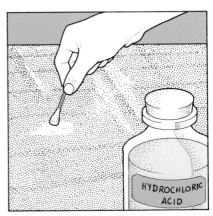

1. Grease, fat and oil stains can be removed with benzoline, benzine, or cigarette lighter fluid. Unfortunately any of these may also affect the glue holding the veneer. So, for veneered or inlaid pieces, spread a thick layer of talc on the grease, cover with several layers of white tissue paper and warm the paper gently with a hot iron—use the "wool" setting and no steam. The talc and paper will soak up the grease. Repeat if necessary. Fuller's earth can be used instead of talc.

2. Alcohol, perfume or medicine leave a white mark on French polished surfaces and the only treatment is to apply new French polish (see Steps 1-6, Page 44). On varnished furniture the damage is more difficult to treat because most varnishes are soluble in alcohol. In this case sand the spot with very fine abrasive paper and touch up with varnish (see Steps 1-3, Page 43) or a proprietary brass cleaner.

3. Wine or fruit stains are seldom very deep. Clean the surface by sanding lightly. Then, with a cotton swab, dab on diluted hydrochloric acid, followed by a few drops of hydrogen peroxide. This method is also effective with very old red ink stains.

Treatment of stains cont.

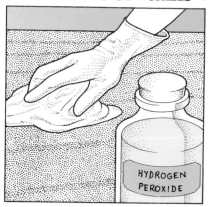 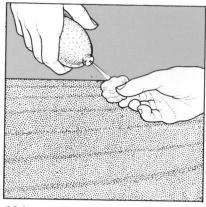 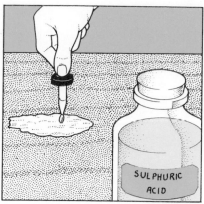

4. Blood can be removed with ordinary hydrogen peroxide or, alternatively, sodium thiosulphate (diluted to 5 per cent). Apply by dabbing on a small quantity at a time, using a corner of a cotton rag or a cotton swab.

5. Ink removal is much more a matter of trial and error. Wash a fresh stain with water, then apply lemon juice to bleach it, using absorbent cotton rags, cotton wool or a paintbrush to apply the juice. However, the treated area may then also need to be treated for water damage (see Step 7, Page 22).

6. If the ink stain is old, sand the area lightly to remove the stain and expose the wood. Cover with cotton wool cut to the size of the stain and pour sulphuric acid onto it. Wait 2-3 minutes and inspect. Repeat if necessary. Oxalic acid diluted with warm water is an alternative and works well on red ink stains.

Repairing drawers and doors

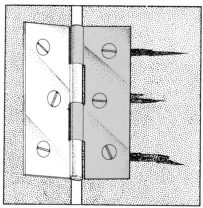 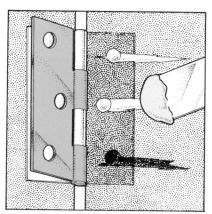 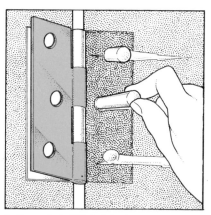

1. Hinges and handles often have loose screws either because the screw hole has become enlarged, or the wood surrounding the screw has been damaged. First make sure that the wood surrounding the hinge or handle is not split, removing the hinge if necessary.

2. Should the wood around the screw hole be split, fill the split with wood filler (see formulas in Steps 4-6, Page 21) and let it dry before continuing the repair. In some instances, it may be necessary to fill both splits and the hole in order to give the screw a firm ground.

3. Alternatively, if the hole has become too big, the quickest remedy is to simply pack the hole with the same length of wooden matchstick, glued into place with wood adhesive, and then replace the screw. If the hole is only slightly enlarged, it may be necessary to enlarge it further in order to pack it. In this case, use a drill bit one size larger than the screw itself, then pack the hole with wood filler or with a matchstick or dowel.

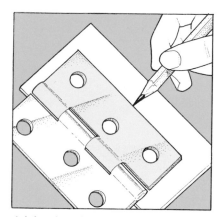

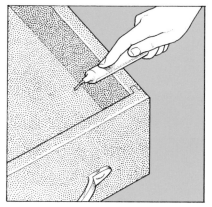

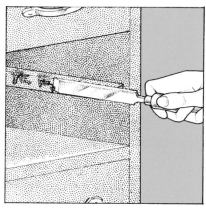

4. A door that will not close is probably caused by a hinge which is too deeply set. Remove the hinge, using a screwdriver to loosen the screws, and then trace around the hinge with a sharp pencil onto a piece of cardboard. Cut out the cardboard, place it under the hinge and reset the screws. This will raise the hinge. If the hinge jams, make sure the screws are flush with the hinge and not protruding.

5. Stiff drawers are usually made worse by damp weather because the wood fibres have expanded. To remedy this, try rubbing the outside of the drawer with soap or a candle. If this fails remove a little of the wood from the side of the drawer with coarse abrasive paper, sanding with the grain.

6. The other possible cause of stubborn drawers, especially on painted furniture, is that old paint drops are often thick enough to clog up the runners of a drawer. If this is the case, remove them with a scraper and paint stripper. If neither of these courses is a solution to the problem, as a last resort it may be necessary to move the article to a room with a drier atmosphere.

Repairing chairs

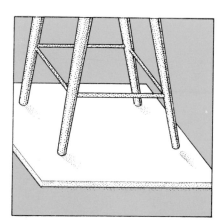

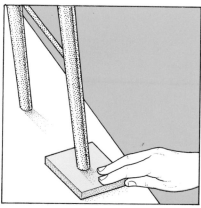

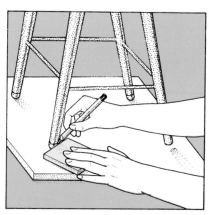

1. A chair (or table) may wobble because either its legs or the floor upon which it is standing are uneven. Place chair on a piece of chipboard or a flat board. If it still wobbles one or two of the legs may be shorter than the rest. (If it doesn't wobble on an even surface then it's the floor that is uneven and the answer is to repair the floor or move the chair.)

2. While the chair is still on a level surface, determine which legs are shorter. Push thin pieces of cardboard under the short leg(s) to see how much needs to be cut from the other chair legs. This treatment is not recommended for antiques, which should have short legs built up - a job for the expert. Even the smallest piece cut off an antique immediately reduces the value of the whole piece.

3. When the chair seems steady, remove the cardboard from under the shorter leg and use it to mark how much must be cut from the others. Saw off the excess with a small saw, making the ends horizontal, whether the legs are straight or angled. Smooth the legs with fine abrasive paper and refinish if necessary.

Repairing chairs cont.

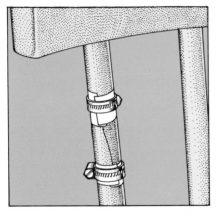

4. Broken fretwork in chair backs should be mended as soon as possible to prevent further damage. Glue the broken ends together using a proprietary wood glue and do not use the chair until the glue is completely dry.

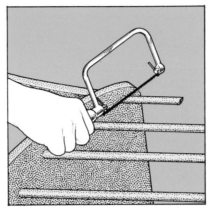

5. If a piece is missing, it must be replaced - either the entire fret or a piece of fret. Cut off the old piece with a coping saw and drill or pick out any wood that remains in the hole.

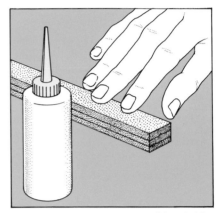

6. If the fret is round, use a length of dowel of the same diameter. If it is square, glue pieces of wooden slatting together to get the right dimensions (a timber merchant will order and cut the pieces for you). If the chair is valuable and made from hardwood, get a carpenter to turn a matching dowel from a block of the appropriate wood, using the colour photographs of different woods opposite pages 16 and 17 as a guide.

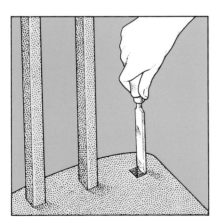

7. Redrill the hole so the diameter is slightly wider than the new fret or slat. Use a chisel for a square hole. Cut the new piece to length, remembering to add the depth of the hole (two holes when replacing a whole slat) at the end.

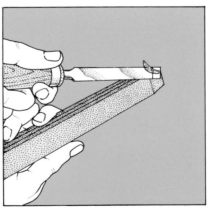

8. Taper the end with abrasive paper to fit snugly into the hole. Apply a drop of cellulose-based glue and set in place. Taper the other end to match the broken piece.

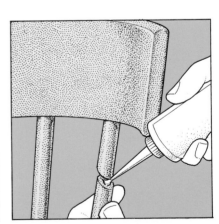

9. It may be best to sand the broken end down to a neat finish before inserting the new piece in the hole. If you do this, remember to take into account that the old piece will be shorter when cutting the new fret to fit. Support the new piece, if necessary, until the glue is set.

Repairing chairs

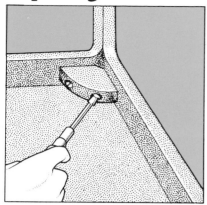
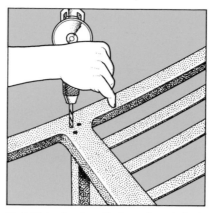
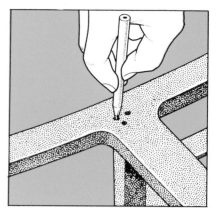

10. If the chair's back and legs are in one piece, as they often are in period furniture, or if there are no slats between the joint and back legs, then the back may work itself away from the chair seat. In this case there will probably be triangular blocks on the underside holding the legs to the seat. On chairs with upholstered seats you may have to remove the bottom cover and webbing, thus exposing dowels holding the chair seat in place.

11. Drill the dowels or blocks out from the back or from inside the seat frame.

12. Measure the depth of the holes with a pencil. Cut new dowels that are a little longer, tap them into place and tie or clamp the chair together until the glue has set.

Repairing tables

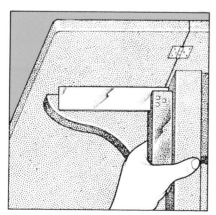
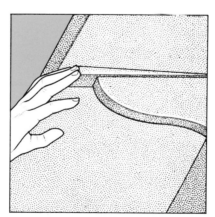
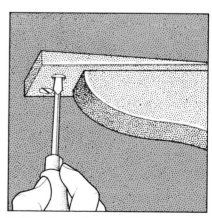

1. Open the leaves of the table, pull out the stays and check if the tops of the stays are in even contact with the leaves. (A T-square or right angle is helpful when doing this.)

2. If the top of the stays and the leaves are not evenly in contact, insert a small hardwood wedge until the angle is perfect and the table top is flat.

3. If the table gets a lot of use, it is better to make a longer wedge so that the leaf is more firmly supported. Screw the wedge in place on the underside of the leaf.

Types of joints

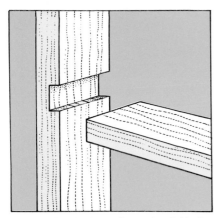

Common housing joint, often used as divider for drawers; they provide good support for heavy drawers.

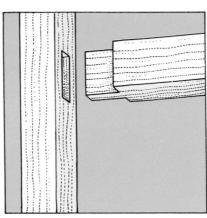

Mortise and tenon joint as used in the eighteenth century; it was always glued.

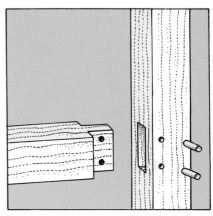

Dowel and stub tenon; used from Victorian times onwards and always glued.

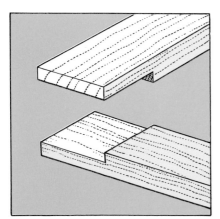

Halved angle joint as used in cheap plywood panel frames.

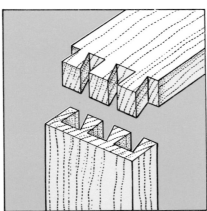

Lapped dovetail joint; used from the eighteenth century onwards and always glued.

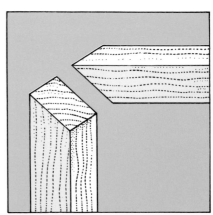

Simple mitre joint, in use from the seventeenth century; it can be glued or nailed.

Bridle joint, one of the many less common joints found in very old furniture.

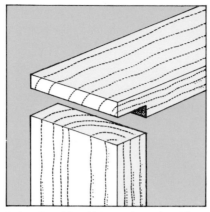

Rebated or rabbeted joint; can be used straight or at right angles, glued or nailed. Found in cheap pine furniture of all periods.

Tongue and groove joint; can also be straight or at right angles. Used mainly from the nineteenth century onwards.

Repairing joints

The following tools and supplies are required for repairing glued joints: blunt knife or scraper, water, alcohol-based glue solvent, wood glue, and a suitable clamp. For dowelled joints, a small saw, coping saw, drill, chisel, and length of dowelling will also be required.

For repairs to tenon joints, tools and materials include: saw, chisel, hammer, wood glue, and pieces of hardwood for wedges.

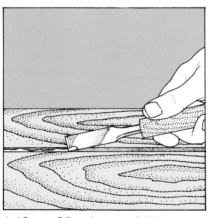

1. After carefully easing apart the joint, remove any old glue with a blunt knife or scraper. Then use warm water or alcohol-based solvent to dissolve any remaining glue. A wooden matchstick can be used to apply the solvent when working with non-water-soluble glues.

2. Always save even the smallest splinters or chips of wood and glue them in place after the main joint has set.

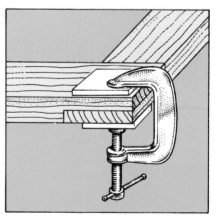

3. Always clamp the work while the glue sets, since a good joint depends on a close fitting of wood to wood, not on the glue itself. Most glues set completely in 24 hours but check the manufacturer's instructions to be sure. (Avoid cheap vinyl glues which separate into layers).Encourage drying by keeping the room temperature at 70°F/20°C.

Repairing joints cont.

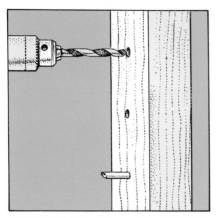

REPAIRING DOWELLED JOINTS

4. Saw off the broken dowel flush with the wood into which the dowel is inserted. Then drill out the remains of the dowel stubs. This generally requires a drill bit of 1/8-1/4in/3-7mm, but in any case, use a drill bit one size smaller than the dowel. (Anything that remains after drilling can be cut out with a narrow chisel.)

5. Cut dowels from a purchased length of a similar diameter, calculating the length so the new dowel fills the depth of the holes just drilled plus the depth of the hole it is to be inserted into. Taper the ends with a chisel and cut a slit in one end using a coping saw. Also cut a small V-shaped channel down the part of the dowel that goes into the hole to allow excess glue to escape.

6. Apply wood glue or general purpose adhesive to each end of the dowel and insert firmly. If the dowel is sound but has come loose, clean away the old glue on the dowel and in the hole with a scraper and warm water, then apply the new glue. Whether using old or new dowels, a C-clamp may be necessary to hold the glued pieces for a few hours; alternatively bind the join with string.

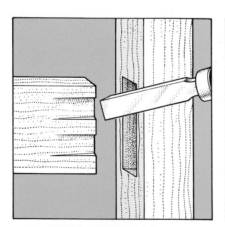

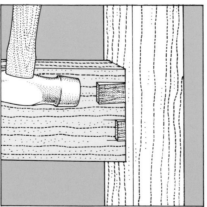

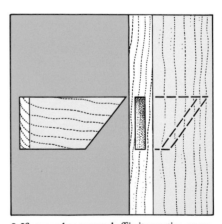

REPAIRING TENON JOINTS

7. If a mortise and tenon joint has become loose, glueing will often solve the problem. If not, cut wedges from a hardwood without a pronounced grain, such as ramin, beech, mahogany or jelutong. Saw or chisel the wedge to the right length and width from an end piece of wood. Cut two or three slots in the end of the tenon with a sharp chisel.

8. Cover the wedges with wood glue and tap them into the slots of the inserted tenon with a hammer. The wedges may stick out slightly, but this excess can be removed with a chisel once the glue is dry.

9. If a tenon has snapped off in its mortise, a new tenon can be cut and fitted. Trim off the old, broken tenon flush with the mortise. Cut a wedge-shaped piece out of the mortise. Cut a new tenon of the same shape, remembering that it must be longer than the piece cut out of the mortise. Glue the new piece and fit into place. When the glue has set the repaired tenon can be fitted and glued in place.

Replacing panes of glass

To replace a pane of glass, assemble the following tools and supplies: soldering iron, putty knife or blunt kitchen knife, cardboard, putty, gloves, gold size and artists' oil paints (optional), and glass cut to size.

1. Remove as much of the broken glass as possible. Use a soldering iron to soften the putty, moving it over a small area at a time. Take care not to burn the wood surrounding the pane of glass (the beading) or you may have to refinish it.

2. When the putty becomes soft, lift it out, a little at a time, with a blunt kitchen knife or putty knife.

3. Remove all remaining bits of glass, tapping them out gently with the handle of the putty knife. Wear gloves when doing this. To replace the glass, cut a piece of cardboard to fit inside the wood and then cut off 1/16th in/2mm around the edge. Get glass cut to this size and be sure to take a piece of the broken pane to match the thickness. Knead the new putty on newspaper to remove excess linseed oil.

4. To make the putty tone with the wood, press a hole in the centre of the putty and fill it with gold size. Knead putty and size until the size is absorbed. Pinch off a small piece of putty and press it along the inside of beading, working your way around the frame inserting a little each time and overlapping the new lengths of putty.

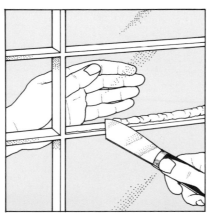

5. Gently press the new pane of glass into the putty, making sure it sits straight and there are no gaps in the putty holding it. Support the glass from the inside with one hand while scraping the excess from the outside with a putty or scraping knife.

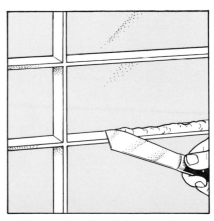

6. Make another thin roll of putty and press it against the glass on the inside, shaping the correct slant between the glass and the wooden beading, again joining lengths as you go. Make sure the putty does not show on the outside. Paint the putty with artists' oil paints to match the wooden beading as closely as possible.

Repairing warped wood

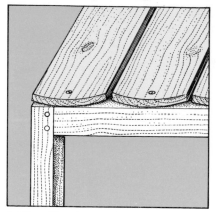

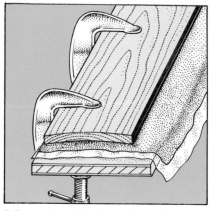

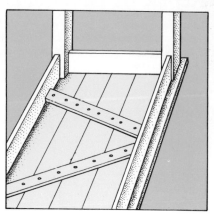

1. Warped boards on a tabletop or as a backing must always be treated individually. Free each from its base using a screwdriver as they are usually only held in place by screws.

2. Lay a piece of plastic sheeting on a length of blockboard, or any other straight piece of wood. Place a length of water-soaked cloth on the plastic and put the warped board concave-side down on the wet cloth. This will enable the fibres on the concave side of the boards to expand. Clamp and leave overnight. If you lack the space and tools for this repair there is a simple alternative: place the boards concave-side down on damp grass overnight.

3. By morning the warp will have gone but it is essential to refit the boards to the piece of furniture as soon as possible once the warp is corrected. However, be sure to fix battens underneath, otherwise the warp will return. The boards must then be allowed to dry out before the necessary finish is applied.

Repairing split wood and replacing moulding

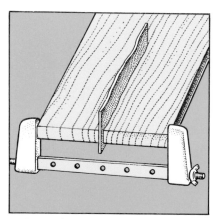

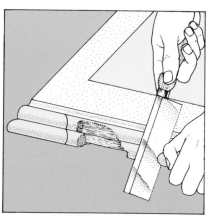

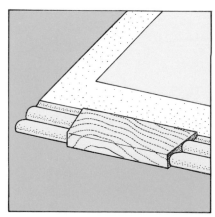

1. If it is impossible to clamp and glue a split piece, it is best to insert a piece of tapered veneer into the crack. Taper the veneer by cutting it with a sharp knife, pulling the wood over a plane blade, or sanding it with abrasive paper. Use wood glue to hold the veneer in place, then clamp or weight it. Once the glue has set, plane (if necessary) and sand the veneer until it is level with the surface.

2. If a piece of moulding is missing, cut the broken end of the original on an angle, using a saw, then sand smooth. Cut a matching length of similar design to fit the gap, apply wood glue along the length and to both ends and insert, holding it temporarily in place with a thin nail.

3. Alternatively, if a similar moulding cannot be found, a length of wood can be glued in place as above. When the glue has set, the new block of wood can be carved with shaped chisels to match the existing moulding.

Decorative finishes illustrated opposite are (from left to right, top to bottom): picture frame in black metallicized faux marble; triptych panel of metallicized glazing; split panel of vinegar painting; glazed and rag-rolled frame with antiqued mouldings *(bottom left); three marbled corners and one antiqued corner; black faux marble box, black box stencilled with metallic powders; mirror frame in faux marble and small picture frame and box in tortoiseshell.*

Replacing missing veneer

If a piece of veneer is damaged and a new piece has to be inserted, follow the instructions for removal above. When selecting veneers to match the original, go for grain direction and type, rather than shade, which can be altered by stains (see pages 40–41).

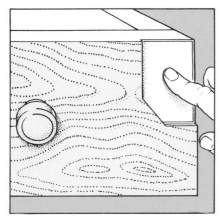

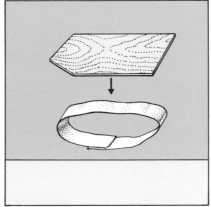

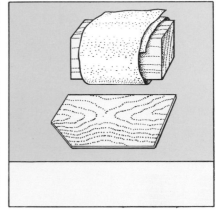

1. Modern veneers are so thin that the new piece may lie lower than the original surrounding veneer. If so, cut a piece of tissue paper slightly smaller than the new piece and glue in place. Let it dry, then glue on the new piece of veneer. Should tissue fail to raise the new veneer enough, it may be necessary to use two pieces of veneer, or place balsa wood underneath.

2. If, on the other hand, the new piece is too thick, sand its underside until the surface of the veneer will lie flush with the surrounding area. To hold the piece of veneer while sanding, make a ring of masking tape, attach one side to the topside of the piece, and press the other side down on the work surface.

3. If the area to be sanded is small, make a tiny sanding block 1½in × 1½in × 1½in/40mm × 40mm × 40mm, from cork or wood, and wrap with abrasive paper. Sand the underside of the veneer piece, going with the grain.

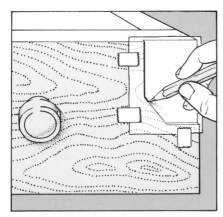

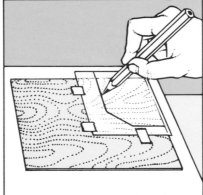

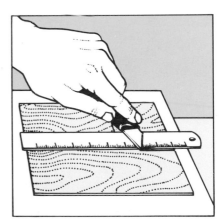

4. If the edge of the surrounding veneer is jagged, which often happens on drawer corners, trim it with the knife to give it a regular edge. Make a template by tracing the area to be replaced with a sharp pencil onto a transparent paper such as tracing paper. (Taping the paper in place with masking tape will make it easier to get an accurate tracing.)

5. Rub the back of the paper with soft pencil until it appears dark grey. Put the paper, traced side uppermost, on the new piece of veneer and go over the shape with the pencil again, transferring the outline to the surface of the wood.

6. Carefully cut around the shape with a single-edged razor, or a knife with replaceable blades, and a steel ruler. Glue the shape carefully into place with wood glue (cellulose-based) or general purpose glue, and weight if necessary.

Decorative finishes illustrated opposite are (from left to right, top to bottom): découpaged nursery screen (in background), gilded casket top resting on a small chest painted with a French tole design, two vinegar-painted panels, lacquered tinware box painted with brushstroke design resting on two round sponged boxes; and, sitting on top of a faux bois blanket chest — lacquered crumb pan, modern lacquered tinket box, round reverse-stencilled box, round-topped stamp box, lacquered English door panel, tortoiseshell box with raised design resting on a bargeware box, and hand-painted tray in foreground.

Replacing missing veneer cont.

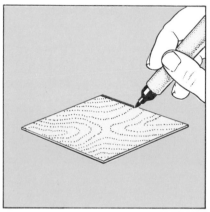

7. Be sure the grain on the new piece is going in the same direction as on the old piece, and if the other inlaid pieces of veneer have dark lines around them, use a dark felt marker to outline the new shape.

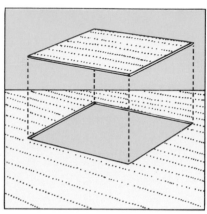

8. When replacing veneer from a central area, follow the same method as when patching a corner. On straight-grained timber straighten the edges of the missing piece into a diamond shape. Make a template as before and transfer the shape to the new piece of veneer. Make sure that the grain of the new piece aligns with the old. Cut out the patch so that its sides are angled inwards, then glue into place.

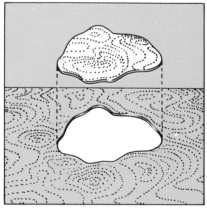

9. To look right, burr wood veneer needs an irregular patch. The method is exactly the same as given above in Steps 1–7. To get an exact fit on an irregular shape, cut the patch a little too large and place over the missing area. Trace round the new piece with a sharp point so the outline of the shape is marked on the original surface. Then cut away the original to fit the patch. Glue as before.

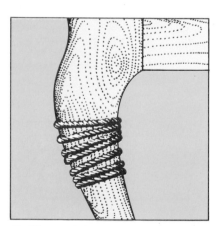

10. When replacing veneer on a concave or convex base, use a contact cement (two-part glue). The adhesion will be instant and difficult to change, so lay the new piece very carefully. For larger areas, apply a cellulose-based wood glue and then wrap wet ropes closely around and over the glued pieces — the wood tightens as it dries, and holds the new piece in place.

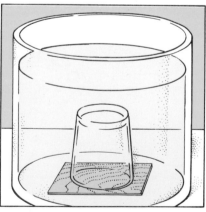

11. Crazing is the word given to the network of tiny cracks that often cover the surface of older pieces of furniture. If a crazed piece of veneer needs replacing you can duplicate the effect by wetting, then drying the piece of new veneer as follows. To saturate the veneer weight it down under water for 15–30 minutes or until it can absorb no more.

12. Then, iron it between pieces of thin paper with a very hot iron which will singe it and produce tiny cracks. Cut out the necessary shape with a scalpel as directed above in Steps 1–7 and glue in place. Alternatively, wet the veneer, hold it with tweezers and drop it into hot clean sand which has been heated in an old pan over a low heat. Leave the piece in the sand until it crazes.

Repairing dented veneer

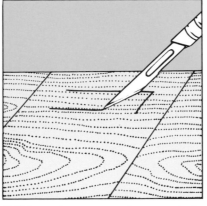

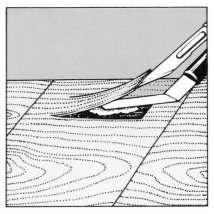

1. If the veneer is dented but the carcase wood is intact, the solution is to make the fibres of the carcase wood swell. Soak a cotton rag or man's handkerchief in water, wring it out and place over the dent. Put a very hot iron over the damp cloth so that a lot of steam is produced. Remove the iron after a few seconds — don't keep it on too long as this may affect the French polish or the glue underneath. Check under the cloth to see if the dent has gone.

2. If the previous treatment does not work, the wood under the veneer is probably also dented. If so, lift the veneer by slitting it above the dent and along the grain. Fold the veneer back carefully, saving any fragments that break off.

3. When the soft carcase wood is exposed, fill the dent with wood filler, using a palette knife, or a matchstick for small areas. Let the filler dry thoroughly; it will shrink slightly as it dries, so always overfill. Let it dry. Glue the veneer back, cover the glued area with cardboard and place weights on top.

If the carcase wood is split, the veneer covering the split will have to be removed so that the carcase can be looked at and filled as above.

Repairing blistered veneer

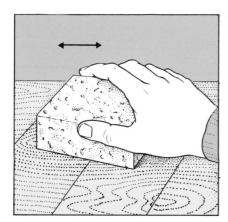

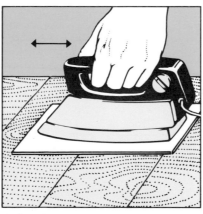

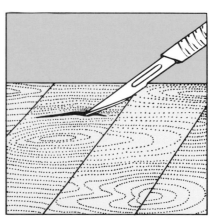

1. Veneers were often glued with water-soluble or animal glue; insufficient glue or damp sometimes leads to the development of small blisters in the veneer. Try rubbing a small cork pad back and forth across the blister. Sometimes the friction heat will level the blister and the finish is less likely to be harmed.

2. If this does not work, put a piece of cardboard over the swollen area and move a hot iron with great pressure slowly backwards and forwards over the cardboard until the swelling has softened. Leave a heavy object on the cardboard for 24 hours and the veneer should be restuck.

3. Should the above fail, it will be necessary to apply more glue under the veneer. To do this, slit the blister in the middle and along the grain with a scalpel, single-edged razor or knife with replaceable blades.

Repairing blistered veneer cont.

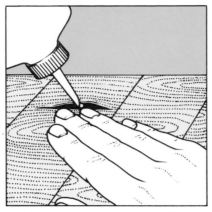

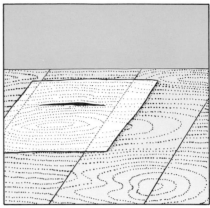

4. If the carcase wood under the blister is dirty or gritty, try to brush out the dirt with the point of a paintbrush.

5. To facilitate glueing, press down one side of the slit blister. This will open up the other side. Insert a dab of cellulose-based wood glue with the container's nozzle or a pinhead dipped in glue, depending on the slit's size. Do the other side of the blister in the same way. Squeeze the excess from both sides and wipe it away with a slightly damp clean cloth.

6. Put a piece of white tissue paper over the glued area and weight with books. If a vinyl glue is used, after squeezing out the excess, put tissue paper over the area and iron with a warm, but not hot, iron. Switch the iron off and leave it in place to cool. The glue will stick as the iron cools.

Removing veneer

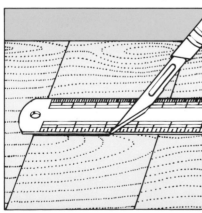

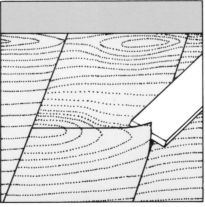

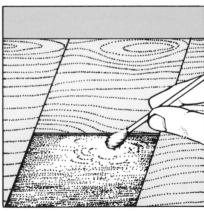

1. Sometimes veneer is so damaged that small patches or large areas have to be removed, then replaced. Remove a small area or a single piece using a scalpel or knife with replaceable blades. Press lightly on the knife at first, then apply more pressure until you meet the carcase wood. For larger areas or stubborn veneer, carefully score around the area first, using a steel ruler, before applying pressure.

2. Cut around the area and lift the piece off gently, working from one corner. Place a chisel under the piece and tap the chisel gently with a hammer. This should lift enough of the veneer so the rest can be gently pulled off.

3. Clean off the old glue using warm water and a small sponge or cotton swab, but don't let any moisture get under the surrounding veneer.

Removing opaque paints

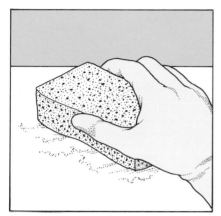

1. A piece must be cleaned before it can be stripped. If it is only slightly dirty, washing with a solution of three parts water to one part vinegar or stale beer should be enough. If it is really dirty, use 2oz/50g detergent to 2pt/1litre warm water. Lightly sponge the surface. Leave for about ten minutes, then repeat the application. Never soak the surface, as the water may penetrate cracked or broken finishes and damage the wood below.

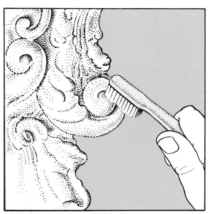

2. Clean dirty carvings with an old toothbrush or shaving brush. Rinse, then dry with cotton rags.

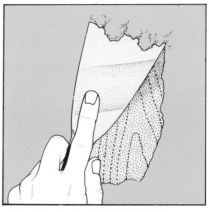

MECHANICAL STRIPPING

3. First remove chipped and peeling paint with the aid of a paint scraper. (Don't confuse this tool with a spatula or filling knife — it is roughly the same shape but has a fairly sharp bevelled edge.) It is possible to use single-edged razors, but these are inefficient over large areas, not to say expensive and dangerous, and should be reserved for awkward crevices. Proceed cautiously with this mechanical stripping, as it is called; it removes paint very unevenly and the wood is easily scraped and gouged, necessitating more filling.

HEAT STRIPPING

4. One alternative method is heat stripping — the quickest way to remove paint, albeit the most dangerous. Its disadvantages are that it can't be used on raised areas since the flame would only affect the highest surface, and that once the last layer of paint is removed, it is easy to scorch the underlying wood if the blow-lamp is held in one place for too long. In addition, the blow-lamp can't be used near glazed panels because of the intense heat. (Both old-fashioned paraffin and modern liquefied gas blow-lamps can be used.)

5. Before commencing, it is a good idea to practise on scraps of painted wood, spreading a fire-proof sheet beneath. Manual dexterity is paramount, because you will heat the paint with one hand, and scrape the melted area with the other. Begin by moving the flame back and forth across the area to soften the paint, turning the torch aside while you actually scrape. Hold the scraper at an angle to prevent the hot paint scraps from touching your hands. If charring occurs, refer to the treatment for burns (see Steps 1 – 6, Page 20).

CHEMICAL STRIPPING

6. Chemical stripping relies on the action of a proprietary paint stripper (liquid or jelly) on the paint, causing it to dissolve and bubble up. It is also ideal for carving, beading and any other areas difficult to reach with a scraper. Spread newspapers under the piece; wear old clothes, rubber gloves and goggles to protect your eyes. Apply the stripper with an old paintbrush, working on a small area at a time. Work in a well ventilated place because the fumes are unhealthy.

Removing opaque paints cont.

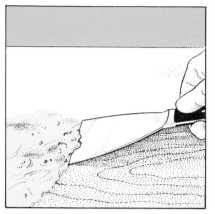

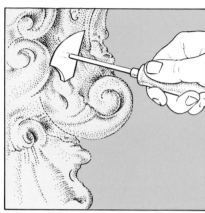

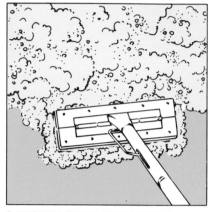

7. When the paint starts to bubble, scrape it off with the scraping knife. You may need several applications of stripper if there are several layers of paint. The paint scraps are caustic and will burn the skin, so after you have finished, wrap them up carefully and throw away. Do not burn. Always be sure to follow the manufacturer's instructions because wood may need neutralizing after some strippers have been used on it.

8. If the piece has many complicated details of carving or beading, or just has many crevices, you will need to use a combination shave-hook, chisel or piece of broken glass with an end taped to protect your hand. Once all traces of paint are removed, rinse the piece with water, then wipe with a rag saturated in denatured alcohol (methylated spirits).

CAUSTIC SODA STRIPPING

9. Caustic soda stripping is spectacular and particularly effective on large pieces. It must, however, be done outdoors with a garden hose handy. Wear goggles, heavy clothes and plastic (not rubber) gloves. Use caustic soda, potash ("lye") or one of the caustic products sold for unblocking drains. Add a handful to 2pt/1 litre of water. (Or make a paste by adding flour and whisking until thick.) Apply with a mop or sponge. Frothing will signify that the chemical is working. If nothing happens, add more water and wait.

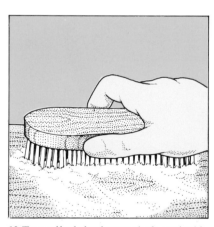

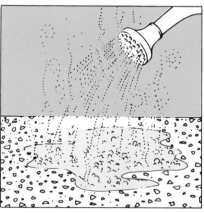

10. To speed both the above methods, scrub with a brush to loosen the paint, but do not let the treated surface dry out. A watering can with a fine rose is perfect for wetting the area. To treat carved areas, lay the object down and remove the paint using a toothbrush and/or blunt knife, taking care not to gouge the wood. Rinse thoroughly, and apply the above paste or liquid to any areas not affected by the first application.

11. A variation on the same technique is to sprinkle caustic soda crystals directly on the surface to be stripped, spreading them evenly. Pour on very hot water, using a watering can with a fine rose sprinkler. The result should be instant effervescence, but beware of the noxious vapours. Repeat if necessary.

12. Rinse the piece very well after both the above caustic soda treatments, otherwise a "bloom" or slight film may appear. Soda will also weaken most glues, so a thorough spray with a garden hose is useful for getting the soda out of cracks and crevices. Finally, rinse with a bucket of clear water neutralized by a cup of vinegar. In addition, it will be necessary to bleach some woods after this process — oak and chestnut will darken, while cherry will redden — and to sand the piece (see Steps 1 – 3 opposite).

Removing clear finishes

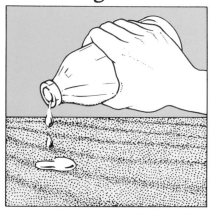

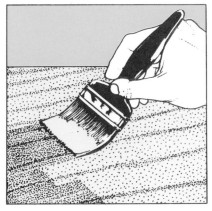

REMOVING FRENCH POLISH

1. French polish must only be removed from a small area at a time. Before starting to work, spread the floor with paper, put on rubber gloves and open the windows. Then apply a drop of denatured alcohol (methylated spirits) to a corner of the piece. Strong liquid ammonia or proprietary paint removers can be used, but the fumes from these are even more unpleasant than those from the alcohol.

2. Rub the finish with a finger-sized piece of fine wool, until a light "gravy" appears. Remember, work with the grain, not across it or in circles. The "gravy" means the polish is yielding; mop it up quickly with absorbent rags, cotton wool, paper towels or toilet paper. The last is probably the best because you can put your gloved fingers in the central hole and unwind lots of it quickly and easily. Continue until the paper or cloth shows no sign of brown stain. Let it dry and go over it again.

REMOVING VARNISH

3. Varnish and shellac removal requires patience because of the number of different types. Work in a well ventilated room, spread newspapers, wear rubber gloves and protective clothing. In an inconspicuous place try the following solvents in this order: turpentine, denatured alcohol (methylated spirits), commercial strippers, acetone, ammonia, caustic soda (or "lye") and a strong borax-and-water solution. Apply with an old paintbrush, then rub or scrape off the old finish using steel wool and/or a stripping knife, working with the grain.

Bleaching and sanding

If, when the wood is bare, there's a stain or the wood seems too dark, it can be bleached. Try commercial wood bleaches, sodium hypochlorite or crystalline oxalic acid. Add crystals to water in the proportions of 1oz/30g to ½pt/0.3 litre. Apply with an old paintbrush. Rinse off with 1oz/3og borax to ½gal/2 litres water followed by a clear rinse. Let dry for 24 hours. An alternative is to add one part .880 ammonia to five parts water, apply with old paintbrush and rinse with one part 100 volume hydrogen peroxide to two parts water. (This will also take the redness out of mahogany.) Be careful — bleaches are strong and some are poisonous.

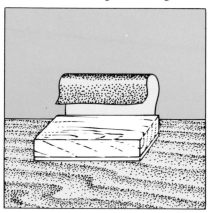

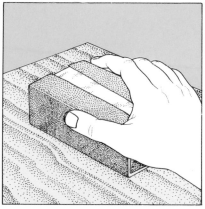

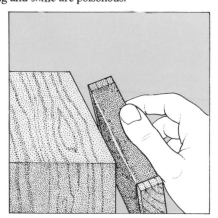

1. Stripping and bleaching will raise the grain of the wood slightly, so a light sanding is necessary. Make a sanding block from a hand-sized piece of cork, rubber, or wood with felt on one side. Wrap the block with abrasive paper.

2. If you have a very large surface to sand use a brick; first wrap in cotton cloth and then with abrasive paper. The weight and size of the brick makes a large job easier. Whichever sized block you use, always sand in the direction of the grain, never across it or in circles.

3. Don't round the corners of the wood, just sand them lightly with fine abrasive paper. First use medium-fine abrasive paper on the sanding block and then a finer grade. When the sanding is complete, the piece is ready to be refinished.

Filling pores

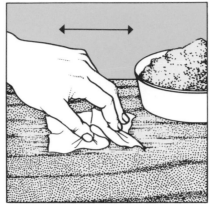

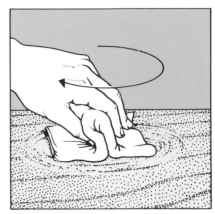

1. In addition to sanding after stripping or bleaching, it is necessary to fill the grain or pores of the wood to get a perfect surface before staining, French polishing and/or varnishing. Do *not* fill before applying a linseed oil, teak oil, beeswax polish or petroleum jelly finish.

Ready-made fillers are available or you can make your own: tint plaster of Paris (unless a "whitened" grain is wanted) with Vandyke brown powdered pigment for use on dark oak, or walnut; use red ochre for mahogany.

2. Dip a damp rag into the tinted plaster and apply it with a circular motion so that it fills the grain. Finish off by stroking with the grain. Allow to dry completely. Make sure pores look and feel sealed — rub your hand across the surface and it should feel smooth. When dry, smooth with very fine abrasive paper, going with the grain.

3. An alternative method, which is ideal for filling the pores before French polishing, is to use powdered pumice: sift it, then moisten a clean cotton pad in denatured alcohol (methylated spirits). Dip the pad into the sifted pumice powder and coat the entire surface using a small circular motion and gentle, even pressure so that you completely cover the grain in every direction, shaking out or folding over the pad as necessary.

Staining

WATER STAINS

1. Mix water stains as directed on the pack, but always start with a light application and test the shade first on a piece of scrap wood — it's easy to apply additional coats to get a darker effect, but very difficult to lighten something that is too dark. Stand the piece on a thick layer of old newspaper. Apply the stain with a clean paintbrush, stroking with the grain. Tilt the object slightly and begin the application at the top so gravity assists spreading. Don't load the brush with too much stain — this causes blotchiness.

OIL STAINS

2. Oil stains are brushed onto raw wood, wiped off and allowed to dry for 24 hours. Sand with abrasive paper, wipe with turpentine substitute and let dry. Repeat for a darker tone. To make your own stain, grind 1-2½lb/450-1100g of artists' pigment (not dry pigment) into 110fl oz/3.125 litres boiled linseed oil. Mix in a drop of turpentine and a few drops of japan drier and apply as above. For a quicker drying stain, grind 1-2½lb/450-1100g of pigment into ⅓ gallon/1.5 litres boiled linseed oil and add ⅔ gallon/3 litres pure turpentine.

HOME-MADE STAINS

3. Home-made stains (see the formulas opposite) achieve the same results as prepared stains but are less expensive. When it's necessary to strain the stain, fit a stocking over an old kitchen wire-mesh strainer. Mix only as much stain as you will need and always add crystals to water until no more dissolve, never the other way round. Always wear protective clothing and rubber gloves, and test the stain on an inconspicuous area first. All of these stains must be French polished, varnished, or waxed afterwards.

Formulas for home-made stains

To stain oak, mahogany and walnut a rich brown, use Vandyke crystals, walnut crystals or potassium permanganate, but use a weaker solution for walnut and mahogany.

Dissolve the crystals in warm water. Apply stain with an old brush, repeating if necessary. Add a drop of .880 ammonia, which fixes the stain to the wood, but take care, the fumes are unpleasant and the fluid stings. Keep stain in a tightly sealed container after adding the ammonia.

Aniline dyes will also stain wood a variety of browns. The dyes come in powder form and are easiest to apply when mixed with water, but they are soluble in turpentine or oil, too. Treat them with care because they are extemely poisonous. Mix Vandyke brown with Bismarck brown or with black for a dark brown stain.

Mix each powder separately in warm water. Add ½tbsp/7ml of glue and a drop of vinegar to each. Mix together to obtain the effect you want; the more water you add, the lighter the stain. Apply with a brush, working as directed opposite.

Green copperas, sometimes called sulphate of iron, gives a blue-grey tone to oak. It will dull the redness in mahogany and, when applied to sycamore, produces a grey tone, becoming what is known as "harewood". However, it is poisonous, so never leave it where children or pets can reach it.

Dissolve the crystals in warm water, which will turn a muddy green. Apply evenly with an old brush, as previously directed. As the wood dries, the effect will gradually begin to show.

To darken oak and mahogany slightly you can use .880 ammonia mixed with water. However, try not to inhale the extremely unpleasant fumes and don't let the liquid come into contact with bare skin. If you can, work outdoors. After an hour's exposure to the air, the mixture will lose its strength, so work quickly or mix a new amount.

To darken mahogany or give a greenish-brown tone to oak use bichromate of potash. Dissolve the deep orange crystals in water until the water will not absorb any more. Dilute if necessary after testing some of the stain in an inconspicuous place and letting it dry. If the result is satisfactory, apply the stain to the rest of the piece with a brush, as previously directed. It is always best to apply stains in daylight, or failing that in a well lit place, but this particular stain has to be applied in daylight to ensure an even spread of colour. The stain itself is a deep orange, but the final results depend on the type of wood.

To "weather" oak, you can use American potash, sometimes known as crude caustic potash. Oak wood treated with this solution will turn a deep brown and the grain blackens.

Dissolve the crystals in water until the water will not absorb any more. Apply the solution to the piece with a paintbrush, as previously directed, then allow to dry.

Fumed oak furniture was popular in the 1920s and 1930s. The following will stain a new piece of wood for use in repairing fumed oak.

Pour some .880 ammonia into a saucer. Put the piece inside an airtight plastic bag with the saucer of ammonia. The fumes will start colouring the wood almost at once. Keep checking the wood until it is the right colour.

To "fume" a larger piece, brush a dilute solution of ammonia and water on the piece, rinsing when the desired effect is achieved.

Protective clear finishes: beeswax

Beeswax is the classic polish for antique furniture, beloved by dealers and collectors everywhere. It can also be used on wood block floors and old-fashioned linoleum, but not on modern vinyl tile floors or furniture with plastic finishes. It gives a lovely soft matt sheen but is slightly tacky and tends to attract dust. By adding some carnauba wax or powdered resin in the proportions one to four, you will get a higher gloss finish and the polish will be harder and less tacky. Purchase bleached beeswax if the polish will be used on light woods; unbleached if it is for darker woods. Apply it after sanding and staining.

1. Use 4oz/100g beeswax to ½pt/250ml of pure spirits of turpentine. Grate the beeswax into flakes using a cheese grater.

2. Put the flakes of wax into a bowl or clean tin and cover with pure spirits of turpentine (*never* turpentine substitute).

3. Put the container into a larger one and pour boiling water into the outer container. Be careful not to get any water on the beeswax and turpentine, and keep the turpentine away from heat.

4. The heat will make the flakes dissolve into the turpentine. To speed the process, stir with a wooden spatula. If the flakes do not dissolve completely just empty the outer container and put in more hot water.

5. Put the liquid into a clean jar or can, but do not put on a lid for 24 hours. Brown polish can be produced by adding dry burnt or raw umber pigments to the liquid before it sets, and mixing well. This gradually darkens the surface it is applied to. Alternatively, you can produce a black polish by adding lamp black.

6. Apply a thin coat of polish to the clean, dry surface and buff with a soft clean cloth. Repeat as often as necessary, remembering that several thin layers are better than the occasional thick one.

Protective clear finishes: natural oils

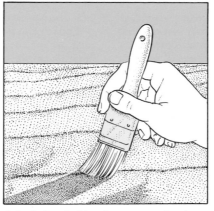

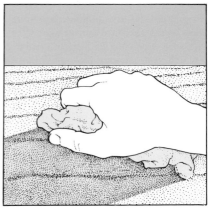

1. Another clear, natural finish which can be applied to bare wood is boiled linseed oil. It imparts a slight sheen, but with successive applications will build up to a pleasing patina. Place boiled linseed oil in a glass or china cup; then put this into a pan of hot water until the oil is warm to the touch.

2. Apply the oil with a clean cotton pad or clean 2in/5cm paintbrush, working in the direction of the grain. Keep applying the warm oil until the wood rejects it — you will notice the excess staying on the surface. Allow to stand for a few hours, wipe off the excess with paper towels and leave the piece until it is completely dry. This will take several days, even in a warm room — the disadvantage of this method. Repeat the whole process if necessary. Finally, rub hard with a soft cotton cloth and then apply a furniture wax if a higher shine is desired. Keep the piece well dusted.

3. Teak oil can be applied to other woods as well as teak; it has the advantages of being quicker drying and more resilient than linseed oil. Apply with a soft cloth or 2in/5cm brush. Wipe off the excess after half an hour and apply a second coat. Rub down 36 hours later, or when dry, with very fine steel wool lubricated with furniture wax. Buff with a soft cloth. Repeat application as necessary. Alternatively, petroleum jelly can also be rubbed into teak and rosewood. Remove the excess after 24 hours and buff with a soft cloth.

Protective clear finishes: varnishes

When applying varnish, work in a warm (70°F/20°C is ideal), clean, well ventilated room, but avoid draughts. Wear clothes of synthetic material and put damp newspapers under the piece to keep the dust down. Varnish brushes are soft, thick and chisel-shaped, oval for larger surfaces. Varnish should be thin, it should not stick when applied, but don't shake or stir it — movement adds bubbles. Seal new wood first with shellac under cellulose varnishes and cellulose under shellac.

1. Apply varnish straight from the can using a brush reserved for this. Clean a new brush in turpentine before use. A clean wire stretched across the varnish tin and wrapped around the sides is ideal for wiping the brush. Don't press the brush against the rim — it causes bubbles.

2. Apply varnish to a square foot or so, then brush back across your first strokes to give an even finish, unless the manufacturer's instructions state otherwise. Drying times vary according to varnish type and weather conditions. Follow directions and never apply the next coat if the previous one is at all tacky.

3. Always sand between coats with very fine abrasive paper or fine steel wool and wipe after sanding with a rag dipped in white spirit or turpentine substitute. For a less hard shine, rub with finest steel wool after the final coat, and apply two coats of beeswax or proprietary furniture wax.

Protective clear finishes: French polish

French polish is the ultimate clear finish, imparting a very high gloss to the surface of sanded wood. You can buy French polish (also called padding lacquer, and sold under various proprietary names). But you can also make your own: Dissolve 8oz/225g shellac, ¼oz/7g benzoin and ½oz/15g sandarac to 2pt/1 litre high quality denatured alcohol (methylated spirits). (Try to get "methylated finish" or methylated spirit white lac, in which case leave out sandarac.) Mix everything in a large tinted glass jar and let it dissolve. Shake the polish well before use.

You can also make a French polish reviver if the surface of a piece has become dull: mix one part linseed oil, one part clear furniture polish, and one part denatured alcohol (methylated spirits) together in a screw-top glass jar and shake well. Another recipe for reviver is: four parts linseed oil, one part terebine (a drying medium), and two parts white vinegar. These, too, should be shaken well together. Use either mixture as often as necessary.

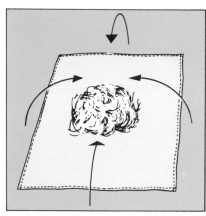

1. First sand the surface until it is perfectly smooth by using finer and finer grades of abrasive paper. Remove all traces of dust with a slightly damp cloth. Then, make a French polishing pad or "rubber" about 3½in/9cm long and shaped to fit your hand. Fold a wad of absorbent cotton into a fine lintless wrapper (a man's cotton handkerchief will do — two will come in handy if the piece of furniture is large). Fold in the opposite sides as shown.

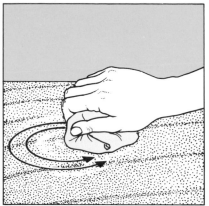

2. Seal the grain of the wood by dipping the pad into fine pumice powder (sieved if necessary). Coat the surface of the piece by working in gradually increasing circles so you go over the grain in every direction. Don't push down on the pad, and shake it out if necessary. To make the pumice powder adhere, add a few drops of the polish. But don't use too much or it will soak into the wood and may cause swelling and shrinking. The surface should be very smooth when dry, but if the pores still show a grain, repeat the process, using a little polish to lubricate.

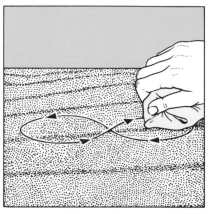

3. Apply the polish sparingly on a clean French polishing pad, in elongated figure-of-eight movements, working with very light pressure. Every stroke of the pad should leave a thin film of polish. Examine your polishing occasionally to make sure that the work is even. Don't polish continuously; give the polish a chance to dry out. After a while you will see that it is having an effect.

4. If sticking occurs, lubricate with a drop or two of boiled linseed oil. After a few layers of polish, little flaws may appear, caused by uneven distribution of polish. These can be smoothed out by buffing. Buy the finest grade wet-and-dry abrasive paper and lubricate it with linseed oil instead of water. Wrap the paper around the wooden or cork sanding block, smear it with linseed or mineral oil, and apply light, even pressure, working with the grain.

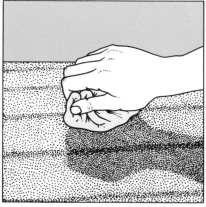

5. Wipe off any excess with a chamois leather or dry natural sponge. Then continue polishing, buffing again if necessary. A high gloss finish will develop. When this seems thick and even the job is almost completed.

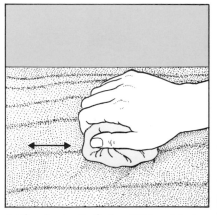

6. After allowing the final coat 24 hours' drying time, you can apply the finishing touch. Make a clean pad and dip it in denatured alcohol (methylated spirits); go over the surface very lightly and very quickly using a figure-of-eight movement first and then using a straight forwards and backwards motion, and more pressure, working with the grain. This should give the surface the desired high gloss.

Preparing for opaque finishes

Sometimes, after stripping a piece, you will be disappointed to uncover unattractively grained or badly disfigured wood. In this instance, there is no choice but to apply a painted-on opaque finish which will completely obscure the tone and grain of the wood underneath. However, the types of opaque finishes are almost infinite, ranging from a thick coat of acrylic paint applied in a hurry, to layers of lacquer applied over several weeks, as described in DECORATIVE FINISHES, pages 47-79.

The choice of paint depends on the desired effect, the painter's skill and patience, and the style of the piece itself. As far as patience goes, bear in mind that the application of all but the simplest plastic-based paint is a time- and nerve-consuming occupation.

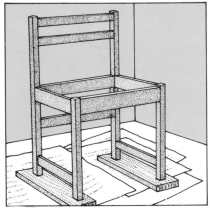

1. Spread newspapers beneath the piece and wear clothes made from synthetic fabrics. Clean a flat 2-3in/5-7cm brush with turpentine substitute or white spirit, then wash it with soap and warm water. Take glass from mirrors, remove top covers from upholstered chairs and lift out drop-in seats or cover with plastic bags taped in place; take off glass table tops (unless the area underneath is not to be painted); remove fittings from chests of drawers, taking the drawers out and standing them face up. Finally stand the piece of furniture on wood blocks so that it does not touch the ground.

2. Sand the piece thoroughly using medium, then fine, abrasive paper wrapped around a sanding block as described in Step 2, Page 39. Dust, wipe with turpentine substitute and let dry. On new or bare wood, it is necessary to treat all knot holes with a proprietary sealer to prevent resin from seeping into successive coats of paint.

3. Prime the piece with an oil-based wood primer (the same shade or one shade lighter than the final topcoat), diluted a quarter with white spirit. Alternatively, use a slightly thinned water-based paint (emulsion). With this and later coats, paint the top of the piece first, then the front, then the sides. Let the primer dry completely. Sand lightly, using fine abrasive paper; dust, then rub down with a soft cloth saturated in turpentine substitute.

4. If you are a perfectionist, seal this primer coat with a layer of shellac, thinned by 50 per cent with the recommended solvent. Follow the manufacturer's instructions or refer to the advice given on the application of varnish (see Steps 1 – 3, Page 43). Then sand again, dust and rub down again with turpentine substitute (white spirit).

5. Next, apply the undercoat, a highly-pigmented paint. It can be thinned to the consistency of cream if desired, but must be well brushed-out. Stroke first one way, then another, with a soft 2in/5cm brush. Let dry, sand lightly, dust and wipe down as before. The piece is now prepared for the application of any opaque paint.

THE QUICKEST WAY TO PREPARE WOOD FOR OPAQUE FINISHES

6. Instead of following the above steps, it is possible to take a less classic approach. Once the wood is sanded smooth after stripping and/or bleaching, apply five coats of ready-mixed synthetic gesso. (Gesso is a plastic-based primer approximating the material used to hide shoddy workmanship in previous centuries, and a perfect base for gloss paints.) Although this sounds more complicated, instead or waiting eight to ten hours for primer and undercoat to dry, each coat of gesso takes only a few hours to set rock hard. Rub down each coat with the finest grade of abrasive paper, aiming for bone-like smoothness. Note: this is also the ideal way to prepare a surface for lacquering (see pages 68-74).

Types of opaque paint

Opaque paint comes in three surface qualities: gloss or high sheen; matt, flat or no sheen; and eggshell or mid-sheen. Gloss and semigloss come as oil-based enamels which dry to a very hard surface in 12-16 hours. Enamels are thinned with white spirit, must be used over a proprietary undercoat, and exaggerate flaws, so immaculate surface preparation is essential. Vinyl (latex) enamel is based on polyacryl resins often referred to as acrylic, and usually comes in a shiny but not brilliant gloss. It may be in gel form for easy application, dries in two to four hours, and is water soluble.

Aerosols or spray paints are pigmented acrylic- or cellulose-based paints, which must also be undercoated. When properly applied they impart a quick and perfect gloss finish and are ideal for coating awkwardly shaped or textured objects, such as tubular or wicker furniture. Their main disadvantage is their expense, because much paint gets wasted during application. In addition, they are difficult to apply evenly.

MIXING PAINT COLOURS

Mixing the desired shade is undoubtedly the trickiest aspect of working with opaque paints. If money is no object, purchase two or more shades, and mix until the desired colour is achieved. But there is an easier and cheaper method of tinting, lightening or darkening and it can be used whenever mixing paints is necessary — even for walls, floors, etc. It will even tint varnishes and shellacs.

First, purchase four tubes of universal stainer — yellow, red, black and blue. These stainers are bound in oil, but can be used to change the colour of oil or water-based paint. What's more they're cheap, highly concentrated and, with a little patience, ensure the most perfect tonalities.

There are other types of tinter: finely ground artists' pigments can be used in the same manner, but they need a protective topcoat of varnish or shellac since they are less durable. Oil colour in tubes can be used to tint oil-based paint. There is a wonderfully large range of shades, although the paints are expensive and slow to dry. Gouache paint can be used, and produces beautiful effects, especially when over the gesso base described in Step 6, Page 45. Acrylics in tubes may also be employed — they are quick to dry, can be used straight from the tube for tinting oil-based paint, or thinned with water for pastel tinting.

1. When striving for pastel shades, add the tinter to white, not the reverse. Squeeze it drop by drop until the desired intensity is achieved. To practise mixing, work with small amounts of paint on white card or artists' palette paper, using a palette knife. Take your time, and mix until the desired shade is reached — the effort will be worth it in the end.

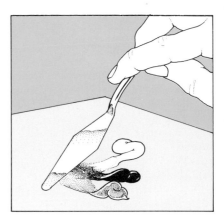

2. To darken or dull a colour, add black or its complement on the colour wheel, i.e. green to red, blue to orange, yellow to lilac, and the reverse. (The latter is an artist's approach to colour mixing, and should not be tried if too confusing.) To achieve interest, three or more colours may be mixed to achieve a precise shade. For example, if a blue-grey is desired, blue paint can be darkened with black, followed by a drop of green or yellow to take the shade toward ultramarine. Additionally, yellow can be warmed with a drop of red, or lightened with white, and raw or burnt umber may add an antiquey shade.

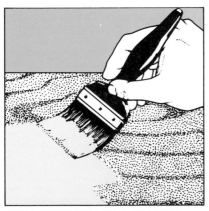

APPLYING OPAQUE PAINTS

1. If using the classic method of priming, sealing and undercoating, follow with a light sanding, dusting and wiping with white spirit. Then apply the first coat of enamel or plastic-based paint. Stir the paint until it is the consistency of cream, unless directed otherwise by the manufacturer. For stirring, an old kitchen whisk is better than a fork, an old fork better than a stick. When the first application is dry, sand again, dust, wipe with white spirit, and apply the final coat.

2. When time is of the essence, and the object has been prepared with coats of synthetic gesso, apply two coats of acrylic paint, thinned with a little water if necessary. Do not overload the brush — paint should never reach the metal ferrule. Sand, dust and wipe down with water-dampened rag between coats, as above, but finish off with a protective layer of transparent polyurethane varnish.

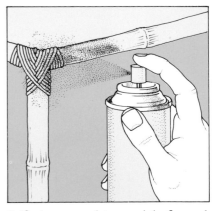

3. If using spray paints, spread the floor and anything else that might be damaged with old newspapers, put on old clothes and tie a handkerchief or mask over your nose and mouth as the fumes can be irritating. Shake the can well and hold 6-8in/15-20cm away from the piece. Press the nozzle and apply an even film in short bursts. The first few coats won't cover, but allow each to dry and apply another. If the paint runs, you are spraying too long in one place.

DECORATIVE FINISHES

If you have no special artistic ability, but want to satisfy a creative urge, here is the ideal outlet. The effects described in this chapter, which have been used virtually since furniture production began, require a steady hand, keen observation and patience, but no special talent. What's more, most of these finishes can be wiped off and begun anew if they go wrong! Decorative finishes are a way of personalizing mass-produced whitewood furniture, enlivening second-hand "finds" and uniting disparate objects in the same room.

ANTIQUING is a trick of the trade from the American colonial period used to give a mellow patina to an opaque finish. The key is subtlety. The finished effect is one of delicate shading and can be combined with spattering or overlaid onto lacquer or stencilling. Tiny paint dots spattered over the surface suggest age or wormholes. A glazed surface can be textured to enhance the antique effect. For a touch of elegance, try lining or striping. A painted line in a contrasting shade accents the contours or gives the impression of mouldings or beadings. If on the other hand you are aiming for a bold and uninhibited effect, like that of children's finger painting, vinegar painting allows plenty of imaginative scope. It is a simple process devised by country craftsmen to imitate the faux graining popular in the nineteenth century. The vinegar medium will take the impression of anything that will produce an interesting texture.

DÉCOUPAGE, the art of glueing cut-out decorations to surfaces, is from the French *couper*, to cut. It probably began in Italy, when frustrated Venetian decorators of the eighteenth century tried to imitate the fashionable "chinoiserie"—oriental-style lacquer more common in northern Europe. Découpage has been called "the poor man's lacquer", but, like lacquer, it was really a hobby of the fashionable classes. The *Ladies Amusement Book* of 1760 gives several motifs to colour and cut. Pillemont, a French engraver, produced the first extensive range of rococo prints to adorn the already ornate furniture of that period. There was a revival in the early 1900s and nursery screens were embellished with romantic prints. Respected découpeurs included Caroline Duer, Carl Federer and Maybelle and Hiram Manning.

FAUX MARBLING was first practised by Mycenean potters 2000 years before Christ and there is a reference to it in a formula from the seventh century A.D. French and Italian artisans used it on windows, shutters and doors where it was impossible to put real marble. Fine examples can be seen at the Borghese Palace in Rome and at Fontainebleau and Versailles in France. In England, Adam used it to decorate pedestals—there are fine ones in the Royal Pavilion in Brighton. Remnants from colonial American floors have also been found. Even if your home is not a palace the most prosaic pieces of furniture can be given importance with this process.

GILDING reflects man's infatuation with gold, which is as old as civilization itself. In ancient Egypt and China the dynastic rulers adorned their temples, palaces, tombs and houses with pure gold. Later Greek and Roman sculptors embellished their statues with the glittering metal, as did many African and South American tribes. In medieval Europe monks used gold to illuminate religious manuscripts.

The fashion for gilt decoration comes and goes. It was at its height in early eighteenth-century France where elaborate rococo interiors were often entirely of gold and not a hint of wood or plaster was visible in an entire room. Even after these excesses were no longer possible craftsmen continued to be inspired by such opulence. When the White House in Washington D.C. was rebuilt after the war of 1812 much of the new furniture ordered from France was of gilded wood.

Now such luxury has virtually disappeared, there are few skilled gilders still practising their craft; many of them are employed chiefly as restorers by museums and art galleries. In precise terms, gilding is the process of covering an object with any kind of metallic finish. Gold leafing, on the other hand, is more specific and means coating a surface with thin sheets of gold, called leaves. Gilding is often used to cover inferior carcase wood as well as to create the illusion of solid gold.

LACQUER was invented by the Chinese before the sixth century B.C.; the Japanese took it up and made their own stylistic changes; the West avidly imported it and imitated it in any way they could. The magnificent appearance of this strange, glossy substance was widely admired and coveted—and puzzled over too, for its precise nature and production remained unknown to its imitators.

The raw material is the sap of the Chinese tree *Rhus vernicifera*, which is extracted by tapping, then purified, mixed with oils and pigments—usually black or red—and patiently applied in numerous thin coats to a basic shape, each coat being rubbed down to a perfectly smooth surface. A damp atmosphere is necessary to harden the successive coats. The piece may then be decorated by carving, inlaying or painting.

Lacquered articles arriving in the West, from the early seventeenth century, consisted of screens, chests, cabinets, and panels which could be applied to a basic framework of European manufacture. These panels were often unsympathetically cut up, without regard for the decoration, for use on smaller cabinets, frames for looking-glasses, and so on. As time went on, the Chinese produced work for export which was not of the best quality. Japan, on the other hand, exported lacquer wares which exceeded the Chinese exports in fine craftsmanship and brilliance of lustre, and this gave rise to the Western view that Japanese lacquer was "the real thing", and that lacquer had originated in Japan. Hence the English term "japanning" to describe the process of imitation that was to spread throughout the West.

The growing demand for Oriental curiosities throughout the seventeenth century, allied to changing international relations and shipping restrictions, encouraged would-be lacquermasters in Europe in their efforts at imitation. There was much experimentation with varnishes; eventually the usual formula included shellac with a spirit solvent. The use of such substances meant that the work had to be done in a warm, dry atmosphere—quite different from the Oriental conditions. Although the standards and finish did not match the results achieved by Eastern craftsmen, by the late 1680s "japanned" furniture had become highly fashionable—and even amateurs tried their hand at it. Bright ground colours were used, as well as black and white, and any decoration with an

"Eastern" look was acceptable, be it Persian, Indian, or the craftsman's idea of Chinese. Those European countries which made little or no lacquer themselves imported it from the others. Extensive suites of furniture were commissioned, and apartments lined with japanned panels; they must have looked splendidly colourful and opulent. The japanning was not durable, however: it cracked, chipped, faded and wore down, and most surviving seventeenth-century examples have been much restored.

The trend continued into the eighteenth century with improvements and stylistic variations. Probably the best-known imitation is the French *vernis Martin*, which was developed by the Martin brothers in Paris and first patented in 1730. In later years the Martins improved their recipe, and their eventual use of copal resin from Brazil probably brought their product closest to the Oriental model. The Martins' work—in particular a certain green they used—was one much admired feature of the rococo style, although several French cabinet-makers were still obtaining and using Chinese lacquer panels, whose glossy black surface and gold decoration accorded particularly well with the elaborate ormolu mounts of the period. Towards the end of the eighteenth century the finer woods – such as satinwood – came into their own and were increasingly appreciated for their polished natural surface; thus japanned finishes on wooden furniture gradually lost favour. But japanning in a different form survived on metal wares.

Japanned metal had been produced from the seventeenth century at Pontypool, in the factory of Thomas Allgood; but various improvements were necessary in both materials and processes before general domestic use was possible. Also associated with japanned metalware was John Baskerville of Birmingham (1706–75), who pioneered various processes and decorative techniques, but is best remembered as a typographer. By the 1770s japanned tinware was widely used in Europe and America—much of it originating in England and France—for all manner of articles such as tea kettles, trays, vases, clock-faces, jardinières, bowls, pots and boxes. The hard, shining surface could withstand heat well. Pontypool ware became a generally used term for all such articles made in England, including the numerous mass-produced items of inferior quality.

Two Allgood brothers left the family factory to start production of hand-painted japanned tinware at Usk in 1763. Pontypool and Usk work was noted for its quality throughout the West, and much was exported; its only serious rival was the work of the Stobwasser family in Germany. *Tôle peinte* was the term for the French equivalent, which tended to be more elaborately and delicately decorated, and the word "toleware" came to be used for similar American products, made mainly in Pennsylvania.

The use of japanning on *papier-mâché*, popularized for small articles by Henry Clay in England from the 1770s, was taken to its fullest extent in the nineteenth century by the firm of Jennens and Betteridge of Birmingham, which made bedsteads, tables, chairs and fireguards, as well as the lesser items, and also exhibited a casing for a pianoforte. This firm specialized in ornamental inlays of mother of pearl in addition to painted decoration, and for a time its wares enjoyed a vogue; but it was forced to close in 1864. By this time both papiermâché and japanned tinware were being superseded by more modern products, and although bright japanned metal kettles, coal-scuttles and buckets continued to retain their place among the possessions of bargees and gypsies for decades to comes, lacquer and its imitations suffered a general decline.

STENCILLING's history is difficult to establish, partly because early stencils were made of perishable materials until the Chinese invented paper around the beginning of the second century A.D. Some experts claim that this process was known 3000 years before Christ in China, whilst others maintain that the first historical accounts are of the primitive Fiji Island women who stencilled geometric designs onto bark cloth through openings cut in dried banana leaves, using vegetable and charcoal dyes. There is also some evidence that the Egyptians may have used stencilling as early as 2000 B.C. to decorate mummy cases. Whatever its origins, stencilling has played an important role throughout history. It was, for example, instrumental in the spreading of Buddhism in China. Religious texts and manuscripts were reproduced by means of stencils and thus made accessible to a greater number of people.

In Japan stencilled silks, fabrics and paper date back to the eighth century A.D. In particular, from the fourteenth century onwards, Nō theatre costumes were decorated with stencilled patterns. Stage costumes were the field of honour for the nation's art; weavers, dyers, painters, gilders all vied to outdo each other. The technique had its heyday in the sixteenth century. The stencils were made from mulberry-fibre paper waterproofed with the juice of persimmons.

The craft reached the West via the trade routes. In Rome, in the first century A.D., Quintilian recommended the use of stencils in teaching boys to write and in 403, Saint Jerome gave similar advice. Imperial rulers such as Justinian, Emperor of Byzantium, and Charlemagne signed state documents with wooden stencils. In medieval times the sacred monogram IHS was stencilled on Church rafters and ceilings in Europe and religious manuscripts were illuminated with the aid of ornamental stencilled capitals.

For the next 300 years stencils played an important part in many areas of everyday life: they were used to reproduce religious pictures and pilgrimage banners, song sheets (popular and religious), ballads and folk tales, illustrated news-sheets providing local history and political squibs and caricatures. Attempts were made to rekindle waning patriotism with stencilled military posters, and popular games like lotto, tarot and dames spread due to the mass production of stencilled boards. In 1688 Jean Papillon invented wallpaper by covering complete walls with stencilled patterns, an innovation which rapidly gained popularity, and which spread to the decoration of furniture, particularly in England and Germany.

In North America stencilled floors were fashionable up till the Civil War. Imagination and improvization were used to compensate for sparse furnishing. Canvas floor cloths, borders for plaster walls, tin boxes, trays portraying flowers, stars, birds and the favourite motif, the eagle and stars. Itinerant stencillers were much in demand until wallpaper took over as the favoured method of decorating walls. Early nineteenth-century ornamental furniture was decorated with stencil motifs and the manufacturer would label the pieces with his name—an early form of advertising. Hitchcock was the best known manufacturer of this period. He was one of the first people to give employment to women, as stencillers. In the 1920s and 1930s Tiffany's extravagant designs adorned the homes of the rich and famous. His creations were imitated by the middle classes but World War Two limited scope for experimentation. But since the 1960s interest in stencilling as a decorative technique has been renewed.

TORTOISESHELLING was developed in response to the popularity of real tortoiseshell, used as an ornamental veneer in the Orient. It was made popular in the West first by Venetian craftsmen, but more importantly by Boulle, Louis XIV's cabinet-maker, who used it as a decorative surface on commodes, desks and table tops, combined with silver, pewter or ormolu.

In the seventeenth and eighteenth centuries the overwhelming fashion for chinoiserie, which had stimulated experimentation in lacquer finishes, also created a vogue for simulated tortoiseshell, or tortoise lacquer, as it was then known. Large pieces of furniture and small decorative objects such as mirror and picture frames were all embellished in this way, and sometimes whole panels, ceilings and cornices were given a tortoise finish. The renderings vary from a naturalistic faux effect to fantastic colour schemes which bear little relation to the natural material.

Antiquing

This technique of subtle shading is used to give a mellow patina to an opaque finish. It may be combined with découpage, distressing or spattering, or overlaid on to lacquer, gilding, striping or stencils. Above all, antiquing requires a good eye. Inspect antique painted furniture and note where it gets worn and where dirt collects. Chair stretchers, table tops, and areas near fittings often appear lighter from constant contact while crevices and mouldings will harbour grime, and appear darkened. Consider also how thickly to apply the mixture — as a rule of thumb, heavy antiquing looks best on rustic pieces, while a finer application suits lighter furniture.

The materials required are: shellac, raw umber artists' oil paint (1 tsp/5 ml of a shade darker than the base coat can be added (optional), or, if the base coat is very light, include ½ tsp/2.5 ml of white flake), a few drops of linseed oil, pure turpentine, clear matt varnish. Supplies will consist of: a glass jar, a stiff old paintbrush, a

1. To begin, isolate the coat of opaque paint with two applications of a clear finish, such as shellac. When dry, rub the final coat with sudsy wet-and-dry abrasive paper.

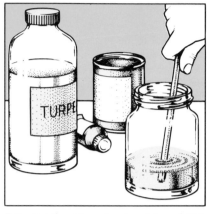

2. Prepare the antique glaze by mixing a dullish shade from 1½ tsp/7 ml raw umber artists' oil paint, 3 tbsp/45 ml pure turpentine, 1 tbsp/15 ml varnish. Shake pigments and turpentine in glass jar, add varnish, and stir slowly.

Alternatively, prepare a more interesting glaze by mixing 1 tbsp/15 ml of a shade darker than the base and ½ tbsp/7 ml raw umber with the varnish and turpentine as above. There are several methods of applying the glaze, as outlined below, but feel free to improvise or combine techniques.

3. "Stroking" or "dragging" relies on applying the glaze with a "ridgy", old paintbrush. Work in one direction only, and do not go back over your strokes, as the overall effect should be distinctly "liney".

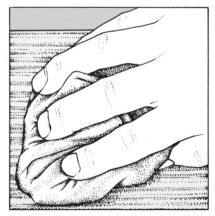

4. Wipe off excess with a piece of old denim, working evenly and quickly, as the formula sets quite quickly. If it dries too fast, add a drop of boiled linseed oil to the above mixture.

5. After the first application has dried, retouch edges, crevices, carvings, anywhere dust and dirt might collect, with the antiquing formula. "Feather" this second application into the first using the brush and piece of fabric so the demarcation is softened. Leave the "antiqued" object for 36 hours, then protect the work with three coats of clear, matt varnish, sanding lightly between coats if necessary.

6. If the glaze looks too dark, lighten it by rubbing the surface very delicately with fine steel wool.

piece of old denim, fine steel wool, finest abrasive paper, a small, real sponge (a make-up sponge is perfect), a 1½in/3.8cm oval sash brush, stencil brush or old paintbrush, stenographer's rubber finger guard and optional mesh screen (for spattering).

First prepare the surface as directed in Steps 1-6, Page 45.

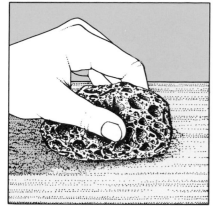

7. While the glaze is still setting, it is also possible to texture even further — it may be daubed with a small piece of real sponge.

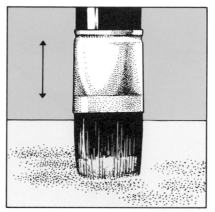

8. It may also be "pounced" or spattered. To pounce, dip an oval sash brush or stencil brush into the antiquing formula, tap the excess out on to a newspaper, then tap or pounce lightly over the surface so the brush bounces along. Cover the entire surface once, then re-pounce edges, crevices and carvings.

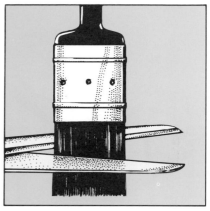

9. Spatters or tiny paint dots can be used to suggest age or worm holes, but should never be large, or evenly distributed. Use a stencil brush, or cut the bristles off an old paintbrush to about 1 in/2.5 cm long.

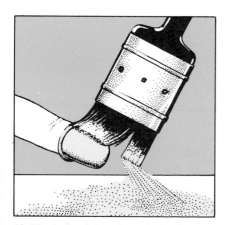

10. Dip the brush into the antiquing formula, and rub your index finger across the bristles to cause spatters (protect finger with a rubber finger guard if desired).

11. To cover a large area, rub the brush over a fine mesh screen — placement of the spatters is crucial, so experiment on a piece of white cardboard before tackling the piece itself. If the effect is unsatisfactory, wipe off the spatters while still wet with white spirit.

12. If the spatters appear too hard, soften the texture by spattering with pure spirits of turpentine. Protect as described in Steps 1-3, Page 81.

Découpage

Découpage, the art of glueing cut-out decorations to wood or metal surfaces, derives from the French word, *couper*, to cut. It should not be confused with collage which means glueing anything to a background and is a fine art technique. Unfortunately, découpage is very susceptible to damage — the glued-on motif loosens and tears, leaving only pieces behind, so the restorer must often find and tint a suitable replacement print. Before commencing the découpage technique itself, make sure that the surface of the object itself is sound, then prepare as directed in Steps 1-6, Page 45.

For découpage, assemble the following tools and materials: aerosol fixative, shellac, denatured alcohol (methylated spirits) vinegar, water-soluble white glue, matt varnish, furniture wax, a knife with replaceable blades, a sponge, a pair of nail-scissors, an old, clean paintbrush, a lintless cloth (or clean, old stockings or tights), wet-and-dry abrasive paper and the finest grade steel wool.

1. If the chosen print is in a book, remove the page carefully. If necessary, run a sharp knife with replaceable blades along the gutter of the book, having first placed a ruler underneath the area to be cut so that the knife does not sever the pages below. If a black-and-white print cannot be removed, a photocopy of the image will do, and can be tinted as suggested above.

2. Carefully select the print so that it is neither too big nor too bold for the surface; small delicate motifs are usually most suitable. The best sources are museum facsimile editions of old books, damaged books with period prints as illustration plates, magazines, old wallpaper books, printed ephemera, catalogues and postcards. Do not cut anything of value. Use already-tinted prints, or for a more authentic effect, shade in black-and-white prints using soft pencils or watercolours.

3. Spray the print with a protective coat of an aerosol fixative, or apply a home-made version mixing shellac and denatured alcohol (methylated spirits) in equal amounts, using a varnish brush.

4. Should the print be too thick to lie flat on the surface of the object, a layer or two may have to be removed. In this case, wet the back of the print with a sponge dipped in a solution of three parts vinegar to one part water, and gently peel off as many layers as necessary. (This same mixture can also be used to soften glue holding a fabric backing.)

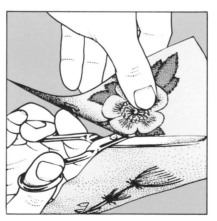

5. Once the print has been removed, tinted (if desired) and fixed, it can be cut out. Use sharp, well-made nail-scissors (those with a slightly curved blade) about 3in/7.6cm long, holding the scissors in one hand while turning the paper to feed the scissors with the other. Use the tips of the scissors for awkward corners. This method of cutting causes the edges to turn under very slightly, and makes glueing easier.

6. Apply a water-soluble white glue with a resin base to the back of the print, using an old, clean paintbrush, starting in the middle and working outwards.

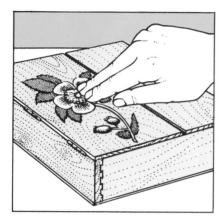

7. Let the glue dry until tacky before positioning the print on the object.

8. When the glue has dried for 24 hours, give the print a protective coat of one part denatured alcohol (methylated spirits) and one part shellac.

9. Let this coat dry for 24 hours, then rub it down very lightly with the finest grade steel wool.

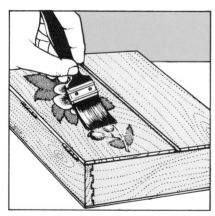

10. Dust with a lintless cloth (old, clean stockings or tights will do) and apply a matt varnish that has been thinned with the recommended solvent. Stroke it on, working in one direction. Let it dry and apply ten more coats, allowing each to dry thoroughly before applying the next. This is imperative or a very irregular surface will result. Apply more coats if necessary – you should not be able to feel the print at all.

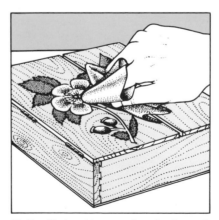

11. Should the object somehow be damaged while the varnish is being applied, or should the varnish cause problems, remove the last coat of varnish with the solvent, let it dry, and begin again.

12. Finally, sand the surface with finest wet-and-dry abrasive paper, then smooth with the finest steel wool. Dust and apply a coat of furniture wax, working in small circles until the desired sheen is achieved.

Distressed paintwork

The following procedure can be applied to darken wood, as age might, and is used as the undercoat beneath the final coat of an opaque finish.

The following materials are needed: abrasive paper, No.8 hog bristle brush, wooden meat skewer, piece of towel or terry cloth, burnt umber japan paint, japan drier, turpentine, shellac, flat or gloss oil-based paint, water-soluble liquid paint remover and high gloss varnish.

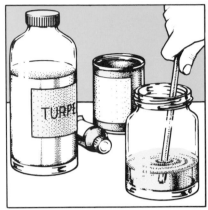

1. Mix one volume burnt umber japan paint to one-tenth volume japan drier and one-half volume turpentine. Apply one coat of the above stain formula to raw or painted wood which has previously been sanded lightly. Let dry for 24 hours and then seal with two coats of diluted shellac.

2. Apply two coats of flat or gloss oil-based paint to the object, allowing each application to dry thoroughly. Sand the final coat with abrasive paper so that the brushstrokes are removed.

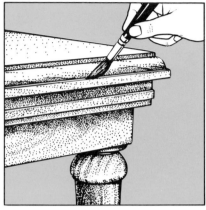

3. Pour liquid paint remover into a flat container and load the tip of the No.8 hog bristle brush. Deposit the paint remover in small patches on the edges, mouldings, carvings of the piece, in fact anywhere you would expect to see the signs of wear.

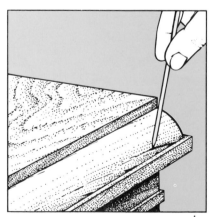

4. Use a wooden skewer or similar pointed instrument to push the paint remover into cracks and crevices along the moulding.

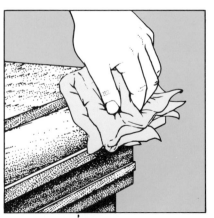

5. When the paint begins to "wrinkle", rub those areas with a piece of towelling in order to lift the paint and remover, and stop the action of the remover before it gets through the brown stain underneath. Do not wipe – use a daubing motion.

6. Rinse off any remaining paint remover with water. When dry, protect the distressed paintwork with a coat of high gloss varnish and proceed to "antique" it (Steps 1-12, Pages 50-51) if you like.

Faux bois

Faux bois is a French term which means false wood, and should be distinguished from the coarser wood grainings of the house painter. Faux bois is used to embellish furniture and small objects, and can be painted on in confined patches imitating marquetry or parquetry, or in larger areas such as drawer fronts and desk tops to give the impression of expanses of a precious wood.

The essence of the process rests on a delightful quirk of nature – the various species of woods have qualities peculiar to them, each one differing in grain, pore and shade. The photographs opposite pages 16 and 17 are a demonstration of this and can be used as a reference when attempting this decorative finish. However, it is not necessary to follow nature exactly, as long as the essential position of the knots followed by the rhythm of the surrounding grain is maintained: the flow of the grain emanates from the knot, gradually straightens and enlarges, and slowly curves again toward another knot.

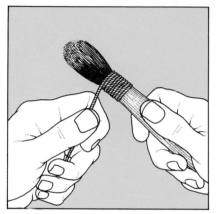

PREPARING THE BRUSHES

1. To execute faux bois expertly, at least two paintbrushes have to be prepared. For the wood knots, bind the end of a round, stiff-bristle brush with strong string about 1in/2.5cm down from the ferrule. Then chop the brush to 1½in/3.8cm length using a single-edged razor and a hammer.

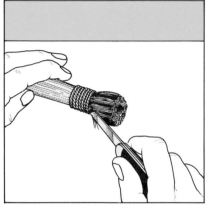

2. Next, the round brush has to be "cored": force a sharp knife into the middle as deeply as possible and turn it around, removing about one-third of the bristles in the middle of the brush. Use tweezers to remove the last stubborn bristles. Then lay the brush on a board so that clumps of the outer bristles can be removed near the ferrule, so that the remaining bristles are of unequal lengths.

3. The brush is then rotated on a flat surface, so that the remaining clumps of bristle can be cut off at the ends in a slanting direction. Finally, the bristles are turned and twisted over a piece of wet carborundum to round their ends. If envisaging several wood knots of several sizes, prepare various sizes of round brushes in the same manner as above.

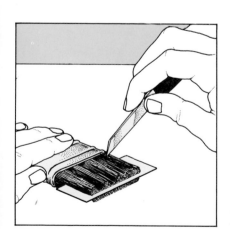

4. To achieve a convincing wood grain, several flat, stiff-bristle brushes of differing widths are used. These too must be chopped off to a length of 1in/2.5cm, using a razor and hammer as in Step 1. The bristles are then divided in the middle with a piece of cardboard or a steel comb, and on one side of this divider, four or five clumps of bristle are cut out near the ferrule using a sharp, pointed knife or nail-scissors.

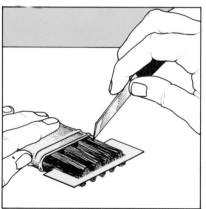

5. On the other side of the divider, additional clumps of bristle are removed, alternating with those already removed. In addition, there must be a small, bristleless space on either side of the clumps.

6. The ends of the bristles are then cut in an irregular slanting way, and the longest remaining hairs ground on wet carborundum.

Applying faux bois

Before starting the actual painted finish, it is advisable to make a pencil sketch of the desired wood pattern. The prepared brushes should be tried out on heavy brown paper, after being dipped into India ink. Other tools required are several pointed sable brushes, No. 3 and No. 6, and a steel comb.

First prepare the surface as directed in Steps 1-6, Page 45.

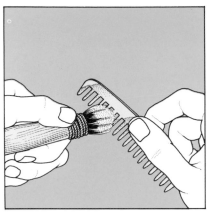

1. Fill the round knot brush with the medium (see Steps 1-5, Page 67), rub it out on paper until half dry and then gently push the brush against a steel comb in a slanting direction to spread the hairs.

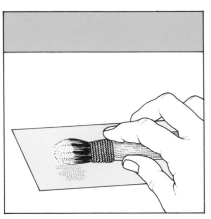

2. Next, round the points of the bristles by rolling them on a piece of paper.

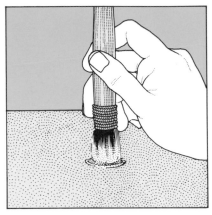

3. The lightly loaded brush is then placed on the surface to be painted and rotated using a slight pressure, thereby producing a knot with an open middle. Dot these knots at irregular intervals around the surface to be wood-grained. Obviously, if the surface is large, a variety of knot sizes will add a considerably more realistic effect.

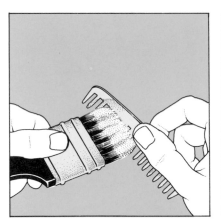

4. The rings around the knot are added next, using the flat, divided brush. Load the brush with the paint and press it against the steel comb to separate the bristles.

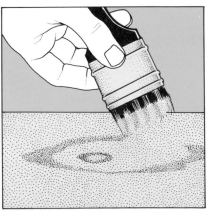

5. Hold the brush at the ferrule between your thumb and fingers, and begin the rings around the knots just completed. The stroke at the top of the knot begins with the brush held in a slanting position with the palm turned toward the surface. A similar stroke is used for the bottom of the knot. Aim for the grains to be more widely spaced the further they are from the knot.

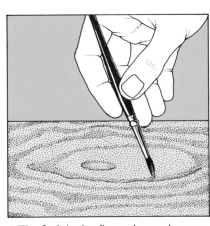

6. The final (optional) step is to paint more pronounced grains using a pointed No.3 or No.6 sable brush. The grain enlarges and widens at the top of the knot and narrows and tightens at the side, as the illustration shows. Additionally, the side of the brush can be used to make thicker lines, which can also be smudged with the graining brush to make them more realistic.

Faux marble

This fake marble finish is applied over three tinted background coats which have been sanded smooth using very fine wet-and-dry abrasive paper and a soapy solution. If a flat paint is used for these base coats, protect them with two coats of thinned shellac. Sand with finest abrasive paper between coats as it is imperative that the surface to be marbled should be satin smooth. Assemble all or some of the following tools and try out each of the techniques on a piece of scrap white cardboard to see which you feel most at ease with. It may help to have a picture or a piece of marble nearby for reference and inspiration.

Possible tools for the application of faux marble are: a stiff brush turkey feathers, two oxhair brushes (¼in and ½in/7mm and 13mm), 12in/30.5cm squares of cheesecloth, small, coarse natural sponges, and/or crumpled newspaper.

First prepare the surface as directed in Steps 1-6, Page 45.

1. Make a flatting oil from one volume boiled linseed oil mixed with six volumes turpentine or paint thinner. Next make the "floating paint": mix one volume japan paint with a solution of equal parts of flatting oil (as above) and mineral spirits, to the consistency of water. Dilute an equal amount of the base shade. Brush the surface first with some flatting oil then immediately with the diluted base shade.

2. Dip any "tool" from the list above into mineral spirits, and then apply the floating paint while the surface is still wet, following the instructions for any of the six methods below.

WAYS OF MARBLING

3. The oxhair brushes, each dipped into a different shade of floating paint, are held at the top of the handles and used as one brush. Pat on, letting the paints mingle.

4. Each 12in/30.5cm square of cheesecloth is twisted into a coil and then each section of the coil can be loaded with a different floating paint. It is rolled over the surface repeatedly. Reload each surface as necessary.

5. Clipped feathers are dipped into the mineral spirits, combed with a fine comb and then each loaded with a different floating paint and used on the broad side to paint on the hue.

6. Each group of bristles on the clipped brush is loaded with a separate floating paint and is then turned and twisted over the surface.

Faux marble cont.

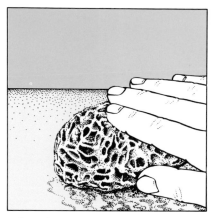

7. Several small natural sponges can be loaded with paint and then rolled over the surface.

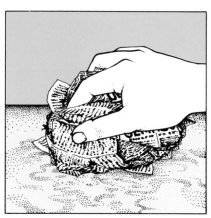

8. Newspaper can be crumpled up, saturated with paint and dabbed over the surface.

9. Any of these methods will produce interesting and irregular effects, but if they are not satisfactory, or if the surface dries too fast, try dipping a small natural sponge into turpentine or paint thinner and squeezing it over the surface. Be careful not to flood it, as this will cause many of the effects to dissolve. If the spirit collects in pools, dab up the excess with absorbent cotton or cotton wool. All areas that resemble marble can now be left to dry, but inadequately decorated areas may need further treatment.

10. Touch up with another clipped feather, crumpled newspaper or cheesecloth dipped again in the floating paint.

11. An additional, final touch is veining. (In its natural state marble has veins which are caused by impurities.) To simulate these, dip a fine brush into the mineral spirits and then a dark shade of japan paint, and hold as shown. Paint fine irregular veins over the surface. This should be done when the surface is still slightly damp, and the thickness of the stroke should be varied.

12. When satisfied with the marbling and veining allow to dry for several days and then protect with two coats of thinned gloss varnish.

Faux porphyry

This special effect is a variation on the spattering technique used in ANTIQUING, Steps 1-12, Pages 50-51, but the result looks much more stone-like. It is particularly effective on areas which you might expect to find in stone, such as table tops. The process involves the application of a base coat followed by one or more contrasting spattering shades.

The following materials will be required: flat white paint, raw umber, yellow ochre and black-and-white japan paints (optional), japan drier, fine grade abrasive paper, pure spirits of turpentine, white cardboard, a stenographer's rubber finger guard, a block of wood, a coarse-bristled brush and optional metallic powders and gold size.

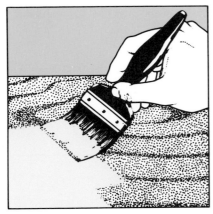

1. Prepare the surface as directed in Steps 1-6, Page 45, then apply two coats of the following grey-beige base hue: six volumes flat white paint, one volume raw umber and one volume yellow ochre. Sand lightly after application, using the finest abrasive paper to remove traces of the brushstrokes.

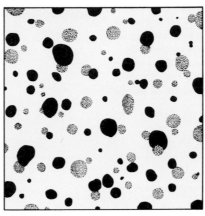

2. Japan paints are used for the characteristic spatters of faux porphyry, and mixed with the following values in mind. The dominant spatter hue should contrast with the base hue given above, i.e. be of a lighter or darker value. If a second shade spatter is desired, this should contrast with the first; in other words if the first spatter was a dark brown, the second spatter might be a pale beige.

3. For each spattering shade, mix one volume japan paint, three volumes pure spirits of turpentine and one-tenth volume of japan drier. Dip a short, coarse-bristled brush halfway into the first spattering hue and rap the side of the ferrule of the brush on a wooden block as the brush is swung over the surface – this will release largish spatters. It is advisable to experiment first on a sheet of white cardboard until you have some control of the technique. Clean the brush in white spirit if a second spatter shade is to be applied.

4. For the second application of finer spatters, run your index finger (protected with a stenographer's rubber finger guard) slowly over the bristles of the brush so that an even spray is directed to the surface below. If the desired effect is reached, stop there, but if you want a richer effect, do a third fine spatter in a markedly contrasting tone, such as a dull yellow or red.

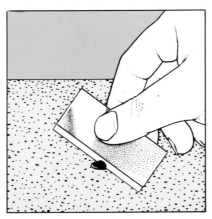

5. If a large or unwanted spatter occurs accidentally, scrape it off when dry using a single-edged razor blade, taking care to remove just the spatter without damaging the base coat. Re-spatter this area once the unwanted spot is removed.

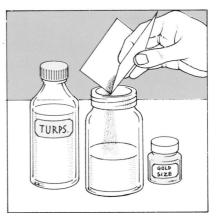

6. The final, optional touch, is a fine gold spatter. Applied as in Step 4 above, it is prepared from: one-quarter volume rich gold metallic powder, one volume gold size and one-quarter volume pure spirits of turpentine. This can be further enhanced by black or white spatters depending on the desired effect. Finally, protect the surface with two coats of clear varnish, applied as directed in Steps 1-3, Page 81.

Gilding

If you are fairly skilled with your hands, there is no reason why you shouldn't attempt to restore small areas of damaged gilding. The instructions on the following pages will enable you to tackle all but the most extensively damaged pieces. However, before beginning any gilding process, it is imperative that the surface should be in perfect condition. To restore damaged wooden surfaces, see pages 20-24.

Gilding is a general term for the process of covering an object with any kind of metallic finish and, like veneering, is often used to cover inferior carcase wood. Gold leafing, on the other hand, is more specific and means coating a surface with thin sheets of gold, called leaves. Certainly, the easiest way to achieve a gilded finish is to use metallic powders, which are far cheaper and much easier to work with than any of the various types of gold leaf. However, powders are not suitable for fine pieces of furniture or picture frames — these have usually been gold-leafed.

When restoring a gilded object, it is important to ascertain what kind of gilding has been employed. Surfaces treated with gold paint or metallic powders will generally be dull and rough. Gold leaf will look much shinier — gold does not tarnish — though burnished water-gilded surfaces will have much more of a shimmer than oil-gilded gold leaf. Also, surfaces which have been gold-leafed will often show vestiges of the dull red ground where the leaf has worn or been damaged. When restoring by either method, it is advisable to treat only the surface which was previously gilded — small highlights are much more effective than large expanses.

Gilding with metallic powders

If you simply wish to introduce some shimmer, the process outlined below using metallic powders is far cheaper though not as authentic as the gold-leafing methods that follow. Purchase good quality metallic powders — these are pulverized metals which come in a tantalizing array of shades from palest silver to darkest bronze, with lots of golden tones in between. They can be used to highlight already painted areas or used for lining, spattering or with stencils as described below.

Prepare the surface as suggested under OPAQUE FINISHES, page 45, i.e. with undercoat of flat or mid sheen oil-based paint. For background hue, it seems that the rich, dark end of the spectrum looks best with metallics, although they have also been used with white and pastels for centuries. Whatever your choice, protect the ground with a coat of thinned shellac or varnish so any mistakes can simply be wiped off. Rub this down with fine steel wool, or wet-and-dry abrasive paper, and wipe with a clean rag moistened with white spirit. Then apply a coat of clear gloss or semi-gloss varnish. Assemble the following tools and supplies: metallic powders, flat or mid sheen oil-based paint, shellac, clear gloss or semi-gloss varnish, white spirit, fine steel wool, wet-and-dry abrasive paper, sable brush, denim or velvet cloth, or chamois leather and cotton wool swabs.

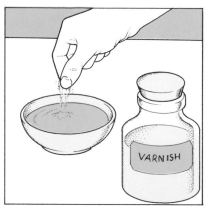

PAINTING

1. When the undercoat is dry, mix powders with thinned varnish and apply with fine sable brush to areas which are to be highlighted – the "gold" will look floated on. Use this treatment on top of areas which are already hand-painted, lined or striped, over stencils or turned chair legs and backs.

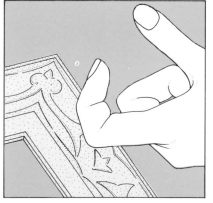

STENCILLING

2. Alternatively, for a very flamboyant look, use the powders with stencils. After preparing the stencil as directed under STENCILLING (see Steps 1-6, Page 76), apply a coat of clear gloss or semi-gloss varnish. Leave the varnish to dry until there is just a touch of the characteristic stickiness or "tack" left — the cut stencil should stick very slightly to the varnished surface.

3. Tip a bit of the metallic powder into a jar lid or shallow saucer. Wrap your index finger in a small piece of denim, velvet or chamois leather, so there are no creases, and dip the covered finger into the powder. Rub finger lightly on a piece of paper towel to remove excess.

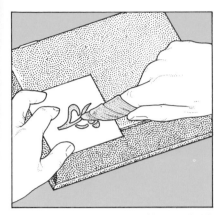

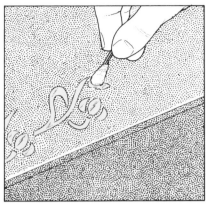

4. Then daub over the cut area of the stencil with the powdered fabric. Work from middle to side so there is less powder toward the edges of the design. Try not to let the powder slip under the stencil — a sloppy edge will result. Obviously, if working with more than one powder, keep the stencil in place, and use clean fabric and saucer for each metallic shade applied.

5. When the motif is complete, carefully lift the stencil and move it along to the next spot. Repeat process until the design is complete.

6. If ragged edges appear, remove excess powder with a cotton wool swab dipped in white spirit, or after drying, scrub away the blotch with mild abrasive on a cotton swab. Leave varnish and powders to set for 24 hours, then gently wash the surface with soapy water to remove excess powders. Protect with a thinned coat of clear gloss or semi-gloss varnish, tinted with a little of the base shade for a less garish effect.

Water gilding

Water gilding produces a rich, burnished effect, though patent gold leaf (see Steps 1-12, Pages 65-6) is easier to lay.

To prepare the surface, assemble the following materials: gold size (a fine clay sometimes called bole, available in several shades, although deep red is most commonly used), and rabbit skin glue grains. Supplies will consist of: purified water, wire strainer, nylon stocking, flat sable brush, spoon, finest abrasive paper, two china cups, pan of hot water, palette knife or paring knife. Avoid wearing wool or rayon because of their static-producing properties.

1. Pour 1 cup/0.3 litre cold purified water into a tall glass. Add ½oz/14g rabbit skin glue grains. Stir with a spoon and let stand for 8 hours.

2. Place the glass in a pan of hot (but not steaming) water and stir the mixture well until the glue granules dissolve. Keep this mixture warm by adding hot water to the pan as necessary.

3. Place 1tbsp/15ml creamy gold size into a china cup, add 3tbsp/45ml warm glue solution and stir well. If necessary, use fingers to push all the size off the spoon.

Water gilding cont.

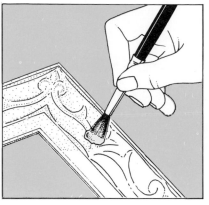

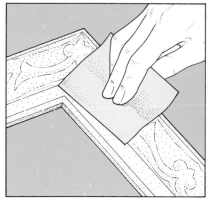

4. Strain this mixture into another china cup by letting it run through a small wire kitchen strainer covered with a nylon stocking.

5. Apply the strained mixture in small, even strokes to a dust-free object using a flat ⅝inch/15mm brush, stroking in one direction. Don't wipe the excess from the brush on the edge of the cup — use the newspapers. Let it dry for 30 minutes, then apply five or six more coats, allowing at least the same time between each coat.

6. Smooth with the finest abrasive paper after the third and sixth coats, then dust well before applying next coat. Sand the final coat with a very gentle pressure, trying not to rub through the red coats or the gold leaf will not adhere. Should you remove the red, be sure to touch up the area with the red size mixture. Next apply gold leaf as below.

Applying gold leaf

To apply gold leaf, the following materials and supplies are required: book of loose gold leaves, gilder's tip (brush) and gilder's cushion, curved agate burnisher, camel-hair dusting brush, plus purified water, denatured alcohol (methylated spirits), cotton wool or cotton wool swabs, talcum powder, scissors, round sable brush, palette knife or paring knife, and old newpapers.

Though usually applied in water gilding, gold leaf can also be applied over the oil-based size used in oil gilding (see Steps 1-3, Page 65).

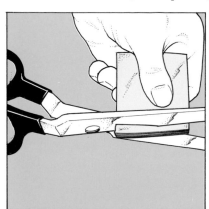

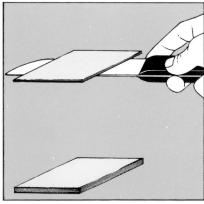

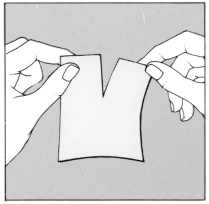

1. First cover the work surface with old, clean newspapers, then dust your fingers with talcum powder to prevent them sticking to the leaf. Cut off the binding edge of the leaf book using sharp scissors, rubbing the cut edges afterwards with your fingers to smooth any crumpled areas.

2. To lift the cover from the book of leaf, use a small, sharp knife with a 4in/10cm blade; there should be tissue underneath protecting the top leaf. Slip the knife under the first four leaves and lift them away from the book.

3. Take the first four leaves in turn, keeping them between the tissue, and tear them very slowly in half, working with about ¼in/7mm at a time. Then tear these pieces in half again. Do not cut — you'll crimp the edges. Keep the resulting four pieces stacked away from the main book, moving them by slipping the knife under the bottom tissues. These small pieces will be used for leafing small areas. (When leafing very highly carved surfaces, it may be easier to apply leaf which has been torn into strips rather than smaller squares.)

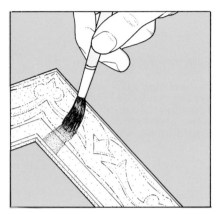

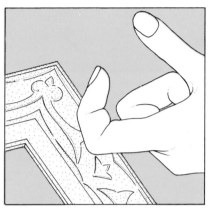

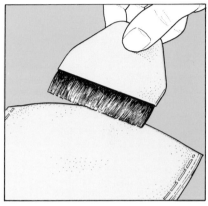

4. Mix "gilder's liquor" in a china cup: 15-25 per cent denatured alcohol (methylated spirits) to 75-85 per cent purified water. Dip the round sable brush into the liquor and brush this on to the spot where the leaf will go. Try to make the area wet with a single stroke; re-wet only when the first application is thoroughly dry.

5. When the liquored area becomes tacky, lay down the loose end of the leaf first. To test for tackiness, touch the area with the knuckle of a bent finger — a clicking sound means that the area is ready to be leafed.

6. To pick up the leaf, move a gilder's brush, referred to as a gilder's tip, lightly across a gilder's cushion to magnetize the hairs.

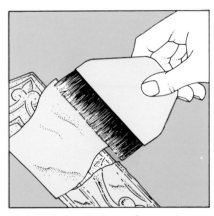

7. Begin gold leafing the large areas first. Don't touch a sized surface with anything other than gold leaf. Pick up the first leaf in the book by laying ¼in/7mm of the tip over the leaf, which will be attracted to the tip. If necessary, transfer tip and leaf carefully to other hand.

8. Leaf small and/or intricate areas with the torn pieces in the separate pile, applying it in the same way.

9. Lay pieces onto the surface one by one, overlapping them ⅛in/3mm as you go, working from the top of the object towards you and tilting the work surface slightly if possible. Lower each successive piece with the gilder's tip, but do *not* let the tip or your fingers touch the sized area. If the leaf crumples, re-magnetize the tip and pick up another piece of leaf before the sized area dries out. Note that if the size gets on to the wrong area and is left uncovered by leaf, it will dull the leaf already applied.

Applying gold leaf cont.

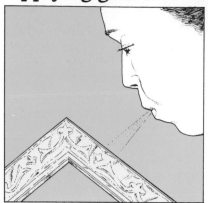

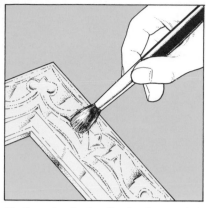

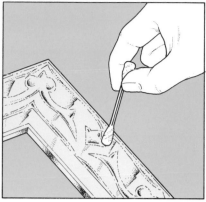

10. If a drop of size should get trapped under the leaf and make a bulge, blow on the bulge to force the excess out. Avoid the temptation to press it out using the brush or fingers.

11. Once the sized surface has been entirely covered by leaf, use the camel-hair dusting brush to remove the loose bits of leaf. If a bare spot is exposed after dusting, tear a bit of leaf to the approximate size and apply as before, using a more diluted liquor — one part alcohol to seven parts purified water.

12. Don't touch a newly-leafed surface for 12 hours; after that, polish with a cotton wool pad or the end of a cotton wool swab, but don't rub very hard or you'll disturb the leaf. If a high gloss is required, burnish as below.

Burnishing or polishing gold leaf

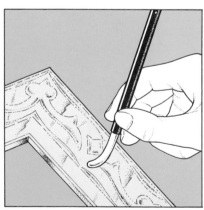

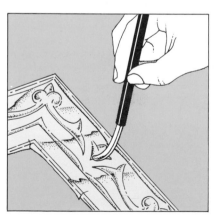

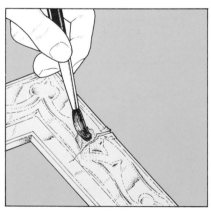

1. To achieve a high gloss, wait at least 24 hours after the final rubbing, then polish the gilded surface with a curved agate burnisher. This is a polished piece of agate fixed to a wooden handle, replacing the dog's tooth used for the same purpose for centuries.

2. Grasp the burnisher near the agate tip and rub the broad curve of the tool back and forth in left-to-right strokes or small circles, depending on the area in question.

3. Work slowly to avoid dull, unburnished lines between strokes. If any of the laid leaf tears or is damaged in any way, relay a new piece with the diluted liquor described above and burnish it immediately.

Oil gilding and applying patent leaf

Oil gilding is a highly recommended method for beginners. To start, follow the instructions in PREPARING FOR OPAQUE FINISHES (see Steps 1-6, Page 45). Then assemble the following tools and supplies: a book of 20-25 leaves of patent leaf, orange shellac and methylated spirits (denatured alcohol), oil-based size, a ⅝in/15mm sable brush, a paring or palette knife, scissors, steel wool, and a china cup.

Patent gold leaf is ideal for flat surfaces and simple convex or concave shapes. It is less difficult for beginners to apply than loose leaf, because the edging paper can be handled with the fingers. The following materials are required: a book of patent gold (or silver) leaf and gold metallic powder (optional).

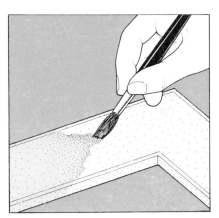

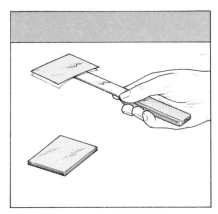

OIL GILDING

1. After the final smoothing and dusting of the gesso surface, apply a sealing coat made from two parts orange shellac and one part denatured alcohol (methylated spirits).

2. Wait two hours or until dry and apply another sealing coat. Wait again and apply a third and final coat. Smooth between coats and after final coat with steel wool to remove brushstrokes which will mar the final surface. Finally, dust the surface as before. Remember that the shellac mixture must not touch the parts which are to be burnished.

TO APPLY PATENT LEAF

3. Open the book of leaves and remove four leaves plus their backing, one by one, using a kitchen paring knife or palette knife. Place on the working surface with gold side upward, but be sure to touch only the margin of the tissue with your fingers.

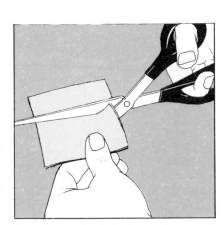

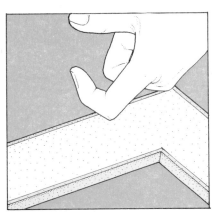

4. Cut leaves to the desired size and shape with sharp scissors, placing the cut pieces near the object to be leafed.

5. Pour ¼ cup/0.05 litre of quick-drying oil-based size into a china cup; apply it evenly with ⅝in/15mm sable brush, sizing only the area which you hope to cover with gold leaf in one hour — probably only 2-3in/5-8cm when beginning.

6. Test for tackiness by touching sized area quickly with a knuckle. A click means the size is ready to be leafed.

Applying patent leaf cont.

7. Slide the knife carefully and slowly under a leaf edge, picking it up by the tissue margin; turn it upside-down, placing the gold side down on the sized area.

8. Rub a finger over the back of the tissue to press the leaf underneath into position.

9. Carefully lift the tissue off and position the next leaf in the same way, letting it overlap the first leaf about ⅛in/3mm.

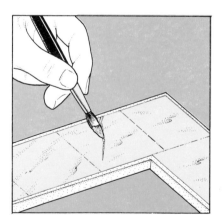

10. Should the leaf crack upon application, patch as in water gilding (see Step 11, Page 64), using instead the oil-based size mixture given in Step 5 above. Incidentally, cracking is sometimes a desired effect in itself, so if you seem adept at laying cracked leaf, accept it — it imparts a more "antique" effect.

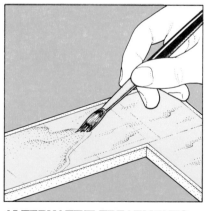

ALTERNATIVE TREATMENTS

11. Slightly cheaper silver leaf will give a similar effect to gold leaf, if varnished over. Varnish is not usually recommended over gold leaf, although it can be employed to protect areas that will be subjected to a lot of use, such as chair legs.

12. For a very glittery effect, sprinkle gold metallic powder on to your first finger and blow the powder on to a varnished and leafed surface. Try to work as evenly as possible, trying it out on an area of varnished newspaper first.

Glazing

This gives a texture similar to ANTIQUING, but the effect is softer and more contemporary. It can be applied to any painted surface. The piece to be glazed should have the usual smooth coats of flat, oil-based paint, applied as directed under OPAQUE FINISHES, Steps 1-6, Page 45.

1. To prepare the surface for the glaze, mix six parts white spirit with one part boiled linseed oil. Wipe the entire piece with this flatting oil.

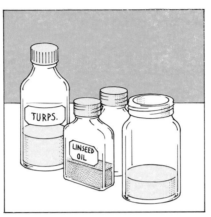

2. The glaze itself can be shiny or matt, and more or less transparent, according to the amount of white pigment it contains. It can be purchased as a thick golden liquid or white cream, or can be made as directed below. Either way, when applied it should appear transparent, unless tinted. To make a glazing liquid, mix one part linseed oil, one part turpentine, one part drier, and optionally, one part whiting. This may be thinned with white spirits, bearing in mind that the thinner the glaze, the faster it will set.

3. Purchased or home-made glaze is tinted with universal stainers or artists' oil paints. Squeeze a blob of the desired shade into a dish or pan, add a drop of white spirit to dissolve it, then add a cupful of the thinned glazing liquid. Stir well and test on a piece of white cardboard. If a softer shade is desired, thin with more glazing liquid.

4. To apply the glaze, take a small amount on the end of a large paintbrush and smooth it lightly over the entire surface. The effect should be "liney" or striated; if the result is undesirable, rub off with a rag saturated with white spirit. However, if the soft dragged texture is pleasing, leave it to dry for two days, then protect as directed in Steps 1-3, Page 81.

OTHER TEXTURES

5. In addition, the mixture can be further textured: sponging is carried out while the flatting oil is still wet. Apply a light glaze immediately after the oil, and texture with bunched-up rags, newspapers, or an old sponge, patting lightly to keep the effect as subtle as possible. If the glaze is drying too quickly, add a teaspoonful or so of boiled linseed oil; if it is setting too slowly, add a drop of proprietary drier.

6. After the initial sponging, another or a deeper shade can also be introduced. Apply this second coat with a larger-grained sponge which will give a sharper texture, to contrast with the underlying mottle. If the difference is too striking, add more thinner to the second shade. At this point, you may stop or proceed to pouncing with an old brush or stencil brush (see Step 8, Page 51). Spattering (see Steps 9-12, Page 51) can also be incorporated after the initial glazing; but bear in mind that this produces a dramatic result and should be used sparingly.

Lacquer

There are three types of lacquered finish: lac, shellac and varnish. Lac is obtained from the sap of the poisonous Oriental tree, *rhus vernicifera,* and is refined to produce seed or grain lac, a crude, granular substance which can be refined several more times to give lacquer of varying degrees of purity, finally yielding flake lac, a glossy but brittle lacquer.

Shellac is derived from the hardening secretions of insects which swarm on trees in India and Thailand. This substance is melted, purified and chipped into small pieces, sold as orange flake or French shellac. A bleached shellac is also available. Both types dry to a clear surface with a slight orange peel effect. They are soluble in denatured alcohol (methylated spirits) or turpentine.

Varnish is a solution of resin (copal, mastic, damar or sandarac) in a solvent. There are two types: spirit varnish, where the resin is dissolved directly in a solvent such as methylated spirits or turpentine; and oil varnishes, where the resin is melted with a drying oil and then thinned with a solvent.

All three finishes rely on the principle that, as the liquid is exposed to air, the volatile solution evaporates, leaving a thin film of resin on the object.

Tools and supplies for cleaning and repair of different types of lacquered objects are given in the appropriate sections. Tools and materials for the lacquering process itself are as follows.

For tracing: sharp pencil, tracing paper, fine abrasive paper, book of motifs.

For repairing the lacquer base: shellac (buy in small quantities), white lead paint (often sold as flake white), pure spirits of turpentine (avoid wood turpentine), japan drier, 1in/2.5cm oxhair primer brush, 1½in/3.8cm white bristle brush, japan paints – a good basic list includes: Liberty red medium (red-purple), signcraft red (orange-red), chrome yellow light, chrome yellow medium, cobalt blue, C.P. green light, C.P. green medium, raw umber, burnt umber, raw sienna, burnt sienna, French yellow ochre, lampblack (a flat black). You could use enamels instead, but the effect is cruder and less "authentic". You will also need: spar varnish, newspapers, palette knives, pieces of white posterboard, palette paper, denatured alcohol (methylated spirits), wire mesh

strainer, nylon stocking, glass jar, small piece of wire, wet-and-dry abrasive paper, non-detergent soap, finest grade steel wool. For *Coromandel lacquer* you will require flatting oil (soybean), refined mineral spirits, gloss varnish, dark green or brown tinted glass jar. For *English lacquer* include: rottenstone, asphaltum, mineral thinner, clear gloss varnish. *French lacquer* requires metallic powders or crushed gold leaf, gilder's tamper, cardboard tube, cheesecloth, rubber band, soft shellac brush, natural sponge, folded paper funnel. For *Italian lacquer* assemble: rabbit skin glue sheets, two pans (one larger than the other) stiff bristle brush, casein paste (deep white), casein emulsion, kaolin powder, pine oil, ox gall, fungicide, gloss varnish, rottenstone, lemon oil. Remember, varnish brushes should always be cleaned in the special solvent named on the can. Dilute gloss varnish 40 per cent as directed on the can. Petroleum jelly around the top of the jar and turpentine on top of the paint inside prevent scum forming. After sanding, always dust the surface of the object with a rag

dipped in turpentine.

For transferring the design: soft rag, ground chalk (for dark objects) or soft pencil (for light objects), masking tape, hard sharp lead pencil, artists' oil paints or casein paints. The ten basic pigments are: opaques – titanium white, chrome yellow (medium or light), vermilion; semi-transparents—yellow ochre, burnt sienna; transparents—alizarin crimson, Prussian blue, yellow lake; toning pigment—raw umber, used as a toner with blues and greens, burnt umber, used as a toner with red and yellow. For highlighting, use gilt paint or metallic dusts. Always purchase the best quality as cheap varieties will darken quickly. You will also need fine sable brushes, sometimes called French quills, Nos. 1-6. For striping, use a long-haired striping brush; for scrolling, a long-haired red sable brush. Prepare small jars of pure turpentine (or water for casein paints), newspapers, palette paper, spar varnish (*never* use plastic/polyurethane-based varnish as a substitute), clean cotton rags, palette knife, cotton wool, linseed oil.

Tracing the motif

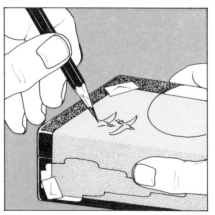

1. First, ascertain that the piece is not a valuable antique, seeking expert advice if in doubt. If the lacquered object is only slightly chipped, it is less time-consuming to touch up the designs with enamel paints available at hobby shops. Where the original motif is indistinct, or if you are decorating a new piece, select a motif from one of the pattern books available. Remember that each period and place has its own style, and that tin, wood and papier mâché designs are not interchangeable. To restore the original motif, proceed as follows.

2. Wear clothes made from synthetic materials to keep down dust. Remove all hardware except hinges from the object. Examine the piece in both daylight and artificial light so as to note every remnant of painted detail. Trace all remaining designs using a sharp pencil and tracing paper, making accurate detailed notes of the precise shades used in order to reproduce them exactly.

3. Alternatively, place a second sheet of tracing paper over the first and write on that. Try to gauge whether the paints were applied thickly or thinly; note any striping or highlighting, and whether this has been gilded or painted on.

Repairing and repainting tinware

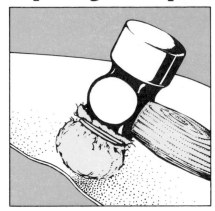

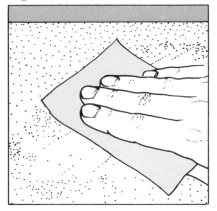

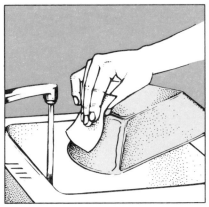

1. Clean by gentle washing in a pure soap and water solution. When dry, unless you are going to retouch the hand painting (in which case, no polish must be used) a beeswax or non-silicone polish should be gently applied with a chamois or soft rag. Having completed the tracing of the original design, or sanded off the old one if it is too obscure to duplicate, pound out any dents with a round-ended hammer, cushioned with a length of cotton wool wrapped around the end.

2. Sand with fine abrasive paper before applying one coat of a flat, rust-preventive primer (usually gray or burnt sienna). Tiny or awkward places can be sanded with a "pencil" typewriter eraser.

3. When dry, sand again, lightly and evenly, with wet-and-dry abrasive paper, under running water. Dry with a rag. Professionals use a "tacrag", but an old stocking will do. The object is now ready for lacquering.

Repairing and cleaning lacquered wood

Lacquer flakes due to the movement of the carcase or basewood, so keep lacquered objects away from extremes of temperature and humidity. Repairing lacquered wood is complicated, even for expert restorers, because the wood used is often a cheap softwood which tends to crack and move, causing the paint to flake.

Assemble the following tools and supplies: proprietary wood filler, a flexible knife such as a palette knife, powdered gesso, small brush, wood primer (for newly-stripped piece), abrasive paper.

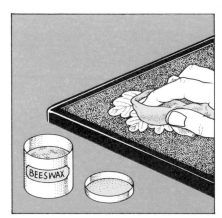

1. To clean and polish a lacquered wooden object (but not before lacquering), use beeswax or any non-silicone furniture wax. Alternatively, mix olive oil and fine white flour to a paste, apply with a soft rag and then gently rub off. Where cracking and flaking have occurred, fill cracks and splits on the underside with proprietary wood filler.

2. If the paint has flaked away leaving a sort of plaster exposed, mix powdered gesso with water to form a stiff paste and remodel and/or refill the damaged part. If the cracks are deep, apply several layers, building up the area gradually.

3. If you are restoring the raised areas on lacquer-work, paint on a thinner version of the mixture above using a pointed paintbrush. Build it up higher than the surrounding raised work to allow for shrinkage during drying. If the piece is newly stripped, apply two coats of wood primer before lacquering, using a shade close to the desired lacquer finish, and when dry, sand until smooth with fine abrasive paper. The object is now ready to be lacquered.

Repairing and cleaning inlay

1. Inlay such as mother-of-pearl requires careful cleaning, because the tiny surrounding crevices tend to trap dirt and polish, eventually loosening the inlay. Very lightly rub each piece of inlay with a cotton wool swab dipped in soapy water (never a strong cleaning solution), then rinse and dry.

2. Should that fail to remove the grime, a gentle scraping of the surface of the inlay using a dull knife usually works, but be careful not to cause further damage.

3. Should a piece become dislodged, apply a dab of clear celluloid adhesive to the back of the inlay and reposition. Always save even the smallest piece, because finding a replacement is difficult.

Repairing papier mâché

To repair papier mâché, assemble the following tools and supplies: synthetic wood filler, fine abrasive paper, japan paints for touching up, pure soap and water solution, clear celluloid adhesive for repairing inlay, cotton wool swabs.

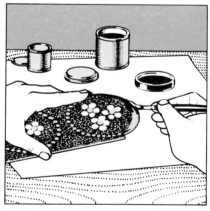

1. First clean papier mâché, following the instructions for cleaning tinware (see Step 1, Page 69).

Repair a chipped or damaged object by building up layers of synthetic wood filler, letting each layer dry thoroughly before adding another. It may help to use a matchstick to support the woodfiller in order to fill a large hole. (Papier mâché is extremely susceptible to chips and splits.) Always overfill slightly as filler tends to shrink while drying. When hard, smooth with fine abrasive paper.

2. The repair must then be touched up with enamel paints before applying a hand-painted design.

3. If you are only touching up a small area, it is worth going to the trouble of blending paints to match the existing background. Black, for example, is rarely pure and often needs to be tinted with red, blue or green. To check, hold a black swatch from a paint store (or from the can of enamel) next to the article.

Applying the lacquer base

Use only japan paints – flat opaque pigments in an oil-free resin varnish – and not the more translucent artists' oil paints. Choose your paints from the list of supplies on page 68 and, after mixing, test for accuracy on white posterboard or palette paper and hold the dried paint against the original shade. Remember that when japan paints are mixed, if the tonal value is above medium, the pigment will appear darker when dry; if below medium value, it will appear lighter. Always replace caps tightly and store japan paints upside-down in a container to keep them moist and easy to mix. Each formula described on the following pages imitates traditional combinations.

The black lacquer described below is used as a base for chinoiserie lacquer, giving depth and contrast to the coloured finish. It can also be used by itself, or applied over the casein base used in Italian lacquer.

1. First mix a black lacquer undercoat from five volumes flat black paint, one-half volume burnt umber japan, one-third volume japan drier and one-quarter volume spar varnish, using a palette knife to blend. The quantity depends on the size of the object, but bear in mind that each article requires four coats of lacquer.

2. Strain this mixture through a wire mesh strainer covered with a nylon stocking, into a glass jar. Clean the palette knife with turpentine and wipe with a rag before mixing paints again. The object should be stood on damp newspapers which will attract dust away from the article being lacquered. It is also a good idea to place the piece in front of a light source, preferably daylight, so that any imperfections are obvious.

3. Dip the 1½in/3.8cm oxhair bristle brush into the lacquer mixture halfway up the bristles, and press it on the side of the jar to remove excess. Don't wipe it on the rim — this causes uneven pressure and results in bubbles. Alternatively, wrap a wire around the top of the jar.

4. Start lacquering in the middle of the object and stroke the brush lightly to one end.

5. Overlap the central starting point and stroke along to opposite end. Brush from end to end with the grain, then across it, then with it again. Depending on temperature and humidity, drying takes between 24 and 48 hours – 70°F/21°C is ideal. When the first coat is thoroughly dry, apply a second.

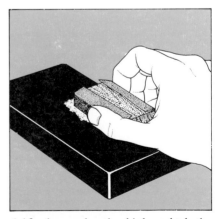

6. After the second coat has dried completely, the surface is rubbed with the finest wet-and-dry abrasive paper, using non-detergent soap suds as a lubricant. Apply another two coats of lacquer in the same way. Protect finally with a mixture half shellac and half denatured alcohol (methylated spirits). Apply two coats of this, smoothing between applications with finest steel wool. (When cleaning shellac brushes, always use denatured alcohol (methylated spirits), never soap and water. Shellac should be stored in a warm dark place, in a glass container.)

Oriental lacquer

The two finishes described here were much used by Chippendale, and suit chinoiserie or Oriental-style objects very well. Coromandel lacquer is an imitation of the lacquer used on elaborate screens imported to Europe from the Coromandel coast of India in the seventeenth century. They were about 8ft/2.5m high, up to twelve panels in length, and combined carved, lacquered and painted scenes.

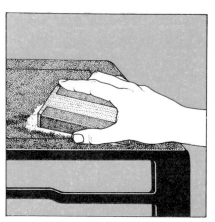

CHINOISERIE LACQUER

To make a red lacquer finish, mix one volume Liberty red (red-purple) japan, one-half volume signcraft red (orange-red) japan, one-quarter volume flake white paint and one-half volume turpentine. Apply one coat. Alternatively, make a yellow variation by mixing one volume chrome yellow medium japan, one-quarter volume raw sienna japan, one-half volume turpentine and one-tenth volume japan drier.

When this topcoat is dry, rub it very lightly using fine wet-and-dry abrasive paper lubricated with a soapy solution. This will reveal traces of the black underneath.

COROMANDEL LACQUER

The base coat is made from one volume Liberty red japan, one-half volume burnt sienna japan, one-quarter volume signcraft red japan, one-tenth volume japan drier, one-quarter volume turpentine. If the gesso or casein base needs repairing, follow instructions given for Italian lacquer, Steps 1-5. Otherwise, apply four or five coats of the above formula, and when these are dry, smooth with fine wet-and-dry abrasive paper and a non-detergent soap solution.

Protect this base coat with two coats of diluted orange shellac, allowing one hour after each coat before rubbing lightly with finest steel wool. For the topcoat, mix the following ingredients: one volume raw umber japan, one quarter volume lampblack japan, seven volumes glazing medium, made from one volume flatting oil (soybean), one volume undiluted gloss varnish, one volume thinner (refined mineral spirits), one to two volumes japan drier. (After use, the glazing medium should be stored in a dark green or brown tinted jar.)

Apply one coat of this formula in a broad-streaked manner. The result is a rich finish which

appears to be a combination of black and mahogany – an ideal background for gold leaf decoration.

English and Italian lacquers

ENGLISH LACQUER

Mix five volumes lampblack with one and one-half volumes burnt umber japan, one-half volume japan drier, one-half volume clear gloss varnish, and mineral spirits for thinning. Apply four or five coats and smooth when dry with fine wet-and-dry abrasive paper and a non-detergent soap solution. Dry with a soft cloth and apply a final coat of the following formula, heated to room temperature (70°F/21°C): three-quarter volume raw umber japan, one-quarter volume lampblack japan, two volumes asphaltum, one volume spar varnish, one volume mineral thinner, one-quarter volume japan drier. After 48 hours, rub with a mild abrasive such as rottenstone or pumice powder and oil, and allow another 24 hours before smoothing with fine wet-and-dry paper and pure soap solution. Protect with one coat of shellac mixed with an equal volume of denatured alcohol (methylated spirits). Rub with steel wool before decorating with a hand-painted motif.

ITALIAN LACQUER

This lacquered effect resembles the Italian method of the eighteenth century. It was usually applied over a gesso layer, which concealed poor workmanship or the bad quality of the wood or plaster beneath. It is a lengthy process, only worth undertaking for extensive damage.

1. Begin by soaking two or three rabbit skin glue sheets overnight in 14 fl oz/420ml water. Dissolve gently over heat by standing pan in another, larger, pan of boiling water, to obtain a size which is applied with a stiff bristle brush and left overnight to dry. Make a casein mixture by stirring 6oz/170g of kaolin powder into 1qt/1litre white casein paste, then add 2½oz/70g casein emulsion, 3 drops pine oil, ¼tsp/1.25ml ox gall, ¼tsp/1.25ml fungicide (crushed in ½tsp/2.5ml water) and 12 fl oz/360ml water.

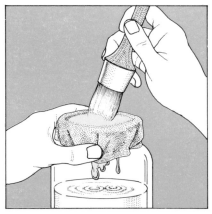

2. Strain through a nylon stocking into a glass jar, forcing it through the mesh with the aid of a stiff brush. The mixture should have the consistency of double cream. Coat the object with an even film of the mixture.

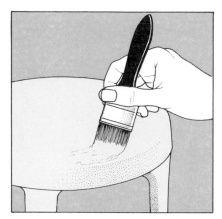

3. After one hour, apply a second coat, brushing the other way. Altogether, apply five coats in this manner, sanding gently after every other coat with finest abrasive paper. Sand again after final coat.

4. Dissolve white aniline powder in hot water. If light tones are required, add cold water.

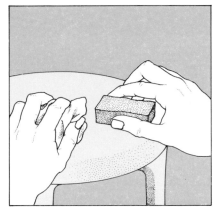

5. Next, rub the aniline solution over the casein base, using a fine-grained natural sponge, and wipe off instantly with an absorbent cloth. When dry, after two hours, coat the piece with thinned white shellac, diluted fifty-fifty with denatured alcohol (methylated spirits). Apply five coats in all, allowing each coat to dry overnight before rubbing with finest steel wool. When the last coat of shellac is thoroughly dry, apply two coats of gloss varnish and rub down the top coat with rottenstone and lemon oil. If desired, a tinted lacquer can be applied over this finish.

French lacquer (Vernis Martin)

This is a modern approximation of the Martin brothers' famous seventeenth-century formula: apply five coats of thinned japan pigment of a middle value, allowing 24 hours between applications. Sand every second coat lightly with fine wet-and-dry abrasive paper and a non-detergent soapy solution. Seal with white shellac solution thinned fifty-fifty with denatured alcohol (methylated spirits), using a soft shellac brush. When dry, rub with fine steel wool.

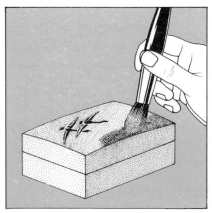

1. Then apply a glazing medium (see Steps 2-4, Page 67), tinted with ½oz/14g japan in a sl le a little darker than the base coat, using a brush or fine-grained natural sponge. Leave to dry for one week. Next apply a coat of thinned clear varnish.

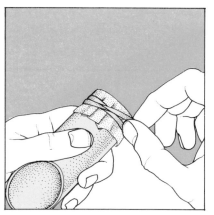

2. Leave to dry for 24 hours and apply a second coat, spattering, when tacky, with metallic powders, or, for authenticity, gold leaf crushed to fine particles. Cut a cardboard tube diagonally at one end, and cover the other with fine cheese-cloth, fixed with a rubber band, to act as a sieve.

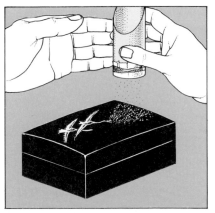

3. With a folded paper funnel, tip the particles into the tube and then scatter them lightly over the tacky varnish by gently tapping the tube. When dry, smooth very lightly with finest wet-and-dry abrasive paper and soapy water. Apply several additional coats of varnish, smoothing each one, until the desired translucency is achieved.

To transfer a design

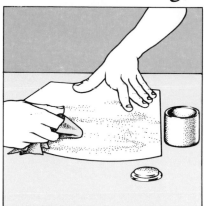

1. Once the base coats of lacquer and a sealer have been applied, the object is ready to be decorated. If the traced design is to be transferred to a dark object, rub the reverse side of the tracing paper with a soft rag dipped in ground chalk. When transferring to light objects, simply rub with a soft pencil.

2. Tape the traced design, chalk or pencil side down, to the object in several places, using masking tape.

3. Using a hard, sharp lead pencil, go over each part of the design very carefully, so that it transfers very clearly to the surface below – it should be visible when the tracing paper is removed.

The hand-painted decoration

When the transfer is completed, you are ready to apply the hand-painted motifs, followed by striping and/or gilding — touches which give lacquer its distinctive charm. Although casein (water soluble) paints may be used, artists' oil paints are recommended; they give the decoration a more genuine, "floated" look. Always try and match the surviving shade, bearing in mind that paint pigment darkens over the years. If gold has been used, purchase a liquid paint from an art store, of the best quality available. If you are restoring stencil work, see Steps 1-9, Pages 76-7.

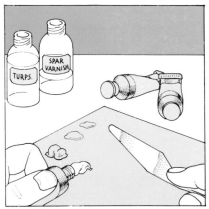

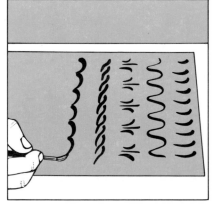

1. The paint can be used straight from the tube or shaded with a toning pigment – raw umber is used with blues and greens, burnt umber with reds and yellows. Apply one pigment at a time, mixing shades according to the notes made on the tracing paper in Step 3, Page 68. Put a drop of paint from each tube on the palette paper, with a drop of spar varnish to one side, and a drop of turpentine to the other. Mix all three to a flowing consistency using the palette knife, but always wiping it clean before adding another shade.

2. Before starting to paint, always try it on a sheet of palette or tracing paper first. Paint in a logical order; for example, if the design shows a blue flower with a red middle, the blue should be applied first. Allow each application to dry thoroughly and clean the brush with turpentine before using the next shade.

3. Professionals obtain most shapes with a single movement. This one basic stroke is varied depending on the size of the brush, the use of the stroke to fill the traced shape, and the amount of pressure exerted.

If you wish to add gilt highlights or stencils, refer to Steps 1-6, Pages 60-61. Striping and antiquing are also optional finishing touches (see pages 50-51 and 75 respectively).

Lining or striping

Lining or striping is applied after texturing but before antiquing. It may also be used alone to add interest to a plain painted finish. In order to remove smudged lines, isolate the finish underneath with a coat of semi-gloss varnish. For transparent, delicate lining, use artists' gouache or acrylic paint diluted with a little water to a creamy consistency; a drop of detergent may also improve the flow. Professionals generally use oil paints or universal stainers dissolved in a little white spirit and clear varnish.

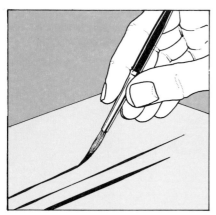

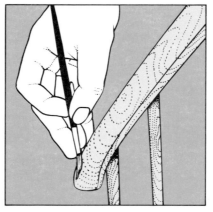

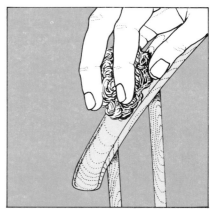

1. To begin, load the brush and try out long, flowing strokes on a piece of white cardboard. The thickness of the line depends on the pressure exerted as well as on the width of the brush itself. Move your eye ahead of the brush, otherwise you may hesitate, and the pause will show in your work.

2. When you feel confident, draw a light pencil line on the area to be striped, load the brush, and using your finger as a guide, glide the brush along one long, smooth, stroke. Avoid using the broad-side of the brush. Correct mistakes with a cotton swab soaked in the relevant solvent.

3. If the line looks too heavy, soften it by rubbing with fine steel wool, but in any case, the line should not look utterly perfect. It should look as if drawn by a human hand, otherwise designer's plastic stripes on a roll could be used. In fact, once mastered, it is easy to get carried away with this process – use it freely on small as well as large objects to make a chic, crisp statement.

Sponging

1. After preparing the object as directed in Steps 1 – 6, Page 45, coat it with flatting oil and make a tinted glazing liquid as directed under GLAZING (Steps 1 – 3, Page 67). If trying to match an object to the walls of a room, it is possible to use the same water-based wall paints to sponge with, but to each cup of paint add 1 tablespoon/15ml of terebine drier, and if necessary, add water to thin the paint to the consistency of thin cream. Oil-based paints such as enamels can also be used if they are prepared in the same way, using white spirit as the thinner.

2. Test the consistency of the sponging liquid by choosing a sponge and dipping it in the paint, squeezing the excess out and daubing the damp-ened sponge on a piece of white card. A fine-grained sponge such as a small make-up sponge will produce a finer texture; an open-grained sponge will produce a coarser texture. The closer the daubs and the more pressure applied, the denser the effect of the sponging will be. Generally speaking, smaller objects demand a smaller sponge texture, but this is only a guideline.

3. When the first application has dried thorough-ly, a second and even third sponging can be added. Prepare the second shade in the same way, keeping it close in value and tone to the first. For example, if the first shade was pale blue, the second might be mint green. Once the final sponge shade has dried, protect the finish as directed in Steps 1 – 3, Page 81. After the sponging is sealed, the piece can additionally be antiqued or even distressed, as directed on Pages 50 – 51 and 82 respectively.

Stencilling

Although time-consuming, stencilling is a cheap and versatile way of enlivening fabric, walls and furniture. Complex designs can be applied without artisic talent — motifs can be copied, enlarged, reduced, and/or adapted from stencil source books or from wallpaper and fabrics. There are also ready-cut stencils.

The layout and coloration of stencils are critical – if you're a traditionalist look at early American or Scandinavian furniture, otherwise, let your imagination go. However, do not be too ambitious. Begin with simple motifs in one shade.

To make your own stencil, the materials needed are architects' linen, acetate sheeting, oiled stencil board, or as a last resort, thin cardboard. (Acetate sheets are particularly useful when applying two or more shades, since they enable precise positioning.) Also assemble the following supplies: knife with replaceable blades, masking tape, a sharp pencil, and plastic cutting board or piece of thick cardboard, plus paint as instructed below.

1. To transfer the chosen design to the stencil material, sandwich carbon paper in between, or rub the back of the design with a soft lead pencil.

2. Tape the design over the stencil material, and carefully trace the outlines of the design using the sharpest, hardest lead pencil possible to ensure accurate reproduction.

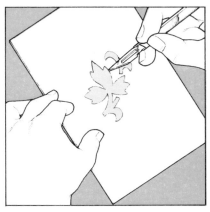

3. Using a knife with replaceable blades, cut out the small shapes first, working on top of a piece of cardboard or plastic cutting board. Aim for smooth, flowing cuts. Slips can be rectified with another cut marginally outside the first, or by sanding the nick with finest abrasive paper afterwards. This cutting process is perhaps the most important step in preparing stencils, so take your time.

ALTERNATIVE STENCILLING

4. Should the combination of location, surface, and/or type of paint present real problems, there is an alternative method of application. It results in a "cleaner" edge because the cut stencil is used as a guide so the design can be traced directly onto the piece using a sharp pencil to follow the outlines of the cut shapes.

5. Remove the stencil, and apply the first shade using a pointed artists' brush and any of the paints suggested opposite.

6. The advantage of this alternative is that the entire design can be traced all at once so that the second and consecutive shades can be applied as soon as you like, taking care not to accidentally brush the first one.

Paints for stencilling

Many types of paint are suitable for stencilling; the only requirement is that they be mixed to the consistency of thick cream to prevent seeping. In addition, they should be quick drying, or mixed with a drop of proprietary drier. Signwriters' paints and acrylic paints are ideal. Poster paints, artists' oil paints, or flat oil-based paint tinted with universal stainers will do too. Similarly, spray paint can be used, although it is not advised for beginners — the effect is softer but the surrounding area needs to be completely masked because of its tendency to spatter.

Avoid mixing too much paint — so little is taken onto the brush that a saucerful is sufficient for an entire piece. Always be sure to have the appropriate solvent close at hand for quick wipe-ups. Drips sometimes occur, especially on vertical surfaces; for this reason, turn the piece if possible so you're always stencilling a horizontal surface.

1. Use masking tape to position the cut stencil, then dip the stencil brush (which looks like a man's shaving brush except that the bristles are far stiffer) into the paint. Sponges or soft cloths may also be used although they are more difficult to work with. Whatever you choose, be sure to keep the paint to a minimum, removing the excess on a piece of blotting paper or paper towel before each application.

2. If using spray paints, apply the paint in short bursts, and at an angle to get the desired subtle shading effect only achievable with these paints. Of course the advantage of using these is that very unusual tonalities can be achieved by spraying the same area with similar shades. For example, in order to achieve a blue green, you might first spray a base green, followed by a second application of blue at the corners for accent.

3. After a few applications, it may be necessary to clean the stencil with the relevant solvent to prevent paint from being transferred to the surface underneath. If smudges do occur, wipe with solvent immediately.

4. Leave paint to dry, then peel off the tape carefully, and move to the next area to be stencilled.

5. Do not move the stencil until the paint has completely dried, or smudges will occur. To speed the process, you may find it helps to work with two stencils. If working with more than one shade, apply each one separately.

6. Finally, protect the work with a coat of varnish — matt or semi-gloss looks best. The varnish may be tinted, as suggested under WOOD, Page 46, to produce a more muted effect. If working with spray paints, use only aerosol spray varnish.

Tortoiseshelling

Painted tortoiseshell is best used on flat or slightly rounded surfaces rather than carved or uneven surfaces which could clearly never be real tortoise. In addition, the tortoiseshelling should not be applied to a section more than 6in/15cm square (the maximum dimension of a tortoiseshell plate) unless the effect is simply intended as a fantasy finish. Use the photograph facing page 32 as a reference for the mottled pattern. If applying this decorative finish to restore a missing section of real tortoiseshell, it will obviously be necessary to use the surrounding intact undamaged shell as reference, attempting to match the tonality and texture exactly. If this is the case, mask the surrounding shell with an application of rubber cement. When the paint process is dry, rub the cement off with your fingers and polish the real shell with a paste made from senna powder mixed with olive oil.

1. The ground hue ranges from ivory to a pale yellow and is mixed by adjusting the proportions of the following ingredients: 8 volumes flat white paint, ½ volume yellow ochre japan pigment and 1 volume chrome yellow light japan pigment. Apply three coats, rubbing each one with fine wet-and-dry abrasive paper and soapy water. When the final coat has dried, protect it with a coat of thinned white shellac. Once the coat of shellac has dried, use a sharp 2H pencil to sketch the desired markings on this ground hue.

2. The first transparent streaks of the radial pattern of tortoiseshell are applied with a 1in/2.5cm oxhair paintbrush or with a small make-up sponge. Cover a little more than half of the background with a wash of: 1 volume each of asphaltum, japan drier and warm undiluted spar varnish mixed with 2 volumes thinner. Apply these markings as if they radiate from a central point. When dry, protect with thinned white shellac.

3. The next shell markings are applied in the same manner. Begin by wiping the surface with flatting oil prepared as directed in Step 1, Page 67 . Then apply a mixture of yellow ochre and raw sienna pigment diluted by half with clear varnish to which a drop of japan drier has been added. Apply with a ½in/13mm brush covering about half the surface, varying the strokes from thin and thick to long and short at irregular intervals.

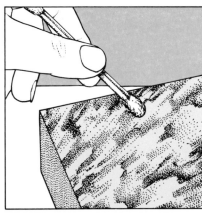

4. After this application of the yellow ochre, blur the end of each stroke using a small piece of cotton wool—this whisking of the strokes makes them more translucent and the blurred edges are more like the actual tortoiseshell. Once dry, protect this first application with a coat of thinned shellac.

5. Second, third and fourth applications of tortoiseshell marks are applied in the same manner, on top of, or beside the previous applications. For each use the formula given in Step 3, using the following shades of oil paints: raw sienna, raw umber and burnt umber. After each application, blur the strokes as in Step 4, then seal with a coat of shellac. Avoid very regular or parallel markings, varying the strokes as much as possible.

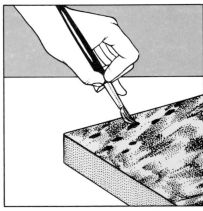

6. Finally, apply lozenge-shaped accents from a mixture of 1 volume burnt umber japan pigment and ¼ volume lampblack. Use a No. 6 artists' paintbrush to dab the accent singly or in groups and at a slight angle to the existing strokes. Protect with two coats of thinned shellac, smoothed between coats with fine wet-and-dry paper and soapy water. After the final rubbing, the piece or the area of tortoiseshell may be waxed.

Vinegar painting

For the same kind of uninhibited effect that children achieve with finger painting, consider vinegar painting. It is a simple process devised by country craftsmen to imitate the *faux* graining popular in the nineteenth century. It must be applied with confidence and boldness, and perhaps looks best where darker shades are applied to a very light ground.

The idea is to let the vinegar medium take the impression of anything that will produce an interesting texture — plasticine, crumpled paper, cork, putty, fingers, feathers, combs, etc. Since the mixture dries slowly, there is plenty of time to experiment, and mistakes can easily be corrected by washing off the mixture. Assemble the following supplies: vinegar, sugar, liquid detergent, glass jar, powdered pigment, semi-gloss varnish.

1. Prepare the piece as for opaque finishes, Steps 1-6, Page 45, i.e. coat with flat, oil-based paint, tinted to the required shade. When dry, rub with sudsy wet-and-dry abrasive paper for perfect smoothness.

2. To begin, make the medium by mixing one-half cup/110ml of vinegar with 1tsp/5ml of sugar and a squeeze of liquid detergent in a glass jar. Shake, then tint a quarter or so of the mixture with powdered pigment. Mix to a paste, then add the rest of the vinegar mixture.

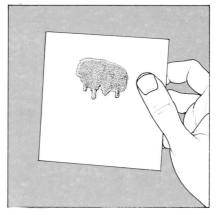

3. Test the shade on a piece of white cardboard, and also check its consistency (when the cardboard is held up, the mixture should run slightly).

4. Experiment with the mixture using various texturing devices before actually beginning. Do plan the pattern before starting – working with the stuff is fun but horrendously crude configurations can result. To relieve the swirls and whorls, you might use the mixture simply as a wash on some areas, or impart a simple texture by dragging a comb or feather through it.

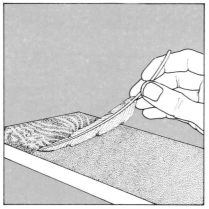

5. When the motif(s) has been decided, wipe the surface with pure vinegar, then brush the mixture over a horizontal surface, and begin texturing. If the mixture starts to dry before the texturing is complete, simply brush on more of the vinegar mixture.

6. When the vinegar painting is completely dry, protect the work with a coat of semi-gloss varnish. Rub with sudsy wet-and-dry abrasive paper to cut shine, then polish with rottenstone and oil as directed in Steps 1-3, Page 81.

Problems with painted finishes

As with any skill, the more practice you have in applying opaque paint, the better the result will be. But until you reach that level of experience, you may encounter the following problems.

1. Bleeding occurs when the stain, filler, primer, etc. oozes into the succeeding coat. It is often caused by using old products, and if it looks really terrible, there is no choice but to strip everything in order to expose bare wood once again. However, before taking this drastic step, let the "bled" coat dry, and apply another coat of opaque paint.

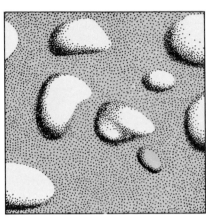

2. Blistering is caused by exposure to excessive heat from the sun, a radiator or blow-lamp, either during or after the drying period. Smooth with abrasive paper, and apply a thinned coat of shellac or varnish before proceeding with the next coat.

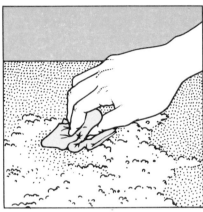

3. Bloom is a whitish or bluish film which may appear on the drying surface of varnishes or enamels. There are many causes. To treat, rub with wet-and-dry abrasive paper and soap suds, or with a fine abrasive such as pumice powder or rottenstone. Rinse. Let the surface dry completely before proceeding.

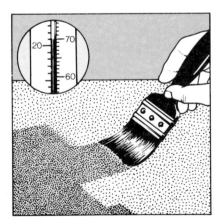

4. Blushing looks like bloom but usually starts to appear when lacquer, shellac, or varnish is applied in too humid an atmosphere *or* when the coat underneath was not allowed to dry completely. To remedy this, flood the entire surface with the recommended solvent, let dry, and start again. As far as temperature goes, 70°F/20°C is ideal.

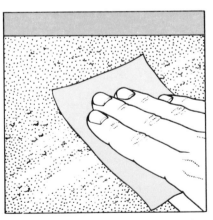

5. Bubbling happens when the paint is not thin enough, or when it has not been properly brushed in. It can also occur on varnished surfaces if the can has been shaken causing air bubbles to stay suspended in the liquid. When dry, sand with the grain, using the finest abrasive paper, and apply another thinned coat of paint.

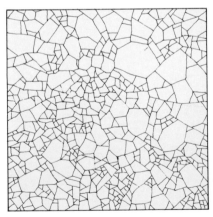

6. Checking, crazing or hard-lining appear as irregular lines on the surface of dried paint. On antique painted pieces they often lend charm, but on newly painted pieces they should be removed. When dry, sand with finest abrasive paper, wipe with white spirit, and apply another coat.

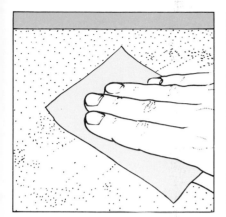

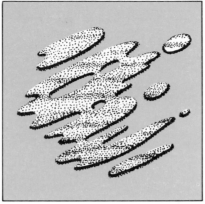

7. Chipping happens if the top coat cannot adhere to a too-smooth coat beneath it. Rough up the surface with medium grade abrasive paper, wipe with white spirit, and apply another coat. (Enamel paints especially need a rough surface to provide "tooth".)

8. Crawling paint seems to shrink from or avoid a certain area because that area is greasy, wet or waxy. Rinse area with white spirit, let dry, and resume painting.

9. Wrinkling is caused by too much paint applied to one place so that the paint piles up on itself. Over-painting is often a problem for amateurs. To remedy, sand the area with fine abrasive paper, and apply another thinned coat. Make sure to brush each stroke in well.

Protecting decorative painted finishes

After the application of antiquing, glazing, stencilling or vinegar painting, it is absolutely imperative to protect your work, otherwise the texture will soon rub off. (It is interesting to note that some specialists put a piece in circulation until some of the finish wears off, and only then apply the protective coats.)

Assemble the following tools and supplies: matt or semi-gloss varnish; rottenstone and fine oil or one of the alternative polishing mediums named below; and non-silicone furniture wax.

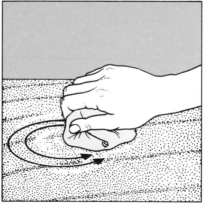

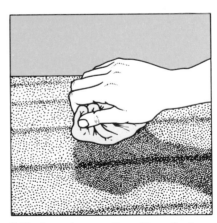

1. The most suitable protection is two or three applications of matt or semi-gloss varnish. If only gloss is available, rub down each coat with sudsy wet-and-dry abrasive paper. Use the varnish as it is, unless you want to emphasize the tone underneath. In that case, tint with a minute amount of artists' oil paint.

2. For an impeccable and authentic looking finish, the last coat of varnish is hand polished. The usual polish is a paste of rottenstone mixed with a fine oil such as lanolin (baby oil), salad oil or lemon oil. Apply in a circular motion, wipe with a clean cloth, and buff with a piece of soft cotton or towel. Alternatively, use powdered pumice, French chalk or flour. Even household scouring powder will do, although it tends to be too abrasive, and needs to be used with a light hand.

3. Finally, apply a coat of non-silicone furniture wax and buff to a soft sheen.

Physical distressing

This process is used to give objects an artificial look of battered old age by means of applying scars, dents, stains and simulated wormholes. It is a rather brutal procedure and cannot be recommended except when trying to age a new unpainted piece which is then going to be stained and waxed, or given one of the painted finishes described earlier in this chapter. It could also be used with the distressed paintwork treatment on page 54.

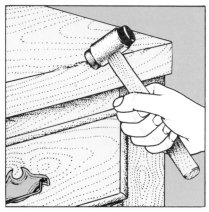

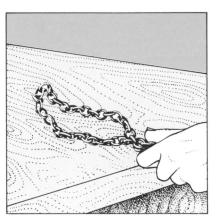

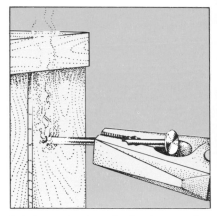

1. A rubber hammer can be used to "soften" the edges of tables and corners of chests of drawers, etc, and to "dent" surfaces.

2. A length of chain or set of keys can also be thrown against the top surface of a piece to cause dents and abrasions.

3. A sharp, pointed metal tool such as an awl or gimlet can be heated red-hot and rammed into the wood to simulate wormholes. Alternatively, a thin nail can be driven into the wood. In both instances, make sure the holes are small and fairly close together.

BAMBOO FURNITURE

Although Europeans had long been fascinated by the East, it was not until the eighteenth century that trade between China and the West developed on a large scale. Demand for Oriental goods became so great that imports were insufficient to meet it and European makers began to produce their own imitations. The taste for chinoiserie reached its peak in the middle of the eighteenth century, stimulated by the publication of pattern books for furniture in the chinoiserie style by Thomas Chippendale and other cabinet makers. Although many of these designs featured imitation bamboo, it was not until the late 1700s that pieces made in real bamboo were first imported.

Chinoiserie received a further boost in popularity when the Prince of Wales, later the Prince Regent, began the creation of the Royal Pavilion in Brighton. The Chinese Gallery was furnished with real bamboo pieces bought in China on the Prince's behalf as well as some London-made simulated bamboo furniture. Other wealthy country house owners soon followed the fashion and bought bamboo pieces to adorn their Oriental rooms. At the end of the eighteenth century the largest importer in England was the East India Company, which sold off its cargoes by auction, while a large collection of Chinese furniture taken to the United States by a U.S. consul at the beginning of the nineteenth century helped to popularize the style there.

Bamboo export furniture included tables, chairs and sofas. Table tops and seats were often in black lacquer, sometimes plain, sometimes decorated with stylized designs of birds and flowers; other seats and tops were of cane, supported by legs consisting of a bunch of thin bamboo stalks pinned together. Curves in the bamboo were achieved by heating and bending but could also be obtained by growing lengths of bamboo in moulds. Such pieces were exhibited widely at international exhibitions throughout the nineteenth century, but such was the Victorian manufacturer's ingenuity — and desire to profit from popular trends — that soon home-produced bamboo was being made and sold in huge quantities, overtaking imports in popularity. Though often less solidly constructed than traditional Chinese furniture, the styles produced in the West were often more in keeping with European needs and tastes than the genuine article.

The fashion for japonaiserie, as distinct from chinoiserie, began in the 1870s and reached its peak around the turn of the century, giving further impetus to the craze for bamboo. It was used for every kind of furniture in ways undreamt of by the Chinese: cabinets, chests of drawers, desks, tables, stands, whatnots, screens, chairs, stools, magazine racks, jardinières, book-cases, gong frames, looking-glass frames, window blinds, lamps, wall-brackets and even larger pieces such as wardrobes, sofas, beds—even pianos! Indeed, some manufacturers even offered to produce to order any article that could possibly be made in bamboo.

The raw materials were imported chiefly from Japan, which did not actually produce bamboo furniture itself, contrary to contemporary misconceptions. Apart from lengths of bamboo the Japanese exported lacquer panels and trays, and rolls of closely woven grass matting, all of which was incorporated into their designs by manufacturers in Europe and America. Methods of construction were similar to the traditional Chinese ones, except that the wooden pegs and wedges originally used in joints were superseded by screws and metal pins, which did not always make for great stability. The best-known and biggest manufacturer in England, W.F. Needham of Birmingham, solved the problem with a metal joint which he patented and named "Ferrumjungo". Bamboo usually formed the entire frame of the piece, and provided decorative additions; flat surfaces were of lacquer or grass matting, as in Oriental designs, but also of tiles, a characteristic Victorian innovation. Heating and bending were employed for curved sections, and the ends of the hollow canes were plugged or capped with metal or wood.

Decoration was sometimes added by brown staining and varnishing and with gold lines painted round the nodal rings. Small scorch marks were sometimes applied to give a tortoiseshell effect. Occasionally the bamboo was stained with shades other than brown, particularly in France, where bright shades were popular. A large section of matting might contain decoratively spaced sections of bamboo, straight or curved.

From the 1860s to the 1930s there were over 150 producers of bamboo furniture in Britain, none so large as Needham(whose output was apparently in the region of 4000 pieces a week), but all turned out huge quantities both for the domestic and export markets. One of the first retailers to specialize in bamboo was Liberty & Co., whose founder, Arthur Lazenby Liberty, enterprisingly set up his own department store to specialize in Oriental goods. Other stores soon followed suit and their catalogues, from the 1880s and 1890s, show large quantities of bamboo ware.

Bamboo achieved a fair degree of popularity in America, although less than in Britain, and there were fewer native producers, imitation bamboo generally being preferred. Bamboo was imported from Britain, and from France, where the largest manufacturer was Perret Fils & Vibert. The style of French bamboo furniture was quite different from the British: as well as being much brighter, it was more commonly used in gardens and on terraces than indoors and was much heavier, with sticks up to 5in/13cm in diameter used for a solid effect.

Although the fashion for bamboo waned after the 1930s, since when it has usually been considered more suitable for garden or conservatory, it is again becoming popular and an ever-increasing range of furniture is being imported, often better made than the Victorian and Edwardian pieces to be found in antique and second-hand shops. But these often have a charm and simplicity which fits well in modern interiors and with only a little attention they can be made serviceable and attractive for many more years.

Repairing bamboo furniture

Because bamboo furniture was considered relatively valueless until fairly recently, it is often found in a considerable state of disrepair. However, since bamboo lengths are still readily available in various diameters, and it is strong and straight except for its growth rings or nodes, furniture made from it is easy to repair.

Restoration of bamboo furniture usually involves attention to one or more of its components: the grass matting used for covering tops and sides, lacquerwork on some of the same areas, and the bamboo frame itself. Methods of construction generally fall into three categories: pegging or plugging, pinning (the least satisfactory) and wrapping with metal strips (the most satisfactory).

Clean the piece before starting repairs: clean the bamboo frame as wood, and, if necessary, remove old varnish (see Step 3, Page 39); clean grass matting as instructed on page 85; and if there are lacquer panels, do not use water-based cleaning solutions—refer instead to Steps 1 – 3, Page 69.

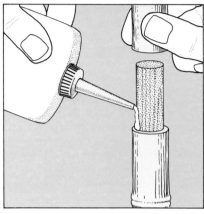

1. Bamboo furniture was often pegged or plugged with thick wooden dowels which were glued into the joints, taking advantage of the hollowness of the bamboo stems. If these are missing, replace with lengths of modern dowels of a diameter which ensures a tight fit and which have been stained if necessary. Glue the dowel into both ends of the bamboo using a woodworking adhesive.

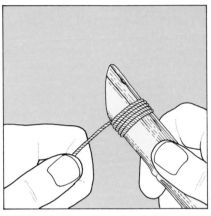

2. If the joints have been pinned, the problem may be complicated by the fact that the bamboo may also be split along its length. In this case, force woodworking adhesive into the splits and bind with wet string. When dry, reinsert a steel pin or brass screw into the hole(s), redrilling the hole if necessary using a fine drill bit.

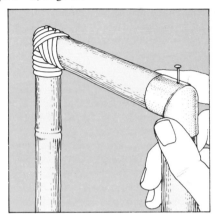

3. The most satisfactory method of joining bamboo is by means of metal covers for all joins. These are made by wrapping a metal strip around the stems and soldering the overlapping ends in place. The join is sometimes additionally strengthened by a small pin or screw as above, then concealed with a wrapping of split thin bamboo. (See Steps 4 – 7, Pages 108 – 109 for instructions on dealing with cane wrappings.)

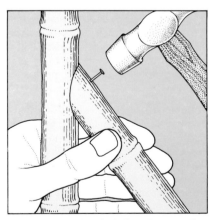

4. The method described above is most often used when trying to make a diagonal join, in which case the ends of the diagonal piece may have to be rasped inwards to fit the curve of the piece it is joining. It can then be pinned or screwed in place, wrapped with metal, then overlapped with cane as in Step 3.

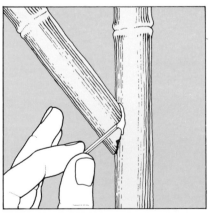

5. Bad joints can be filled with a paste made from sawdust and water-soluble woodworking adhesive. The resulting filler may be varnished to match the surrounding shade. Lengths of bamboo with damaged varnish or with protruding filler may need to be smoothed afterwards with fine steel wool, followed by an application of varnish.

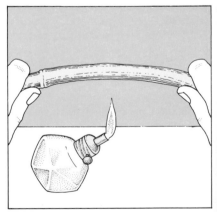

6. When repairing the bamboo frame, and before joining, it may be necessary to replace a bent length of bamboo. Small diameter bamboos bend more easily than large ones, and old bamboo does not bend as easily as new. If possible, make the bend between knots. Warm an 8in/20.5cm section at a time, moving it back and forth over a smokeless flame at the point where you want it to bend. Do not let the flame touch the bamboo for too long. The bending job should be done slowly or the bamboo will split. (There may be some loss of cylindrical shape at the bends.)

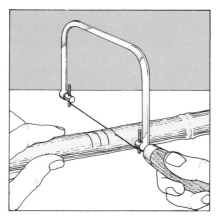

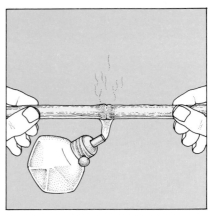

7. When working with large diameter bamboos and when trying to make sharp curves, it may assist bending to make a number of shallow cuts using a saw with a fine blade, such as a coping saw, across the inner curve of the bamboo.

8. When the bamboo is sufficiently bent, rub the bend with a wet rag until cool, using the left hand to hold the cane in its bent position. When a sharp bend is required, it is best to cool the bamboo when the bend is only half done, then resume the heating and bending.

9. Heat can also be used to apply the small decorative burn marks like small darkened patches found on much bamboo furniture. To do this, hold the bamboo still over the flame until the surface is singed. Singeing was often done at the area around the nodes. Reapply at least one protective coat of thinned varnish afterwards.

Repairing and replacing grass matting

The various types of grass matting used in bamboo furniture can be scrubbed using a soft, natural bristle brush and a little soapy water, and rinsed thoroughly afterwards. After cleaning, let matting dry completely before starting repairs.

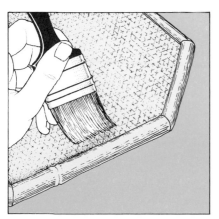

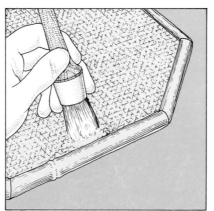

1. Occasionally, the grass matting is intact, but its protective varnished surface has worn away. In this case, simply dust the top with a stiff paint-brush to remove accumulated dirt, rinse with turpentine substitute on a soft cloth, and reapply a non-synthetic varnish, tinting it if necessary with artist's pigments or purchasing a tinted shade close to the existing one.

2. If the matting appears to be in perfect condition, but is painted over, apply a proprietary paint remover to the surface and scrub gently with a stiff, natural brush and/or a paint scraper to remove the layers of paint. However, before applying the stripper, make sure that there are signs of the characteristic grassy texture; if not, the piece may have been lacquered, in which case paint remover must not be applied. Instead, the paint should be scraped off mechanically (see Step 3, Page 37).

3. After the paint has been removed, rinse the matting with a turpentine substitute, and apply varnish (see Steps 1 – 3, Page 43) to protect it. If the matting is still paint-encrusted after this there is no choice but to remove it as follows.

Repairing and replacing grass matting cont.

4. If the matting is merely stained, brush on a proprietary wood bleach to the stain using an inexpensive brush. Repeat until the stain is gone, let dry and seal the surface of the matting with two coats of clear, semi-gloss varnish.

5. Often the matting has been painted over, or is damaged by burn marks or bald patches, in which case it must be replaced. To begin, carefully lift off the thin bamboo strips holding it in place along the edges, using a flexible knife such as a spatula or filling knife. Bear in mind that bamboo splits very easily along its length, so the utmost care is required.

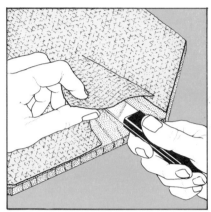

6. To remove the matting, apply warm water to the surface which should soften the glue holding it in place. Use the filling knife to scrape off the matting.

7. Once the matting has been removed, the undersurface can be sanded smooth and a new top cut. If it is still intact, use the old matting as a pattern, tracing around it on newspaper with a felt-tip pen; if only pieces remain, turn the table upside down on the newspaper, trace around it in the same way so that a matrix is made. Tape or pin the newspaper pattern to the purchased matting and cut out the shape, noting that the matting ought to extend to the edges of the tabletop but not overhang them. Trim if necessary.

8. Apply clear-drying fabric glue or water-soluble white glue thickly to the top of the table using an old paintbrush and carefully position the new piece of matting. Allow to dry.

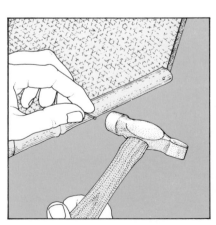

9. When the glue has dried, the bamboo pieces removed from the edges previously must be replaced. If their varnished surface has been chipped, it may be necessary to smooth them with fine steel wool and to repaint them before re-positioning. If not, simply tap the pieces in place with small steel panel or veneer pins, oiling the pins lightly to ease insertion if necessary.

GLASS

Glass is a unique substance in that, contrary to appearances, it is not a solid. Its scientific definition is a liquid in suspension, or a super-cooled liquid, a fact which accounts for its particular qualities of brilliance and fragility. The principal constituent of glass is silica which in its pure form has an impractiably high melting point and so is made workable by the addition of about 15 per cent soda (sodium oxide). Lime is also added to reduce the water solubility of the glass to make the ordinary soda-lime glass used in windows. Although the basic ingredients—sand, limestone and soda-ash (from the burning of hardwoods)—have always been easily obtainable, the ability to make glass was restricted to a very few primitive cultures, although many had mastered metalworking and some form of pottery.

The earliest glass object known is a rod found in Mesopotamia believed to date from about 2600 B.C. A piece of Mesopotamian blue glass dates from about 2200 B.C. while glass vessels are known to have been made in Egypt from the time of the eighteenth dynasty—from 1490 B.C. In these early vessels, glass was built up on a core of clay and decorated by winding on threads of coloured glass—yellow, white, green or red—which were afterwards re-heated and combed, then rolled to a flat surface. Primitive glass was always more or less blue or green in colour, because of contamination with iron oxides, and such glass is still made for domestic purposes in some Mediterranean countries.

From these beginnings, glass-making soon developed to a fine art; the components were tinted to resemble semi-precious stones such as lapis lazuli, jade and turquoise and melted together in small pots. When they had been cooled, the blocks were cut, rubbed, engraved and polished to make decorated vessels. Small pieces of glass were sometimes placed together in the kiln to fuse and form patterns during firing. This method of cutting objects out of a solid block of glass was current in Mesopotamia from the eighth century B.C. From here, glass-making spread to Greece and the Aegean, and by the first century B.C. Alexandria had become the great centre of glass production. By this time the technique of using glass "canes" had been developed—glass rods in strands of many colours were cut across to reveal a mosaic pattern. Metallic oxides were used to tint glass. Moulded glass was also made in Alexandria by pressing glass into moulds or by coating the moulds with layers of glass powder which was then fused. Such pieces could be "fire polished" by reheating in the furnace, polished by abrasives, engraved or cut. The craftsmen of Alexandria also invented enamel painting in which powdered coloured glass was fused to the surface by a separate firing.

Some time around the beginning of the first century B.C. the new technique of glass-blowing was discovered, probably in Syria. This was a revolutionary development since blown glass was a totally different material; thin, transparent and highly versatile. Glass gathered at the end of a blowpipe could be blown into moulds, so that shapes such as flasks could be made more quickly and easily than by cutting them out of blocks. Glass thus became a viable medium for large-scale commercial production of bottles and jars for storing oil, wine, cosmetics and food, and their use spread throughout the Roman trade area. Early blown glass was pale green, semi-transparent and surprisingly light in weight, although some of the original thickness may have been eroded by centuries of burial. The greenish tinge comes from the iron oxide in the sand.

By the first century A.D. glass-making had also become well established in Italy, where cameo glass was first produced; in this an outer layer of one colour, usually white, is cut away to reveal a design in a lower layer of a different colour. In the post-Roman period glass-making was widely distributed around the Mediterranean littoral; advances were made in Syria in the techniques of gilding and enamelling, primarily for decorating Islamic mosque lamps.

During the Middle Ages, elaborate designs disappeared except for the so-called "forest" glass—primitive vessels for domestic use produced in small local glass-houses. Although they can be clumsy or rough, the best beakers have a certain sturdy elegance.

It was further south, in Venice, that glass production was to be revolutionized. It had long been an established craft when, at the end of the thirteenth century, the furnaces were moved to the island of Murano, primarily to reduce the fire risk to the city. The great advance of the Venetian guilds was the discovery of additives which decolourized the glass (though it was in fact left with a slight brown or grey tinge). All types of glass techniques were employed, but the Venetians specialized in elaborate and fantastic forms on thin and fragile glass. By the fifteenth century the guilds were blowing stylized drinking glasses, ornamental plates, dishes and cups, all richly tinted and intricately decorated with enamels and even precious stones. For the next two centuries Venetian *cristallo* was unequalled in virtuosity and exported throughout the known world. The glass-workers of Murano were forbidden to leave or pass on the secrets of their art to foreigners, but despite severe penalties many did slip away to establish rival glass-houses in other cities, notably Altare, Antwerp, Paris and London.

In England primitive glass had been made during the Middle Ages but it was the arrival in 1570 of the Venetian Jacopo Verzelini and his creation in London of a glass-house for the making of thin tableware—"Anglo-Venetian glass"—that gave fresh impetus to glass manufacture. In 1615 the Vauxhall glass-house near London was founded for the making of drinking glasses, window glass and mirrors; with only one interval it continued until 1745.

Glass made from the traditional constituents of sand, lime and soda-ash was not strong enough to withstand everyday wear and tear as its use became more and more widespread among the rapidly expanding middle classes. In London, the Worshipful Company of Glass Sellers engaged George Ravenscroft to experiment with ways of making a stronger type of glass. By replacing sand with crushed calcined flint and by adding lead oxide as the flux to stabilize the glass (which was otherwise subject to spontaneous cracking) he was able to produce a greatly superior mixture, known as flint glass. By 1700 lead or flint glass had more or less replaced *cristallo*. Today it is usually called crystal or lead crystal and remains the finest type of glass available. Its particular qualities are heaviness and durability and an exceptional brilliance which lends itself to display because it can be engraved or cut into facets or into fluid, sculptural shapes.

The imposition of a tax on glass by weight in 1745 resulted in the production of lighter and more slender drinking glasses often with an air-twist stem (the tax persisted until 1845). Irish glass escaped the tax and was heavier than English, though indistinguishable in style. Glasses were enamelled or gilded, especially by the Beilby family in Newcastle. However, the distinctively English and Irish contribution to glass decoration lay in cutting. This was assisted by the introduction in the 1740s of the tunnel lehr or furnace, which enabled the glass to be annealed and toughened by heating and cooling. Cutting became ever more elaborate until the middle of the nineteenth century. Much admired and sought after, it was extensively copied on the Continent.

In the United States attempts were made to establish a glass-making industry in Jamestown, Virginia, in 1608, but without success. However, by 1739 Caspar Wistar had established a glass-house in Salem County, New Jersey, and in 1763 Henry Stiegel started one in Lancaster County, Pennsylvania. Both were devoted primarily to making bottles and window glass. After the war of 1812, when the production of lead glass had been mastered and mechanical pressing introduced, a thriving industry grew up. In pressing, the molten glass is forced into a mould by a mechanical pump, enabling quite realistic copies of cut glass to be made, although lacking some of the brilliance of the original.

Paperweights show off the decorative qualities of glass in a different way. Invented by French stationers around 1850 as a desk toy, their production was taken up by the great French factories such as St Louis and Baccarat. Today they are much sought after by collectors and correspondingly expensive. Small slices of millefiori-patterned glass rods and fantastic lace and animal figurines in the best Victorian tradition were enclosed in clear glass domes and then sometimes surrounded a second time with red or blue layers with windows cut out to show the scene inside.

The manufacture of flat glass has also progressed enormously in the last hundred years or so. Until the nineteenth century the only way of producing it was by means of the blowing-iron; a globe of glass was blown, flattened, reheated and spun until it flowed outwards into a huge round sheet called crown glass. It could then be cut into panes, the centre of the disk forming the bulls-eye sometimes seen in old windows (and now often deliberately copied!) Later, a cylinder of glass was blown, slit lengthwise and allowed to flatten on an iron table. If a truly flat sheet of glass was required, it could only be made by polishing a sheet of spun or cast glass, a very expensive process before the arrival of cheap mechanical power. Today flat sheets are made by rolling, by floating the glass on the surface of molten metal, or by drawing vertically a kind of curtain of molten glass.

In many ways glass-blowing has changed little over the centuries, although the kilns are now electric. The tools are traditional: a blowpipe to make the first bubble, a heavy flat surface of metal or marble to roll the bubble into shape, metal or wooden forms to help make uniform designs for each glass, shears to cut off the lip and a solid iron pontil rod to hold the glass by the foot while the finishing touches are applied. The work is usually carried out by a team, although as in many modern crafts, studio glass is also made by individuals working on special decorative pieces with techniques adapted from every glass tradition.

The history of stained glass is inextricably linked with Christian art and architecture. Although its technical origins may lie in Classical mosaics, the art was perfected by medieval craftsmen who used it in churches and cathedrals to illustrate and glorify their faith.

Little of the earliest stained glass has survived, although it is known that the windows of the church of St Martin at Tours in France were glazed with coloured glass in the sixth century. The golden age of stained glass began with the emergence of the Gothic style, epitomized by soaring vaults, sharply pointed arches and flying buttresses, which spread throughout Europe in the thirteenth century. Window areas became much larger, increasing the scope for craftsmen in stained glass. The colours used became darker and more dramatic, with deep, intense blues and violets, in particular, used to create a mystical atmosphere.

The end of the great age of stained glass came with the Reformation in the sixteenth century when the imagery of the medieval Catholic church was rejected as idolatrous by the Protestants. Calvinists in the Netherlands sacked churches, and in sixteenth and seventeenth-century England there was wholesale destruction of windows and other church art. The eighteenth century saw a minor revival but this was limited by the religious climate and by the architectural styles of the Baroque and Rococo, to which stained glass was little suited.

The next flowering of the art of stained glass occurred in the nineteenth century. On historical grounds this was largely due to the Victorian obsession with medieval myths and legends which led to the Gothic revival in art and architecture; on technical grounds there was enormous improvement in the quality of glass being manufactured. At its worst, Victorian stained glass suffers from excessive sentimentality and a very imprecise understanding of the Middle Ages, but at its best, in the hands of masters such as William Morris and Edward Burne-Jones, it can stand comparison with the work of earlier centuries.

The Art Nouveau movement also had a marked influence on stained glass: it introduced a new feeling of lyrical naturalism into the designs and also established stained glass, perhaps for the first time, as a valid secular medium for artists. At the end of the century many famous artists and designers were working successfully in stained glass: Charles Rennie Mackintosh in Scotland, Gustav Klimt in Austria, Horta in Belgium, Gaudi in Spain and Louis Comfort Tiffany in America.

The twentieth century has brought many changes in both style and technique. New architectural materials such as concrete and steel have provided spectacular opportunities: thick slabs of glass, known as *dalles de verre*, can be set directly into stonework to become an integral part of a building's structure, and pieces of coloured glass can be fused together onto plain glass to form a design, dispensing with leading altogether. Abstraction as a fine art movement has been echoed by artists in glass, with brilliant results. Freed from its traditional religious and representational roles, stained glass is today an exciting medium which deserves to be used more widely in architecture and decoration.

Cleaning and repairing glass

Glass can usually be cleaned by washing in warm, soapy water, followed by a clear rinse. If the glass article is particularly dirty, add a drop or two of vinegar or ammonia to the detergent solution, or use a proprietary window cleaning liquid in the water. For extra sparkle, the rinse water can also have a few drops of vinegar added. A stronger cleaner can be made from: ¼pt/140ml denatured alcohol (methylated spirits), ¼pt/140ml household ammonia and ½pt/285ml water. After rinsing, dry glass with a clean, lint-free cloth (linen is ideal) or water spots will remain. Do not rub painted or gilded glass to dry; instead pat dry.

1. If the bottom of a vase, decanter or similar narrow-necked vessel has become very grimy, and washing in the above solutions fails to affect the dirty deposit, try the following: place a spoonful of sand in the bottom of the vessel, using a funnel if necessary.

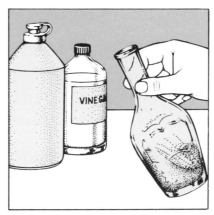

2. Add a drop of liquid detergent, a few drops of white vinegar and enough warm water to cover the bottom of the vessel. Swish the abrasive mixture around the base, rinse and repeat if necessary, then dry as above.

The amateur can successfully clean glass, but not so successfully repair it. The following simple repairs can be attempted, but badly damaged glass must be sent to an expert restorer, especially if the piece is valuable. Experts will be able to buff out scratches, smooth chipped edges but can't join a break invisibly, since the translucency of glass shows up the line.

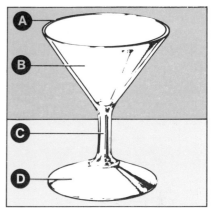

REPAIRING A STEMMED GLASS

3. The most common breakages are to stemmed glasses, which are made up of rim (A), bowl (B), stem (C) and foot (D). The directions below refer specifically to these, but can also be applied to other repairs. When attempting restoration, work in a warm room and avoid applying too much pressure to glass to avoid additional breaks. Remember, glass is not a solid, but a liquid in a suspended state. The illustration shows parts of a stemmed glass.

4. Mending a broken stem is one of the trickiest repairs, even though the bowl usually snaps off fairly cleanly. After washing and drying both pieces as directed in Step 1, turn the bowl upside down, resting it on a soft cloth. Carefully rotate the stem until it rests in the correct position on the bowl, along the break line. If the stem is broken in two or more pieces, position the piece nearest the bowl first.

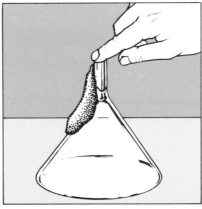

5. Take a small glob of modelling clay or plasticine and make a roll about 1in/2.5cm long, thick enough to support the stem. Push one end firmly but not too hard onto one side of the bowl, just below or to one side of the break, but do not press it against the broken stem yet.

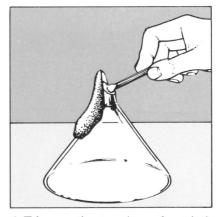

6. Take away the stem piece and coat both surfaces of the break with a drop of synthetic-based glue – choose one that's transparent and waterproof. Try not to let the glue slip onto the sides of the stem. A wooden matchstick is a very useful applicator if the glue's pin or spreader has been lost.

Cleaning and repairing glass cont.

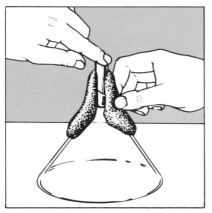

7. Quickly fit the stem in place on the bowl again. Hold it firmly in place for a minute, and, while keeping the stem straight with one hand, push the clay or plasticine against the top part with the other.

8. For a very straight break which won't easily balance, or a heavy stem, use an additional clay support on the other side, but be sure not to push the top of the stem out of place. For breaks near the foot, the clay will probably have to to to be a little more generous so that the piece balances. Leave the supports in position while the glue sets – at least 24 hours – and make sure the surface the glass is standing on is steady and will not vibrate. The same procedure can be followed for large chips and broken pieces of all kinds.

9. Alternatively, masking tape can be used to hold the pieces in place. Tape from one unbroken area right across the break to an unbroken area on the other side. With a multiple break, glue and tape one piece at a time, waiting at least 24 hours before adding each further fragment.

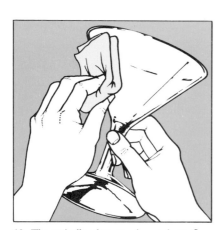

10. Theoretically glass can be made to flow enough to cover small scratches. If you have the time and patience, take a chamois cloth and rub in one direction only, until the scratch fades. However, note that scratches on the base of any glass piece should never be erased or ground away unless they disfigure the object. Such markings are the sign to any valuer that the glass is old and has survived a certain amount of wear and tear.

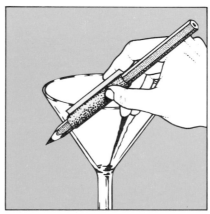

11. A small chip can be smoothed over with abrasive paper – use a medium grade wet-and-dry paper wrapped around a pencil or piece of wood so that it can rub the edges evenly. Alternatively, the edge of the rim can be removed from the glass by a professional glass cutter, although the appearance of the glass may be somewhat changed. However, this is worth doing when the chip is really bad, or there are radiating cracks which may cause more pieces to break off.

12. Have the cut made below the damage. Thicker glass may be cut with one of the home bottle-cutters which are available in many large stores, but any fine and/or valuable glass requires professional attention. After cutting, the rim must be smoothed. In the glassworks, this would be done by slightly melting the rim, but amateurs should only use fine abrasive paper. There will be a slightly frosted effect, but by using progressively finer grades and then polishing it well, the clouding should be minimal.

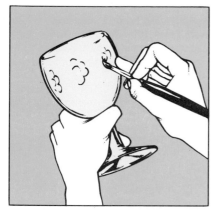

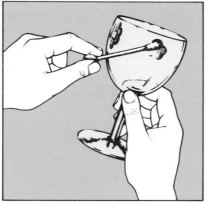

13. Hold the glass up to the light. Paint usually leaves a slight residue and you should be able to trace the missing parts easily, using a pointed brush or felt-tip pen. Paint over the markings in the same shades that are already on the glass, using special glass paints. If they are not available, acrylic or enamel paints will do. No paint that is not fired or semi-permanent will resist much washing and daily use – so it's better to keep such decoration for ornamental articles. Use a very small brush and try to work as evenly as possible. Do one shade at a time, letting the paint dry completely between each coat.

14. For step-by-step instructions on painting a new motif or design, see Steps 1-3, Page 74. If you want to use a pattern from a straight-sided glass but put it on a funnel bowl, it will need adapting. It's best to start with fairly simple, freehand designs, but avoid geometric borders as such patterns are very difficult for a beginner, and show up clumsy brushwork immediately. For badly placed strokes, dip a cotton swab in paint remover, and wipe off the error at once.

CLEANING AND RESTORING MIRROR

There are several reasons for not replacing old mirror with new: the pleasing, irregular tonality, the fine bevelled edge, even the imperfections add to the value of an antique mirror. However, it is advisable to clean mirror periodically. Follow the instructions in Steps 1-2, Page 89, or rub the surface with a ball of paper dampened with denatured alcohol (methylated spirits). If only a patch of silvering has worn away, smooth a thin layer of finest reflecting foil on the back, and tape in place.

Restoring reverse glass paintings

Because the smooth surface of glass makes it difficult for the paint to adhere properly, these charming paintings are often badly damaged. If the paint is flaking away then the glass panel should not be touched except by an expert restorer, who may advise that another sheet of thin glass backing be placed over the flaked paintwork to hold it in place.

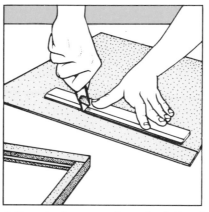

1. If the glass appears to be merely dirty and the paint is quite stable, it is advisable to clean the panel front and back and replace the backing board with acid-free cardboard. To do so, prise up the small nails which hold the backing board in place using needle-nosed pliers, taking great care not to scratch either the frame or the paintwork. Lift the glass panel. Discard the backing board and carefully dust the panel on both sides. Wash with soapy water, then rinse and dab dry with a linen cloth.

2. Dust the frame, restoring and polishing if necessary as directed in previous chapters. Then, cut a piece of acid-free cardboard the same size as the original backing, bearing in mind that the shade of the board will be seen through the glass when viewed from the front – white or off-white boards are usually best.

3. Return the glass panel to the frame, insert the card backing and push the small nails back down so they hold the backing and glass firmly in place.

Restoring and repairing stained glass

Old stained glass may only need cleaning and some of the simple repairs described below to enhance its appearance and stabilize its condition. Stained glass panels in doors and windows can often be repaired in situ by amateurs if the only problems are discoloration and minor cracks. However, if there is any doubt about the age or value of a glass panel, it is essential to consult an expert before attempting restoration.

When working with glass, remember that, once removed from their setting, the panels are very fragile—apart from the pieces of glass themselves, the lead strips are likely to have become brittle with age and the putty may have powdered away, with the result that the whole panel could easily fall apart.

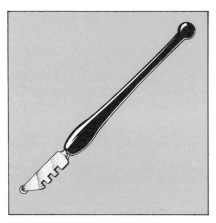

GLASSWORKING TOOLS

Glass cutter: an ordinary single-wheel cutter will probably be adequate, though specialists use a heavier type of cutter with a knob on the handle and a replaceable wheel. A tungsten wheel cutter stays sharp longer but costs more. Keep the cutter lubricated when not in use by storing it in a small jar containing an absorbent fabric pad moistened with white spirit or light oil. Once blunt, a cutter is useless, and should be discarded unless the wheel is replaceable.

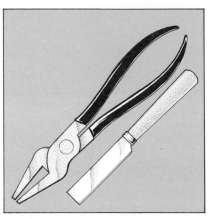

Pliers: glazier's pliers (known as "grozing iron") are available from specialist suppliers, but ordinary flat-nosed pliers can be used instead to trim glass to shape.

Leading knife: it is possible to make one by cutting short an old-fashioned non-stainless table knife and sharpening the butt end. Use it for cutting lead, and also to lift up the flanges of lead and lever the glass into position.

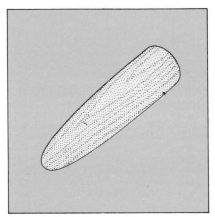

Lathekin: this is used to press the leads down into the glass and run along the groove of a lead to straighten it. Glaziers usually make their own from boxwood or bone, but any thin, hard wood will do—part of an old wooden ruler, the lid of a cigar box or good thin plywood. The lathekin should be 4 – 5in x 1½ x ⅛in/10 – 12.5cm x 3cm x 3mm. One end is gently curved, the other more pointed; all edges must be smoothed with fine abrasive paper. Keep the lathekin well polished.

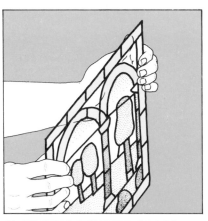

HANDLING STAINED GLASS

1. Take great care when handling panels of glass as lead bends easily and the weight of the glass can impose a strain on the joints of the panel, causing it to sag in the middle or even fall apart. For this reason, a leaded panel should always be carried vertically, never horizontally like a tray.

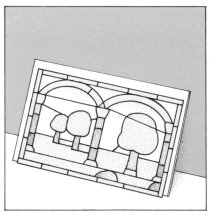

2. If stored flat on a table or shelf the whole area of the panel must be supported, and nothing placed on top. If leant against a wall, a supporting board should be placed behind it at the same angle.

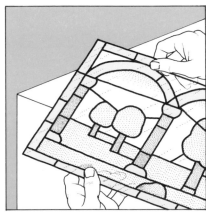

3. When lifting a panel from a flat position, slide it halfway over the edge of the table, holding the front edge of the panel with one hand and lifting up the far end with the other, so that the middle is supported by the edge of the table. The panel can then be tilted upright without placing a strain on the glass. It can be laid flat again the same way.

Cleaning and repairing stained glass

To clean a stained glass panel and repair small cracks and breaks, the following tools and supplies are required: small paintbrush, water, ammonia, liquid detergent, adhesive (two-part transparent epoxy resin, silicone cement aquarium sealant or a glass bond adhesive that sets in ultra-violet light), single-edged razor blade, clear adhesive tape or soft modelling clay, self-adhesive lead strips (used for imitation leading and obtainable in rolls from hardware stores), and scissors.

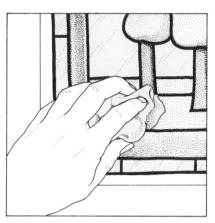

CLEANING THE GLASS

1. First brush off any loose dirt and dust. If the outside of glass from a window is covered in a layer of sticky grime, wash it in a strong solution of liquid detergent, then rinse well with clear water.

2. Wash the panel carefully with hot water to which a few drops of ammonia have been added. The inside of a window should be easier to clean and should be treated very carefully—this is the painted side of stained glass. If there is any sign of flaking paint, consult an expert and do not attempt any further treatment.

REPAIRING CRACKS AND BREAKS

3. Any cracks will be revealed by cleaning; very small ones need not be touched but larger ones can be treated using any of the above adhesives. (When mixing a two-part epoxy resin, follow the manufacturer's instructions carefully regarding proportions: too much hardener will produce a yellow effect.) Paint the adhesive over the crack with a small paintbrush and leave to sink in.

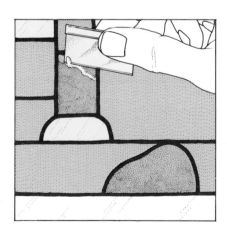

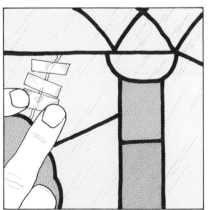

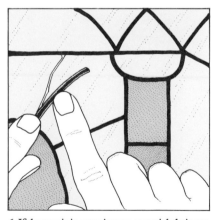

4. When it is completely dry and hard excess adhesive can be scraped off the surface with a single-edged razor blade.

5. If the crack is actually a clean break, join the two pieces of glass using the same adhesive. (See Steps 6-9, Pages 89-90, for directions on glueing broken glass.) Use clear adhesive tape or soft modelling clay to hold the pieces together until set.

6. If the repair is conspicuous or unsightly it can be masked with imitation leading. Cut a self-adhesive lead strip to the right length, using scissors, and press firmly in place over the crack. Repeat on the other side of the panel. When the panel is against the light, the new "lead" should be barely distinguishable from the original ones.

Replacing broken glass

If a piece of glass is badly cracked or broken it will probably need to be taken out and replaced. It may not be possible for the amateur to do this with stained glass as the broken piece has to be matched with a new piece of painted glass which must be fired in a kiln. But plain white or coloured glass can be replaced at home if the right type of glass can be found.

Assemble the following tools and supplies: soft pencil or crayon or "heel-ball" (a block of wax and lamp black used in brass rubbing), heavy brown or cartridge paper, leading knife, lathekin, small pliers, glazier's or flat-nosed pliers, cardboard, white paper, felt-tip pen, glass cutter, small file or fine abrasive paper, linseed oil putty, black powder paint, putty knife.

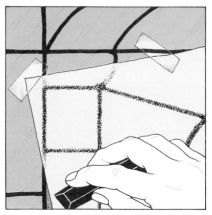

1. First, take a rubbing of the area around and including the damage, using a soft pencil or crayon or a heel-ball, and heavy paper. This will indicate the position of the leads and enable a template for the replacement glass to be made.

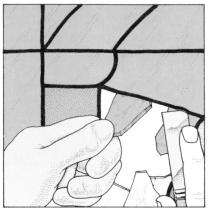

2. Remove all the broken glass, using the leading knife and the lathekin, and, if necessary, small pliers to prise back the flanges of the lead. It may help to cut gently into the corners of the joints so that the lead can be turned back neatly. Do this on one side of the panel only—if treating a window, always work from the inside.

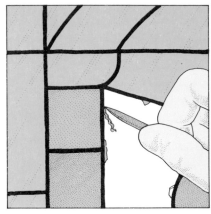

3. Scrape out the old putty and any remaining fragments of glass with a sharp pointed stick or other small slim tool.

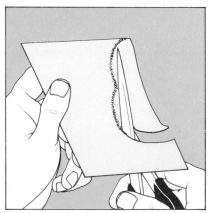

4. From the rubbing, cut out a template from a piece of cardboard, and try it for fit in the hole, trimming if necessary. It should fit fairly loosely, as the glass itself, being rigid, will be harder to insert.

5. Place the template on a piece of white paper and draw an outline around it with a felt-tip pen so that the line will show clearly through the glass to be cut.

6. Place the outline under the glass on a flat surface and cut out the piece. Hold the glass cutter between the first and second fingers, with the thumb as extra support behind the tool—it is *not* held like a pencil. Keep it almost upright, with the teeth facing towards the body. Using firm pressure, either push the cutter along the line to be cut or pull it forwards. As the wheel runs over the glass it should make a slight crackling noise, showing that it is biting into the surface effectively.

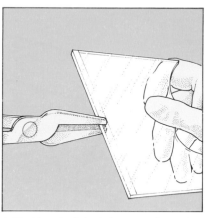

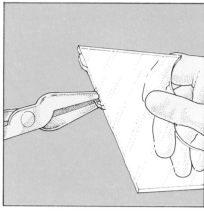

7. When the cut has been made properly, the glass can often be snapped apart easily by hand, but it may be necessary to tap along the line of the cut from underneath, using the teeth of the cutter (not the wheel, which would be damaged). This starts a crack running along the line and the glass should then break.

8. If a thin strip of glass is being cut, pliers will be needed to break it off.

9. Try the replacement glass in the hole — it will probably need to be trimmed for a good fit. Use glazier's or flat-nosed pliers to "nibble" away gradually at the edges, removing sharp corners or bumps. This must be done very carefully and gently; hold the piece of glass firmly in one hand near the edge to be trimmed and ease the pliers along with the other.

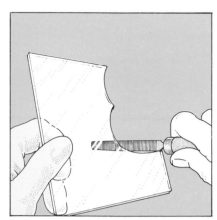

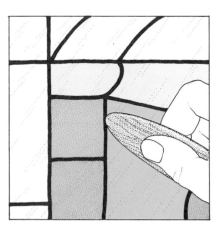

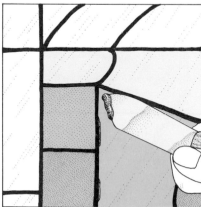

10. Finally, use a small file and/or fine abrasive paper to smooth off the edges so that the glass will slide more easily into place. If it is a tight fit, it may help to lever it into position using the leading knife.

11. When the glass is in place, the flanges of the leads must be gently but firmly pushed back over it, using the lathekin. Good quality lead may be stiff and difficult to bend, but it is important to press down as smoothly as possible.

12. Seal the glass in place with linseed oil putty darkened with black powder paint to the same shade as the lead. With the putty knife, push it under the flanges of the leads on both sides of the panel; carefully remove any excess from the face of the glass.

Repairing other kinds of damage

Depending on the repairs to be undertaken, the following tools and supplies may be required: leading knife, wire brush, linseed oil putty, black or brown powder paint, gold size, solder and a soldering iron. Either a gas or electric soldering iron can be used (minimum 65 watts for electric), with lead "blowpipe" solder and a flux. The traditional flux is tallow, but a soldering paste or a proprietary substance called Baker's Fluid can be used instead. It is possible to use a multi-cored solder (obtainable in strips on a reel) without another flux, but this tends to leave a hard resin deposit that is difficult to remove.

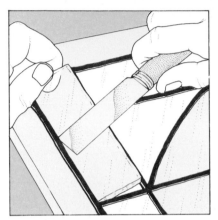

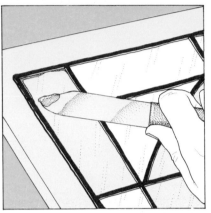

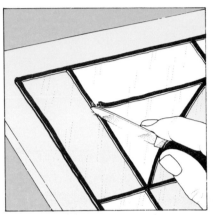

1. Sometimes the glass will have been pushed out of the leads and these will have become twisted. If so, lay the panel flat on a board and ease the glass back, using the leading knife. Then push the leads back into their original position with the lathekin.

2. Scrape out all old putty and replace it as above. It is much harder to do this if the panel is vertically in situ in a window or door — if so, it helps to have someone else assisting on the other side.

3. If any of the leads are actually broken, it may be necessary to resolder the joins, using the equipment detailed above. Clean the surface very thoroughly by scraping with a knife blade or brushing with a wire brush before applying the flux.

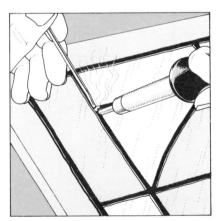

4. Then apply a drop of melted solder on the join, pressing and smoothing it with the soldering iron. The new join will look very bright at first but will darken with time as it oxidizes; it can be toned down initially with black lead or black shoe polish. (It is almost impossible to solder joins vertically so if the leads in a window need attention it is best to take the whole panel out and repair it flat.)

5. Old putty may have dried out and turned to powder. If the leads are still firm, scrape out all the old putty and insert new linseed oil putty that has been darkened with black powder paint. If, however, the leads have become very dry and brittle with age, the whole panel will need re-leading; in this case, it must be taken to an expert.

6. Flaking paint on old or valuable glass must only be tackled by an expert, but to restore the appearance of a newer glass panel, it is possible to reinforce the fading outlines of paint. Mix black or dark brown powdered pigments with gold size, until the desired shade is achieved; then apply using a fine artists' paintbrush.

Opposite: An Arts and Crafts ladderback chair with characteristic rush seating, photographed before restoration (see also overleaf).

BASKETRY AND CANEWORK

Basketry is one of the most ancient crafts, pre-dating both pottery and weaving, and is practised all over the world. Containers which nowadays are often made from paper, plastic and metal were from earliest times made of willow, roots, rushes and grasses. The natural plant material found near at hand was used to make containers for transport, storage, and many other purposes, the nature of the materials available dictating the techniques employed.

Fragments of pottery bearing the impressions of basketwork, and dated before 8000 B.C., have been found in Africa, and some of the earliest baskets found in the Middle East date from 6500 B.C. The type of plaited and coiled work found in Egypt, and made about 3000 B.C., is still made today, and the stake and strand techniques employed in some of the earliest examples of British basketry, found near Glastonbury and thought to be more than 2000 years old, is quite familiar to the modern basketmaker.

The use of basketry has always been far more extensive than simply making containers for food, goods, or livestock. Basketwork served man quite literally from the cradle to the grave, as the new born baby would be rocked to sleep in a cradle made of willow, rush or grasses, and the dead were once buried in coffins made of wicker. It was used to build houses — in the form of "wattle and daub" (interlaced twigs plastered with mud) — and to thatch them, and in warm climates it formed walls, floors, and doors.

Baskets were thus once an essential part of almost every aspect of daily life. They have been used as fish, game and bird traps, as containers of seed before sowing and grain after harvest, for gathering fruit, for marketing, for hauling materials up the sides of buildings, for letting miners down into mine shafts and for hauling coal up, for holding fleece in wool mills and bread at the bakers. The domestic baskets used to contain food and drink, household goods, and clothes, have always been much more than strictly utilitarian objects. In many parts of the world their beauty of design and execution was an indication of social standing. The American Indians made some of the most beautiful baskets found anywhere in the world, and the position in the tribe of their maker (usually a woman), would depend on their excellence. Often her best work would be burned after her death, or buried with her.

In times of war basketry had many important uses. The Romans had wicker shields (the Dutch police still use wicker riot shields), and there were basketwork chariots as well as wooden ones. The basketwork shell cases, so necessary to Charles II's army, were still being made in World War I, and in World War II every British basketmaker had to make his quota of hampers, in which vital supplies were dropped by parachute to battle areas.

In more peaceful times the war chariots became carriages, reaching great heights of elegance in the nineteenth century, with panels in both basketwork and canework; but these materials were also used further down the social scale for governess carts, farm carts, and the small willow handcarts used until quite recent times by postmen. Boats, too, were another means of transport for which basketmaking materials were used successfully, from the reed boats constructed and used by the Kon Tiki expedition, to the coracles — frame boats covered in hide — used in Britain before the Romans came, and still occasionally to be found in use in Ireland and in Wales.

The first men to fly successfully, the early balloonists, used a gondola, suspended below the balloon, made of basketwork because of its strength and lightness. Their baskets were tiny, some only 2ft 6in/76cm long and 12in/30cm deep, but modern balloonists use huge strong baskets with plywood bases. Early aeroplane seats were cane chairs, for both pilots and passengers.

Floor covering, hammocks and bedding were all once made of rushes, sedge and grasses, and furniture made from willow and cane has never lost its appeal. The Romans had basket chairs; coiled rush and straw chairs, often with overhead canopies, were popular in England as well as in the Orkneys, and hooded willow chairs were found in the West Country as well as in Wales. All these are still being made by specialists. Rush seated chairs came into general use in Britain in the seventeenth century, but there is a 4000 year-old Egyptian stool in the British Museum, seated with coiled rushes or palm. William Morris designed some beautiful rush seated chairs in the late nineteenth century, based on traditional country styles, and many attractive modern Scandinavian and Spanish chairs have rush seats. Chair seating in rattan cane from the Malay Peninsula became popular in Holland and France in the seventeenth century, where it was used in furniture of great elegance. It was one of the fashions brought over to Britain by Charles II at the time of the Restoration of the Monarchy. But the techniques used in cane seating are many thousands of years older, and perhaps the earliest example is the beautiful caned daybed which was among the treasures found in the tomb of Tutankhamun.

Although cane furniture has been in and out of fashion several times since the seventeenth century, it has enjoyed times of great popularity, and combined well with many styles, such as the japonaiserie-style bamboo furniture, and the beautiful shapes of bentwood furniture designed by the Austrian Michael Thonet in the nineteenth century. Oriental influences on domestic design proliferated in the latter years of the century and by 1870 there were 150 producers of japonaiserie in Britain alone, manufacturing an incredible 5000 objects a week — a range that included everything from penholders to entire bedroom suites. Most of the second-hand bamboo, lacquer and cane pieces to be found today were produced during the period from 1840 to 1930, and many of them will need repairing.

Time, dirt, dryness and the ravages of woodworm and other insects are the enemies of all natural materials, and the owners of working baskets sadly give little thought to their care. Willow can safely be washed with water, with a soft brush for crevices, and allowed to dry in the open air, though not in direct sunlight. Other hard basketry such as cane and bamboo can also be washed. Cane and rush seating will benefit from a wipe over with a damp cloth, but do not allow it to become too wet. Soft basketry such as rush, sedge and straw will also benefit from sponging with warm water. All baskets deteriorate if they are kept too dry, and an old willow basket will be improved by a good soak, but soft basketry must not get too wet or it will go mouldy.

Opposite: An Arts and Crafts ladderback chair with characteristic rush seating, photographed after the damaged rush seat had been replaced with new rushes (see also previous page).

Restoration of caned seats

It is seldom possible to patch a damaged cane seat or back and *always* more satisfactory to renew it. The "six-way standard" pattern described on the following pages is the one most commonly found on antique furniture. It comprises two vertical "settings", two horizontal "weavings" and two diagonal "crossings" and gives a strong, attractive and hardwearing seat when done properly.

Before cutting away the old canes on the seat, make a drawing of any caning still intact, noting the number of canes in each hole, and their direction. Then remove any beading left and knock out the old pegs, working from underneath with a clearing tool. Cut out the old seat, keeping it intact if possible, and retain it for reference. Then clear all remaining holes. Finally, do any necessary repairs or restoration to the chair and seat frame before recaning (see pages 25 – 7).

Assemble the following materials: chair cane may be bought from wholesalers in large quantities or from craft shops in small

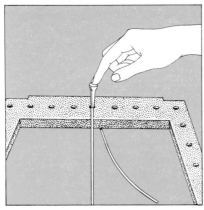

1. Cane may be worked dry or damp, or rubbed with beeswax to make it supple. Begin the first "setting" by finding the central holes on the front and back rails. Mark each with a dowel or golf tee. Thread a length of No. 2 cane through the middle back hole to half its length; peg firmly with the dowel or tee. Bring the end on top forward and down through the middle hole on the front rail, smooth side uppermost; peg it. Thread this end up through the hole to the left, with the smooth side showing under the rail; peg firmly. Take the cane across and into the hole to the left of the middle back hole. Continue until the left side is filled.

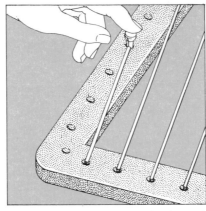

2. When the cane runs out, peg the short end leaving a 3in/8cm tail under the rail. Start a new cane in the adjacent hole, leaving a 3in/8cm tail and pegging it firmly. Proceed as above. Fill every hole on the front and back rails except the corner ones. If the chair is irregularly shaped, i.e. with a wider front than back, fill up holes on the front rail using short settings connecting to holes on the side rails. Keep the settings parallel. When the left side is complete, pick up the second half of the original cane and complete the right side in the same way. Make sure that the short settings match on each side.

3. Begin the first cross-wise "weaving" with No. 2 cane, starting at the second hole from the back on the left, and working from side to side on top of the first setting; fill in every hole except those at the corners. Keep the tension fairly firm. Note: for a bow-fronted chair, it will be necessary to use short weavings at the front to fill in the space; the front "corner" holes will then be those with the shortest settings. Leave them free of weaving if this is necessary to keep the weaving evenly spaced.

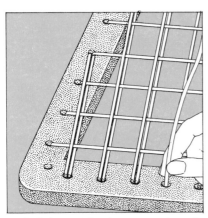

4. Work the second setting on top again, and to the left of the first. Start from the front of the chair, working in the opposite direction to the first setting, so that the canes fill in the blanks between the holes under the rail left by the first setting. This will avoid a lumpy appearance after the later stages have been completed. Peg carefully to ensure that the two settings lie side by side as they come up and down through the same holes. As before, join in a new cane by pegging the end of the old one, then pegging a new one in the adjacent hole, again leaving a 3in/8cm tail.

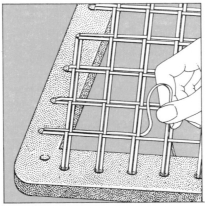

5. The second weaving uses the same holes as the first weaving, but goes from right to left so the canes are alternate to the first weaving under the rail. Begin from the second hole from the back, always keeping the second weaving behind the first, i.e. nearest to the back of the chair, interweaving it with the settings. It goes under the first setting and over the second, i.e. under the right hand setting and over the left. Use the cane in the direction in which it pulls most smoothly; to find this, run your finger along the edge.

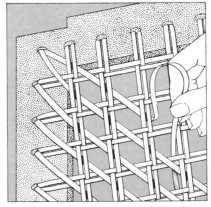

6. Diagonals, or "crossings", are worked in No. 3 cane. The first goes from the back left corner to the front right corner. Peg the cane into the back left corner hole, then take it under the settings and over the weavings. Continue towards the front, taking the cane over the tip of the last weaving before going down into a side hole. Come up through the next hole in front, and work towards the back left corner. Each corner hole has two crossings or "doubles". Each short setting will need a double in one of the holes in front of it to keep the crossings on a true diagonal.

amounts sufficient for one chair. When purchasing cane take a piece of the old cane with you so the size can be matched—especially important if the chair is one of a set. As a general guideline, cane in sizes No. 2 and No. 3 is used when the holes are closer than ½in/13mm; No. 3 and No. 4 if they are wider apart. No. 12 is used for pegging holes; No. 6 for beading. One half pound/250g of each size will be enough for one chair. The tools required are: clearing tool, such as a steel knitting needle or a sawn-off 3in/8cm nail; knife with replaceable blades; a hammer; some small wooden dowels or plastic golf tees; secateurs or strong scissors; side cutters; and shell bodkin (a curved and channelled bodkin) for threading canes into awkward places.

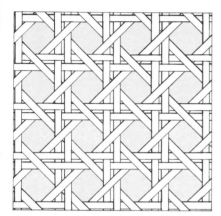

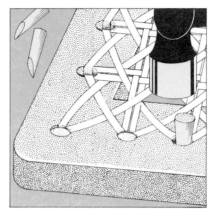

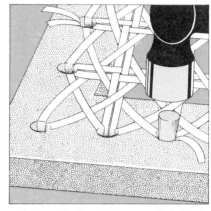

7. After completing the crossings on the front half of the chair, begin the back half. Where there is a double on the left hand side, the corresponding hole on the right must be left empty. (Each hole must have an even number of crossings in it, and a double on the left hand side in the first crossing must be matched by a double on the right in the second crossing.) When the first crossing is complete, start the second crossing from the right hand back corner. This goes over the settings and under the weavings, from back right to front left. The corner holes are doubled and there will be doubles in side holes left out in the first crossing.

8. Chairs made before 1850 will usually be finished with a peg in every hole. To make pegs, cut a short length of No. 12 cane, making a point at one end. With a hammer, tap the pointed end into a hole, then cut it off with secateurs just above the rail. Tap it home with the clearing tool until it is very slightly below the level of the rail. The pegs should fit very tightly and should not project under the rail. When all the holes are pegged, the ends of cane under the rail can be trimmed so there are no sharp protruding ends. There should be no loops or bulges underneath.

9. Chairs made after 1850 are usually finished with a beading of No. 6 cane laced down over the holes with No. 2 cane. Before beginning the beading, all ends of cane must be secured in alternate holes with pegs. Canes in unpegged holes can be brought up through the adjacent holes and held firmly while pegs are driven in to just below the surface of the rail. Cut off closely. Leave all corner holes plus those on either side of them unpegged; if there is an even number of holes, leave the two holes in the middle of the rail unpegged too.

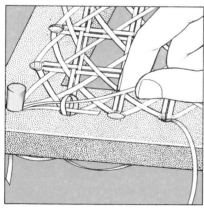

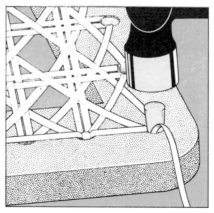

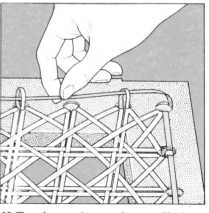

10. To begin the lacing, push the end of a piece of No. 6 cane down through a corner hole. Bring one end of a piece of No. 2 cane up through this hole, just enough to reach beyond the next hole. Bring the long end of the No. 2 cane up through the second hole, over the No. 6 cane and its own short end, and down through the same hole. Continue to lace through the unplugged holes, keeping the canes tight and flat, with the smooth sides showing above and below the rail. If another No. 2 cane needs to be joined in while lacing, secure the old and new ends as above.

11. When a corner is reached, push the end of the No. 6 cane down through the hole. Push a new piece of No. 6 cane down the same hole, and turn it back while a peg is driven in.

12. Turn the new piece over the peg and begin to lace it down, bringing the No. 2 cane across the corner, underneath the rail. When the last corner is reached, bring the No. 2 cane up through the hole, and push the No. 6 cane down. Put in a peg and tap it home. Cut off all ends neatly. (For a bow-fronted chair the beading cane runs from back corner round the front to the other back corner in a continuous length.)

The finished seat should be tight and firm, with all settings and weavings in the correct order so that the crossings bed in properly.

Restoration of caned seats using sheet cane

Many chairs of modern manufacture have seats and/or back made of pre-woven cane called sheet cane. The sheet cane is glued into a groove around the perimeter of the chair seat or back, then the groove is filled with a strip of round cane, referred to as finishing cane or centre cane. However, this type of caned seat is not nearly as strong as the six-way standard pattern described on previous pages, but because of its increasing use, its repair is covered below.

Assemble the following supplies: a sheet of pre-woven cane about 4in/10cm larger all around than the area to be caned; some round cane, No. 12 (about ⅛in/3mm dia), long enough to go around the chair base and/or back in the groove; woodworking adhesive or glue. Tools required are: a narrow chisel or pointed tool, plus hammer, scissors, knife with replaceable blades and a few toothpicks for forcing glue into the groove; and twelve hardwood wedges, approximately 3in/8cm long × 1in/2.5cm wide × ¼in/5mm thick, tapering to a rounded point.

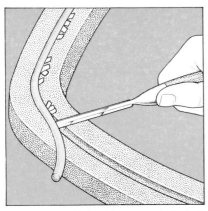

1. Cut away all the old canes with the knife. Using the pointed tool or chisel, scrape the remains of the finishing cane and sheet cane from the grooves making sure that the groove is completely clear. Soak the new sheet cane in cold water for about 15 minutes or until pliable.

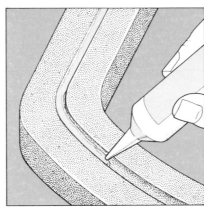

2. Run the woodworking adhesive or glue into the groove all around the chair base or back, making sure that both the sides and the bottom of the groove are covered with glue, using a toothpick to force the glue into the groove if necessary.

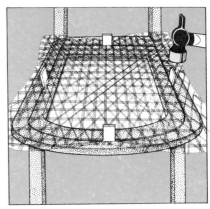

3. Lay the sheet cane over the area to be caned, making sure that the strands of the cane run parallel to a straight side of the chair. Using the hammer, tap a wedge into the groove at the centre back of the chair, forcing the cane down into the groove. Smooth the cane over the seat, then tap a second wedge at the centre front—this will stretch the damp cane from back to front across the seat. Next tap in two more wedges, one in the middle of each side. This should stretch the cane from side to side.

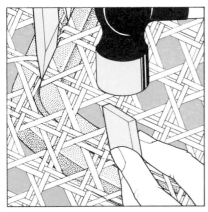

4. Tap in more wedges, working in pairs on opposite sides of the chair, making sure that the canes remain parallel to the straight sides of the chair. When all the wedges have been inserted, remove one of them, and work all around the chair using this wedge to press the remaining areas of sheet cane into the groove. Take care at the corners, trying not to damage strands of the cane—if this should happen, glue the broken end in place. Next, remove all the wedges, and the cane should remain in position, although the glue may not yet be completely dry.

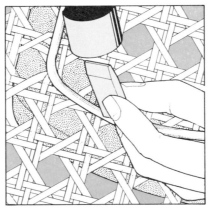

5. Run more glue into the groove on top of the cane. Then cut a piece of finishing cane the length of the back of the seat. Using the hammer and the wide end of one of the wedges, tap the finishing cane into the groove until it is level with the surface of the seat. If the chair is bow-fronted, finish it with a single piece of finishing cane cut to the length of the curve; if it has straight sides, use a separate piece of cane for each side, cutting with the knife to the exact length.

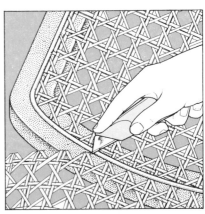

6. To finish, use a sharp knife to trim away the surplus sheet cane, pointing the blade of the knife against the outside edge of the groove while resting the flat of the blade on the finishing cane. Cut carefully around the sheet, making sure that no ragged or sharp edges of cane are left sticking out.

Repairing rush seating

Rush seating is formed by twisting two or more rushes together (depending on the desired thickness) to form a coil. Five coils to the inch is the standard width, but deciding on the thickness of the coil is a matter of aesthetics. Use the original rushing as a guide unless it looks wrong — as a general rule country chairs have thicker coils; more delicate furniture has thinner ones. The coil is then wound around the seat's frame in a continuous strand and extended by twisting in new rushes as needed. Even if only part of the original seat is damaged, it is advisable to remove the entire seat and start

afresh, as attempts to replace a few broken coils are seldom successful. The English method described below will look good and wear well on most rush-seated chairs. However, a closer look at various rushed seats will show a variety of techniques employed and patterns (for example, some rushwork will be coiled in a clockwise direction throughout). If you want to copy any of these methods, take the seat apart very carefully and study the techniques used. Make a careful diagram before you unpick the seat.

1. Before cutting away the damaged rushing, make notes and/or take a photograph or make a sketch of what remains, so you can match the pattern. Also do any renovation to the chair frame before re-rushing—the rails underneath the rush must be smooth or they will cut and scrape the new rushes, weakening them eventually. In addition, there may be a wooden strip covering the edges of the rush between each leg. Prise it off with a chisel or the claw end of a hammer and slice the rush open along the rail. Keep the rush seat intact for reference.

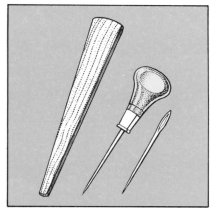

2. Rushes are bought by the bolt, each bolt weighing about 4lb/2kg, the average chair taking about two-thirds of a bolt. Prepare the rushes by dampening them with a hose or shower attachment, or by dipping them in water for one minute. Next, wrap them in a thick cloth for about three hours, so that they become supple. You will also need a stuffing stick, i.e. a smooth, wedge-shaped piece of wood about 9in/22cm long and 1½in/4cm wide—a wide kitchen spatula will do, as will a wooden spoon. To thread the final coils through at the centre of the seat, use a football lacer or carpet needle with a large eye.

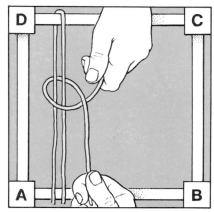

3. To begin rushing a square or rectangular seat, loop a rush over the back rail, and bring both ends up, so they lie on the front rail. If a thick coil is desired, add another rush by its butt end (thick end) using a half-hitch knot as shown, working halfway along the coil. To tighten the knot, pull the butt end of the new rush towards the back of the chair with the left hand, and pull the long end forward with the right hand keeping the knot in its original halfway position.

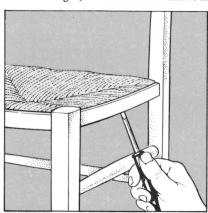

4. To begin coiling, gather all three long ends together and twist in a clockwise direction, working away from the corner and towards the middle of the front rail. Twist and smooth with the right hand, using the left to squeeze out any air or unevenness. Don't twist one rush around the other, rather work them all together to make one smooth, firm coil. Coil enough to go over the front rail and enough to extend about 1in/3cm underneath the chair. (Rushes are coiled on the top of the seat, but left uncoiled underneath.)

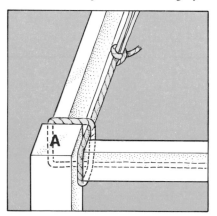

5. Lay the coil over the front rail, aligning it against corner A and pulling it tight. Then bring the coil up inside the chair frame, and using the left hand, coil it anti-clockwise. Lay it to the left, over the side rail to make a right angle over the first coil. It is often easier to coil to the right on the first half of the corner, then turn the chair, and coil the second half to the left.

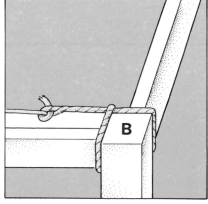

6. Bring the coil up across to the opposite rail, half-hitching in a new rush by its butt end halfway across the seat should the original coil become too thin, and in time to start coiling for the second corner. Take each rush as far as it will go to the tip or thin end, letting it drop out of the coil into the centre of the chair when the tip is not long enough to wrap over the next rail. For corners B, C and D repeat the process for corner A above.

Repairing rush seating cont.

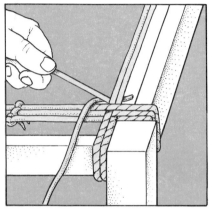

7. It will sometimes be necessary to join in new rushes at the corners. To do this, lift the working rush before forming the right angle, and tuck in the butt end of a new one underneath it, so that a 2in/5cm tail of the new rush protrudes downwards. Smoothly coil the old and new rushes together to form the new working rush. As this coil passes under the seat, bring it under the protruding butt end, which will then be hidden, keeping the weaving tidy on the underside.

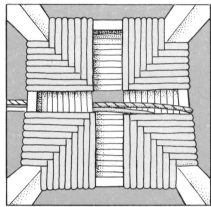

8. When the seat is nearly filled in with rushing, there will be no room to add new rushes using half-hitch knots. Instead, lay the rush to be joined in across the centre of the chair, tuck the butt end in the coils underneath the seat at the back of the opening on the corner just completed, and start coiling where the old and new rushes emerge in the centre. This method will hold the new rush firmly in place.

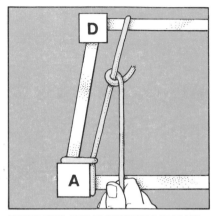

IRREGULARLY SHAPED SEATS

9. To rush seats with a wider front rail, it will be necessary to fill in the extra space on the front rail. Work the front corners as directed in Steps 3, 4 and 5, and tie in the coil temporarily on the side rail between corners B and C. Using the half-hitch knot again, tie in enough rushes to make a new coil onto the original coil between corners D and A, and work the front corners A and B again.

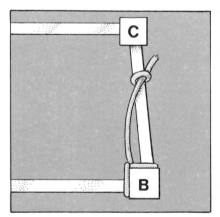

10. Untie the first coil and take in enough rushes from the first and second coil to continue with a single coil over the back corners C and D. This results in two coils over the front corners for every one over the back. Trim off any unwanted rushes between corners B and C, saving any waste rushes for stuffing (see Step 13).

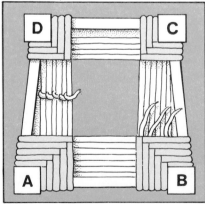

11. Continue working like this until the gap between the completed corners on the front rail measures the same as that on the back rail. Measure only when you have completed a round of rushing, i.e. after wrapping corner D.

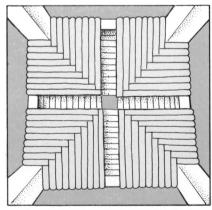

12. Continue around the chair, as directed in Steps 5 and 6, taking care to make right angles with the coils (thus preventing the problems outlined below.) Work until the gap between the coils on the side rails is about 1½in/4cm wide. Note that most chairs with wider fronts than backs, and all rectangular stools,will have larger gaps on the front and back rails than on the side ones, whereas square seats should have similarly-sized gaps on all four rails.

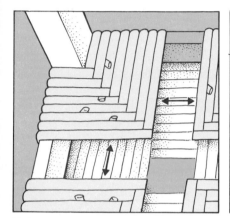

THE STUFFING

13. Allow the coils to dry before beginning the process known as stuffing. (If the seat is stuffed while still damp, the coils will stretch and provide a weaker and looser seat.) At this point, turn the chair upside down so the "pockets" (spaces between the top coiled rushes and the uncoiled rushes on the underside), two to each corner, are visible.

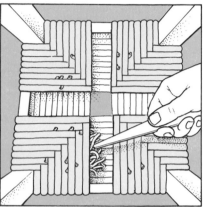

14. Pack these pockets with loose, dry rush, forcing it into the corners with the stuffing implement. This raises the coils slightly above the rail on top, tightens the work and helps the seat to last far longer. When the pockets are full, pack more dry rush into the centre spaces, tucking this stuffing under the coils on either side to hold it in place. This will provide stuffing for the final coils. While working save any waste rush for stuffing.

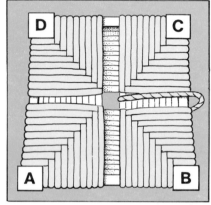

15. After stuffing, the coiling can be completed. The final coil for a square seat will be over the back rail at corner D; as a result the seat and rails should be evenly filled with coils. On rectangular stools and most chairs, the side rails will be filled first. Occasionally, unsightly "grins" appear between the last coils on the side rails. When corner C is complete and before commencing the opposite rail, cover any grins by repeating the wrap over the right hand rail, keeping the coil flat in the centre. Then cross to the left side and make two wraps before going to the back rail at D.

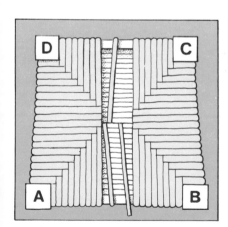

16. The central space is filled by coiling in a "figure eight" pattern going over the front and back rails. After completing corner D, work from left to right, coiling towards the right hand rail as you cross both back and front rails. Press these final coils together tightly, using the threader to bring the last coils through. Pack in as many coils as possible, bearing in mind that they shrink as they dry.

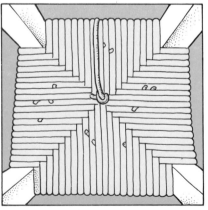

17. When the final coil has been wrapped over the back rail, turn the chair over and take this last coil to the middle of the work. Thread half of it to the right and half to the left, threading it under the opposite coil from the front rail. Tie the ends in a knot and tuck them out of sight into the coils.

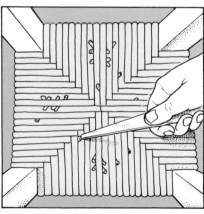

18. Using the stuffing stick or threader, push all other protruding ends into the work, so that the underside of the seat is smooth, and tight, with no ends showing. To make this easier, it may be helpful to dampen the underside of the seat slightly with a wet sponge, to avoid damaging the rushes while tucking in.

Problems with rushing

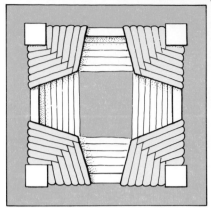  

1. If obtuse angles are allowed to form, the rails will be filled, but there will be gaps or "grins" in the centre of the seat, exposing the coils underneath.

2. If acute angles are allowed to form, the middle of the chair will be filled with gaps on the rails, resulting in the coils lying on top of each other in the middle of the chair as you try to fill up the rails.

3. Accurate right angles at each corner, with the coils running parallel from the centre of the seat to the rails, will ensure that the seat builds up evenly. There should be no "grins" in the centre, and the coils should lie evenly side by side. Keep the underside of the chair tidy by pulling firmly on the coils as they are brought up inside the chair frame, using your free hand to press them flat.

Basketry

Baskets are usually made from one of four materials—cane, rush, willow or raffia—and most are made by the traditional "stake-and-strand" technique: strands, or "weavers" are woven over and under a skeleton of stakes. Careful examination will enable you to follow the pattern of the weave when doing repairs.

Any basket badly affected by woodworm should be burned immediately. If there is only a sprinkling of holes, treat as directed in Steps 1 – 3, Page 22.

The following tools and supplies may be required: awl or large sacking needle for rush (D); sharp knife or knife with replaceable blades for cutting willow and cane (E); secateurs for trimming willow and cane (A); scissors for cutting rush and raffia (I); thin string for repairing stitched plaits (B), plus a bodkin (H) or awl, a hammer (F), and small tacks (G) for securing handles.

To identify the material a basket is made from, study the photograph facing page 112.

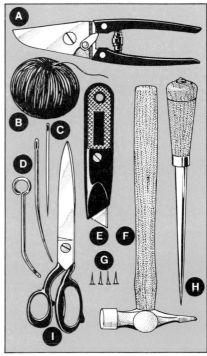

CANE

Cane comes from the tropical rattan creeper. The thorny outer bark is discarded, and the hard, shiny inner bark is used for chair cane, which is flat. The inner core of the plant becomes centre cane which is round and is available in several different diameters. Lapping cane, which is flat but wider than chair cane, is used for wrapping and securing basket handles. Other kinds of cane such as Kooboo and Palembang are used for handle bows and for very large baskets.

When purchasing, choose No. 3 and No. 6. To prepare cane, soak it in water for about ten minutes, then wrap in a damp cloth to keep it pliable.

WILLOW

Willow is cut in winter and graded by length. When purchasing, choose 3ft/91cm or 4ft/120cm rods, which will be adequate for most repairs. Buff willow is the most common. To obtain it, the rods or stems are boiled for about eight hours so that it becomes stained with tannin from its own bark, which is then stripped off. White willow is stripped in the spring, having been stood in water all winter so that it sprouts, making it easier to strip. Brown willow has the bark left on and is a dark tan shade.

To prepare willow, soak it in water for about two hours, then stand it upright to drain for about 30 minutes. Wrap it in a damp cloth so it becomes pliable, preferably overnight. Use within 24 hours or else let it dry out, and then resoak.

RUSH

Rushes grow in rivers, ponds and marshlands and are harvested in July, when they are cut close to the roots, tied into bundles or "bolts", and dried in the open air. The bolts must then be stored away from damp and strong light.

To prepare the rushes, lay them on the ground or in the bathtub and dampen them well, turning them over so they are evenly moistened. Next, wrap in a thick damp cloth for at least three hours or until pliable; use within 24 hours, or let them dry out and re-moisten as above.

RAFFIA

Raffia comes from the leaf of a tropical palm, and is very commonly used in European, Asian and African basketry.

It is usually purchased by the skein in natural or dyed shades, or in synthetic form. A cheaper, natural raffia is sold as garden raffia, and can be used to repair many kinds of soft basketry.

PARTS OF A BASKET

The base sticks (I) are made from the thickest material; and the side stakes (F) are the next thickest, cut to a point and driven into a woven base. The "upsett" (G) is a strong band that has been woven over the upturned side stakes to give the desired shape at the base. On the bottom of the basket is a ring of woven material providing a firm base for it to stand on, referred to as the "foot track" (H). The "siding" (E) incorporates thinner material and a variety of weaving patterns, while the "waling" (D) consists of several rows of thicker weave to give strength at the top of the basket. The border (C) is made by turning down the side stakes and interweaving them. The "handle bow" (B) is formed from a thick rod, which has been pointed and pushed into the siding, and then overwrapped or "roped" (A).

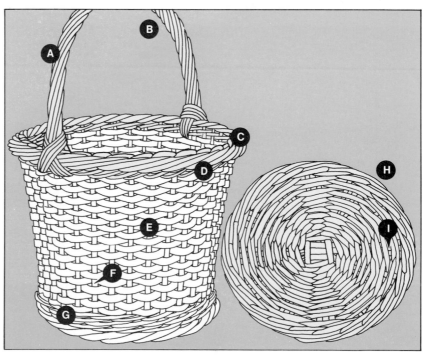

Repairing willow and cane baskets

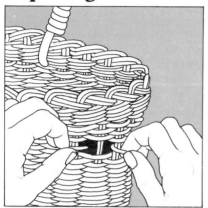 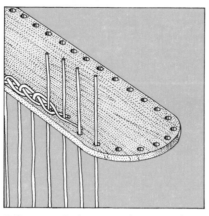 

1. Prepare the material as previously explained, and soak the basket for two to three hours, as working on a dry basket will only cause more damage. Remove the broken pieces, where possible. If the damage is to the weave, 3ft/91cm rods or No. 3 cane will be needed; if the stakes are broken, use 4ft/1.20m rods or No. 6 cane.

2. Some cane baskets are made on a wooden or plastic base, with the stakes threaded through holes drilled in the base, then woven into a border to hold them in place.

3. If only a few of the stakes are broken or missing, replace them by threading a new stake up through the hole in the base, extending it a few inches into the weave above it, before reweaving the foot track. However, if too many stakes are replaced or repaired in this way, the bottom will be weakened.

To repair a woven base

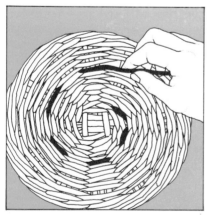  

1. To repair the base of a willow or cane basket, replace the damaged weavers by threading in a new 3ft/91cm rod or No. 3 cane, making sure to follow the pattern of the weave. Willow rods taper from the butt (thick end) to a thinner tip, and are joined butt to butt or tip to tip, in order to avoid gaps in the weave.

2. Broken base sticks can be replaced with 4ft/1.20m rod, or a piece of No. 6 cane, both with a sharpened point at one end. In both cases, push the new stick in from the outside edge towards the centre of the basket, alongside the broken stake, using a bodkin or similar pointed instrument to make a hole for it through the weave. Once firmly in position, cut off the end of the new stake using secateurs, making sure it does not protrude and is level with edge of the basket.

3. If a side stake has been broken at the angle where it bends up between the base and the siding of the basket, it can sometimes be strengthened with a short piece of cane or willow, which has been sharpened to a point at both ends, kinked at the point you want it to bend, then pushed into the base and siding at the same time.

Upsett and siding repairs

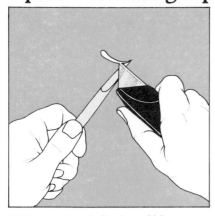

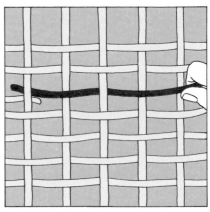

1. The upsett (near the base) uses thicker weavers to support the siding above it. To replace willow upsetts, choose very supple 4ft/1.20m rods, and follow the pattern of the weave that is still intact. Bear in mind that once willow has kinked or bent, it will *not* straighten, so curve it gently into place. "Slype" or slice the butt or thick ends at a long angle with the knife, making them easier to insert. For cane upsetts, use No. 6 cane.

2. The weave used for the upsett is similar to the waling; it involves three weavers at a time, although only one of the three may need replacing. For each stroke, the left hand weaver goes over two stakes, behind one stake, and out in the next space along.

3. The siding may be woven in any of a number of different patterns, so look at what you are trying to copy before commencing the repair. With willow, put in butts and tips in the same way as the existing joins, using 3ft/91cm rods, and trying to use the curving tendency of the willow to make the weaving easier.

Cane baskets are usually sided with No. 3 cane. Don't use too long a length of cane, or it will become rough and "hairy" while weaving, making the task more difficult. Follow the weave, then pick off all ends with secateurs, cutting at an angle so that nothing protrudes.

Damaged border stakes

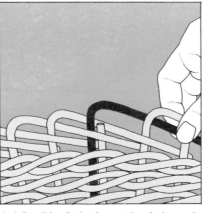

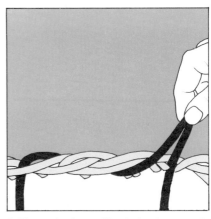

1. If the border stakes are broken or missing, trim what's left level with the top edge of the weave, then pick out the broken pieces. Use a thick rod, or No. 6 cane, and slype the butt. Make a space or channel with the bodkin on the left of the old stake, then push the new stake well down into the weave. Kink the new stake level with the top of the border, and thread the tip away into the border, following the pattern, using the bodkin to make room for it in the weave.

2. A "trac" border is where each stake in turn is kinked an inch or so above the waling, and then passed in and out of the stakes. To replace a damaged stake, insert a new one as above, then make a space in the border with the bodkin and draw the new rod or cane through, trying not to let it kink. Pick off the ends at an angle where they rest against a stake — on the inside or outside of the basket depending on the type.

3. The repair of a roped border involves complicated weavings of two, three, four or more rods or canes, giving varying degrees of width and solidity. The number of rods or canes in a rope border also affects the number of stakes which each one goes in front of. Basically, each rod or cane comes down behind the one to its right and on the outside of the basket, then crosses in front of two (or more) stakes to the inside, finally going behind another stake to the outside again.

Handle repair

The handles of baskets seem to suffer more damage than any other part. Before beginning the repair, soak the basket for two to three hours, then remove all the wrapping to see if the core of the handle bow is broken. If so, a new bow can be made from handle cane (a thick cane sold by the bundle and available from craft shops), a thick willow rod or a length of ash or hazel.

1. Cut a new bow from one of the above materials, if possible measuring the old handle to make sure that the new length will reach at least 4in/10cm into the basket's siding.

2. Slype each end of the new length with a sharp knife so that a long, angled point is produced. Rub a bar of soap along the bodkin before using it to enlarge the channel that held the previous handle bow — this will make it easier to slip the new length into place.

3. Soak the length for the new bow for a few minutes before beginning the insertion. Then, bend it carefully, trying to match the shape of the original handle. Push the new bow as far down as possible into the siding, i.e. at least 4in/10cm on each side.

When the new bow has been inserted, the handle's exterior wrapping can be replaced. There are two very common types: those which are roped (i.e. covered with willow rods or centre cane), and those wrapped in glossy lapping cane.

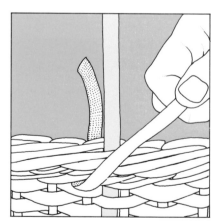

4. To repair a handle wrapped with lapping cane: after soaking the cane, push one end a short distance through the siding towards the inside of the basket, below the waling on the left of the bow. Bring this short end up against the bow. Wrap the longer end over the border to the right of the bow, bringing it from the inside to the outside below the waling.

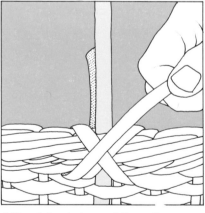

5. Next, bring the long end diagonally across to the left of the bow and over the border, forming an "X", then thread it through the border below the waling, to the outside. Repeat the process.

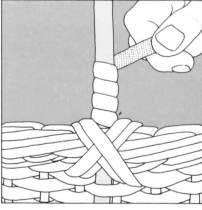

6. After the second "X" has been formed, wrap the soaked lapping cane tightly around the handle so that it is edge-to-edge with each round, completely covering the bow.

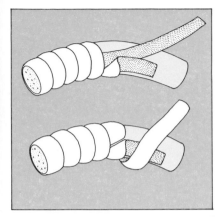

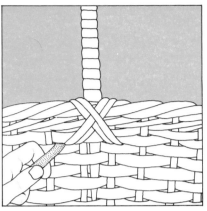

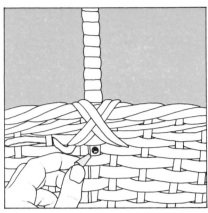

7. If it is necessary to introduce a new piece of cane avoid having the join in the centre of the handle where it will be a weak point in the wrapping.

While there is still enough cane to complete several more wraps, lay in the new piece, glossy side down, against the bow on the underside of the handle. Wrap over it. When there is only about 2in/5cm left of the first cane, turn it at a right angle, laying its glossy side down. Then turn the new cane so that its glossy side faces outwards, and start wrapping with it, over the end of the first cane.

8. Once the handle is completely wrapped with new cane and the other side of the basket has been reached, take the lapping cane over and through the border in the manner described in Steps 4 and 5, finishing on the inside. The end is then threaded sideways into the weave, lacing it in front of and behind a few stakes, but finishing on the inside of the basket.

9. For this kind of handle, a peg will be needed to secure the bow. Drill a small hole through the handle cane below the wrapping, and tap a small peg of willow or cane into it, leaving the ends of the peg protruding slightly so they lodge against the weave. Alternatively, a small steel tack can be driven through the waling into the bow from the inside.

Repairing a roped handle

To repair a roped handle, use 4ft/1.20m willow rods or No. 6 centre cane; four on each side of the basket will be sufficient. Slype the ends and drive all four down into the space to the left of the bow, on the outside of the basket.

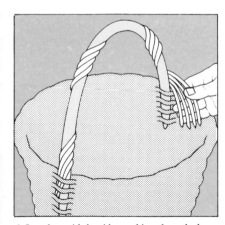

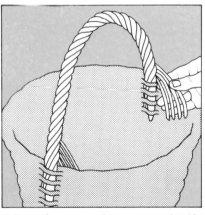

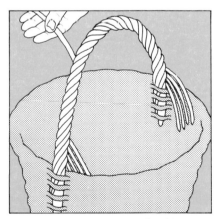

1. Lay them side by side, working along the bow from left to right, bringing the tips under the bow. Do not let them kink or cross each other. Repeat this twice, making three wraps across the bow, leaving gaps between the wraps as shown. Once the opposite side is reached, leave the tips dangling on the inside of the basket.

2. Insert four more rods or canes on the side where the first four were, and repeat the process, filling in the gaps left in Step 1.

3. If any gaps or "grins" occur after this second wrapping, put in an extra rod on one or both sides and wrap it as above, making sure that it lies in, and fills, the gaps, so the handle has a pleasing, even appearance.

Repairing a roped handle cont.

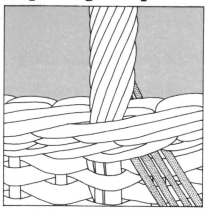

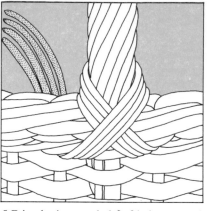

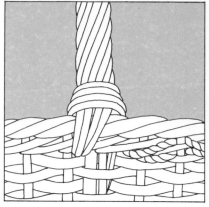

4. To finish, thread the tips through the sides of the basket, under the waling and to the right of the bow on the outside, making sure to keep them in the same order as wrapped.

5. Bring the tips up to the left of the bow, around behind it and then diagonally downwards to the left, pulling them tight as you work. Next, thread them back under the waling to the inside of the basket.

6. Twist the tips into a rope and thread them sideways into the weave to secure them, taking them in front of and behind several stakes, finishing on the inside. Trim the protruding ends against a stake. Finally, the handle may be pegged or nailed as mentioned in Step 9, Page 109, although this should not be necessary.

Repairing rush baskets

Repairing baskets made of rushes is fairly easily accomplished by threading new stakes or weavers into place with an awl or sacking needle. Prepare the rushes as directed on page 105, but do not soak the basket itself or it will lose its shape.

Rushwork baskets can be repaired using raffia, chair cane, rush, straw or even string, but choose a material that matches the original as closely as possible. Dampen the material as necessary, but do not soak the basket unless its fibres seem to be breaking.

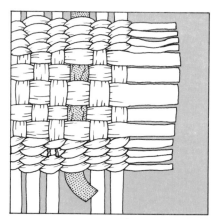

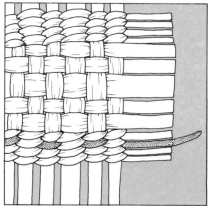

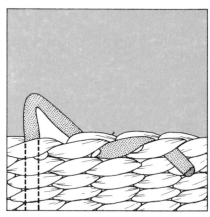

REPAIRING BROKEN STAKES

1. In rush baskets, the stakes run through the basket from one border to the other. A broken stake can be repaired by threading a thick rush into the weave so that it overlaps the break by several rows. The ends are trimmed at an angle when dry.

2. Broken weavers can be replaced by threading a thinner rush into the weave, overlapping the break by an inch or so on each side of the damage.

3. A damaged border must have the broken stakes replaced by threading them well down into the weave, before following the pattern of the border.

Replacing the handle

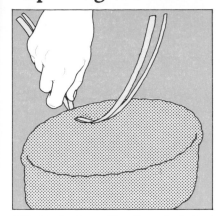

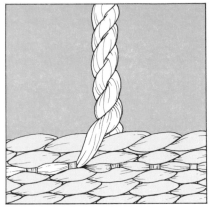

1. Rush baskets have soft handles made of twisted rush. Remove the damaged handle completely. Then take an even number of rushes, alternating butts and tips, and thread them through the original hole on the side of the basket, several rows down in the weave. Pull them halfway through and twist each half to the right until they meet above the border.

2. Lay the right hand coil over the left hand one. Give this group a twist to the right, then lay it over to the left. Keep twisting the right hand group one turn to the right, then laying it over the rushes in the left hand, so a new rope will be formed. Continue until the handle is the correct length.

3. To finish, bring the ends of the two coils to the opposite side of the basket. Thread one coil to the inside and one to the outside, inserting them each into the hole for the original handle. Following the pattern of the weave, thread the ends of each strand into the wave, lacing one to the right and one to the left of the handle. Weave the ends in and out several times, finishing on the inside. Finally trim all ends with secateurs.

Other common repairs

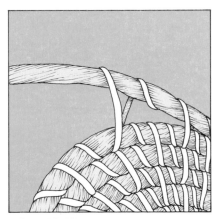

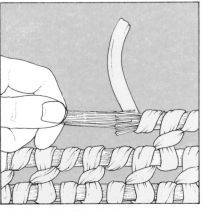

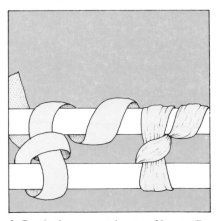

COILWORK

1. Coilwork mats and baskets consist of a pliable material such as raffia or rush wrapped over a core of string, reed or cane. Coilwork is always wound from the centre outwards, each coil stitched on to the one before. Dampen the weaving material and, using a large needle, follow the existing stitch pattern—usually a simple figure-of-eight or the "lazy squaw" stitch shown above. Start and finish by threading the weaver into the coil.

MARIPOSA WEAVE

2. In mariposa weave, corn or maize husks are wrapped around a core of cane, reed or straw. The coils are joined with the knot illustrated in Step 3. Rush, raffia or reedmace can be used to repair the weave. To begin, damp the basket and unpick any badly damaged weaving. To reinforce or replace a section of a damaged core, cut several strands of No. 3 centre cane to the appropriate length and force them into the stronger parts of the existing core.

3. Repair the weave using a sacking needle, drawing the ends of the new weave through some sound stitching to secure it. Working from the back, bring the weaver up and then down over the top coil. Bring it up again and wrap it over the top and bottom coils, then bring it out between the coils to the left of the "stem" just formed, and wrap this stem once or twice. Next, take the weaver out to the back and to the right of the stem, bringing it up to wrap the top coil as previously. Thread the weaver away once the repair is made.

Other common repairs cont.

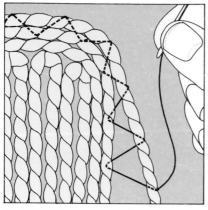

MATTING

4. Mats made from plaited or braided rush are usually joined by string, but this often wears out. To replace the string, use a soft loose twine—a stronger twine will tend to cut the rushes. Thread a strong, large-eyed needle with the string, and re-sew the rushes using a "V"-shaped running stitch as shown. Once the rush is secured, thread the ends of the string into the rushes and knot. If the rush itself is damaged or missing, dampen new rushes and lace in new lengths, attaching them to old lengths.

STRAW WORK

5. Straw work baskets are usually fairly large and often come with a matching top. They are made by stitching coils of straw together with chair cane. If the cane has broken, it can be replaced; use an awl or thick needle to make holes in the coils for the cane to be threaded through, then stitch, following the existing pattern —a simple "up-and-over" stitch is most commonly used. Secure the ends by knotting them on the inside, finally tucking the knotted end into the straw.

6. If a straw coil is damaged, damp the basket with a fine spray of water and damp the new straw before packing it into a tight roll, then stitch in place as in Step 5. (Always purchase straw in long lengths if possible.) If the damage is on the sides of the basket, interleave the new straw with the old, making sure that the new is very tightly packed.

Opposite: A selection of baskets in various materials (from left to right, top to bottom): coiled grass lidded basket from South Africa with geometric designs of coloured grasses; thick-coiled basket from Ghana with lid attached by wrapped loop; green-and-white leaf-shape basket in split bamboo resting on an English rush work basket with lid next to a small, coiled African basket on a shallow, white willow basket; large buff and white willow basket with handle and rod border, inside which are a plaited rush basket and a split bamboo and rattan basket with lattice sides; in the foreground a white willow basket with plaited border rests on a willow basket with plaited sides and coiled handles.

LEATHER

There is no doubt that Ice-Age man clad himself in skins, but skins in the sun have a short life, are hard and crack easily. In order to be converted into useful leather they must be cleaned, tanned for preservation and finished to give suppleness and elasticity. The principles of tanning and finishing are simple, and so were among man's earliest discoveries. Although leather is an organic material inherently subject to decay, it can survive for a long time when protected from light, heat and destructive bacteria, so that ancient leather articles have been recovered from bogs, rubbish pits and similar sites. Specimens from all periods back to 5100 B.C., usually sandals or other footwear, have been found in Europe, the Middle East, India and China. From early times leather was used for many things—clothing, harness, containers for wine and water, tents, boats, drums, writing parchment, bowstrings, shields and armour, beds, curtains and cushions. Some of the more unlikely uses have lingered until comparatively recent times, for instance leather buckets (in gunpowder magazines), Japanese armour, and the leather-covered coracle. So-called gilt-leather work in which hangings, screens, altar frontals, vestments, pouches and caskets were made of embossed leather covered with delicate and intricate designs in gilt and colour, was made from the thirteenth to the eighteenth centuries in large quantities.

The processes of leather manufacture are adaptable and similar, whether made by hand with simple implements, or by sophisticated industrial methods. The first necessity is to remove unwanted hair and flesh. This was probably first done by scraping it off with flint knives. It was then discovered that hair will fall off a partially rotted wet hide. From the Middle Ages onward, lime was used, or the skin was pulled over a fixed sharp knife. Lime is still used, but the fixed knife system has been succeeded by machines with moving knives.

Once the hair and any traces of lime have been removed, the skin is then tanned. In some parts of the world this was done by smoking, or by rubbing in certain oils. Another early tanning agent was alum, which was originally used by mistake instead of salt for preserving skin; alum tanning is called "tawing". But usually tanning was done with barks or roots or other vegetable products. One method was to form the skin into a bag and fill it with the tanning agent and water so that the tan liquor slowly permeated the skin. The traditional English method is to put alternate layers of skin and oak bark into a pit, cover them with water, and leave them for some months, a process which generates a distinctive and very unpleasant smell. In the second half of the nineteenth century chemical tanning was introduced after the discovery in about 1860 of the tanning value of chromium salts; chromium tanning is very rapid, taking only three to four hours, and the resulting leather is tough and has high resistance to heat and water.

After tanning the skin may be shaved, or split to make thinner grades of leather, the outer side is grained, but the splits are smooth and show no grain. Then, if required, it may be dyed. The leather must then be lubricated, as otherwise it dries hard and will quickly crack. The lubricant may be vegetable, fish or mineral oil, animal or vegetable grease, paraffin wax or soap, with additives such as colloidal graphite, sulphur or mineral salts. The leather is then dried, which may make it shrink or change colour. Finally, it can be lacquered, glazed, rolled, or embossed in a press.

Almost any skin may be tanned and turned into leather: cattle, sheep, goat, horse, camel, buffalo, pig, together with the near relatives of each, are the commonest. Then there are others such as seal, whale and shark, alligator and crocodile; deer, kangaroo and ostrich, although since some of these are today protected species, trade in their skins is illegal in many countries.

Suede is the most common of the special leathers. It is a split skin which has been buffed to raise the nap. Shagreen is a tough, waterproof thin leather, often dyed green, used to cover wooden instrument and jewel cases; it was originally made from wild asses' skin, and later from the skin of shark-like fish with the scales filed down to make the characteristic irregular surface; it has been imitated by pressing. Morocco is a fine-grained goatskin, originally Moorish, tanned with sumac and dyed red, green or blue; it has been used for book-bindings, and from the eighteenth century for desk tops. Roan is a soft flexible sheepskin used for cushions and upholstery. Russia-leather is made from calf-skin, and is impregnated with birch-bark oils; it was much used in the nineteenth century for camera bellows. Chamois leather has nothing to do with deer, but is prepared by an ancient process known as shammying which was described by Homer in the *Iliad*; it gives the leather an open structure so that it can be repeatedly wetted and dried. The process includes stretching the leather and pounding it with fish oils, and then hanging it in a heated chamber to oxidize the oil; it was used to make much of the Greeks' best clothing, called "shamoy".

Owing to the rapidity with which leather becomes brittle and cracks in comparatively few years when not regularly "fed", leather items of any age are rare and such things as gloves and screens from the sixteenth and seventeenth centuries survive mainly in museums. Apart from old parchments and vellum, and book-bindings which may survive in more or less cracked condition from the seventeenth century, it is rare to come across things more than about a hundred years old, and these are likely to be limited to articles of hide such as luggage, screens and upholstery, and perhaps the odd leather bucket or blackjack, which is a drinking vessel waterproofed with pitch.

Opposite: A selection of leather bindings: on top, a binding in hide from the seventeenth century, in the stack on the left Watts's Logick *in hide from 1773, opposite that, a turn-of-the-century binding in tan suede, on the bottom of the right-hand stack, a half binding with tooled morocco spine and marbled paper front; on the left,* In Darkest Africa *from 1890 with a black morocco spine and vellum front; to the right,* The Great White South *showing signs of leather deterioration and in need of restoration.*

Cleaning, restoring and simple repairs

Leather is specially-treated animal skin. It retains a high proportion of water, which is lost if the leather is not kept sealed by oils or polishes. The leather will then crack. When this happens, or the surface is rubbed off and not replaced with more polish, the action of the atmosphere will weaken the leather further.

To prevent this, or any other damage, *never* keep leather objects in direct light, because leather can fade just like a fabric; *never* keep leather anywhere hot, because it will dry out; *never* keep leather in a damp atmosphere, since it is organic and rots easily; and *never* dry wet leather quickly in a hot place — pack it with absorbent material, and allow it to dry naturally. In addition, *never* clean or relubricate leather wall hangings or any leather that is painted or gilded, as these are highly skilled conservation jobs; *never* glue patches onto leather objects to repair tears, this, too, is a job for the expert; and *never* try to clean or relubricate leather that is in association with textiles, this is a job for the textile conservator.

1. All leather items should be dusted regularly, whether or not they are going to be repaired. Use a large soft artists' paintbrush and dust gently. Then remove the loose dirt with a small hand-held vacuum cleaner with the nozzle covered with net (see Step 2, Page 140).

2. Wipe the surface with a swab of cotton wool wrung out in white spirit BS245 (Stoddard's Solvent). This is the only solvent that can be used on leather because it does not dry out the natural oils. The leather will darken as the solvent is applied, it will lighten again as the solvent evaporates.

3. Leathers that have dried out need relubricating. For heavy, thick leathers with highly polished surfaces, apply hide food, following the manufacturer's instructions. (Hide food is a specialists' preparation, and is not the same as neatsfoot oil or saddlesoap.) Polish when dry. Lighter-weight leathers can be treated with baby lotion. Moisten a swab of cotton wool with the lotion and dab all over the surface. When the leather will absorb no more, let it dry and then seal and polish the surface with a specialist's micro-crystalline wax.

4. If a leather object has been attacked by insects, seal it in a plastic bag with an insecticidal strip. Leave it there for two to three weeks. Take it out, leave in normal conditions for three weeks and then put it back in a plastic bag with the insecticidal strip again. Leave for another two to three weeks. It is essential to repeat the treatment in this way to kill any eggs which might have hatched since the first treatment, because most insect eggs are completely unaffected by insecticides. Clean the object well after the treatment, as directed above.

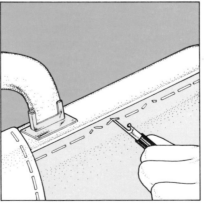

5. When stitching has become broken or weak it must be replaced. First remove the old stitching — a dressmaker's stitch unpicker is the ideal tool.

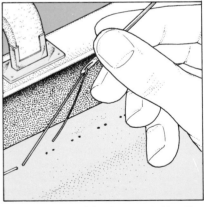

6. Use linen thread for the new stitching, first waxing it by running it through soft beeswax. Then thread a glover's needle and make the new stitches. A glover's needle is best because it has a cutting tip that does not damage the existing holes as much as a blunt needle.

Repairing leather-bound books

For repairing leather bookbindings, the following tools and supplies may be required: eraser, wide tapes, large soft artists' paintbrush and a small paintbrush, cotton wool swabs, white spirit BS245 (Stoddard's Solvent), duster, flour and water or wallpaper paste, tissue paper, sharp knife or scalpel, waxed paper, bulldog clips.

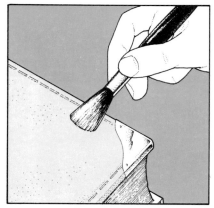

1. Leather bookbindings that are not very dirty will only need the occasional light dusting. Use a soft duster or else a large, soft artists' paintbrush, dusting both the binding and the edges of the book.

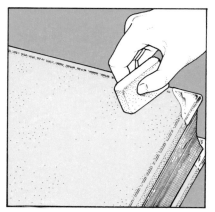

2. Pigskin, vellum or parchment bindings should not be washed, not only because they will absorb water, but also because any gold stamping may be damaged or removed. To clean the surface of the binding, wipe down with a swab of cotton wool wrung out in white spirit BS245 (Stoddard's Solvent). A clean eraser is also effective and can be used on alum-tawed (see the introduction to this section) vellum or pigskins.

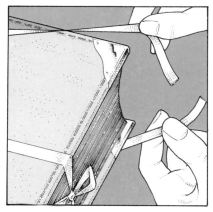

3. If board bindings covered in vellum or pigskin have warped, they can often be flattened during a spell of humid weather. Wrap wide tapes around the book and tie them so that the boards are flat. Do not weight the book, because that will stop air reaching the leather, preventing it from reabsorbing moisture. Keep the book in this position until the end of a period of dry weather, by which time the boards should have flattened and dried out again.

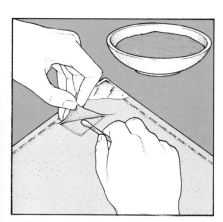

4. The loose edges of tears and holes can be glued down with flour and water paste (see Step 1, Page 181) or wallpaper paste. Apply the glue sparingly with a small paintbrush or matchstick. Wipe off the excess, cover with tissue paper and weight down to ensure that the leather adheres closely and smoothly.

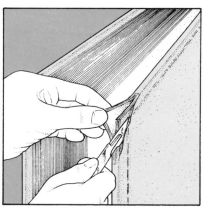

5. Corners, often worn through to damaged paperboard, can be rebuilt with flour and water paste as above, or wallpaper glue. First separate the layers of the board with a scalpel or sharp knife, then apply the glue with a small paintbrush or matchstick.

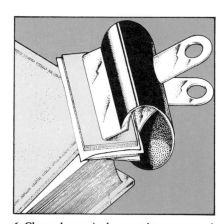

6. Clamp the repaired corners between waxed paper and firm board, using bulldog clips to hold them in place. Do not leave them clamped for more than 15 to 20 minutes, or the moistened leather may darken. When all repairs are finished, relubricate the leather binding with hide food or baby lotion as directed above, paying particular attention to the head and tail caps, and the turn-in of the leather at the hinges.

Replacing leather-covered surfaces

Assemble the following tools and supplies: sanding block and abrasive papers of various grades, white spirit, wallpaper paste and old paintbrush, acid-free masking tape, cork pad or rounded piece of softwood (optional), waxed paper or tracing paper, scalpel or knife with replaceable blades, metal rule, brass embossing wheel, and gold leaf (optional).

1. Rip off old, damaged leather. Wash off old glue and any remaining pieces of leather with warm water. Try not to let the surrounding wood get too wet.

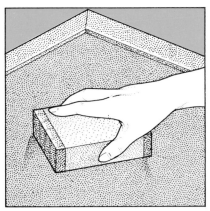

2. Fill any dents or splits in the surface of the table or desk following Steps 5 – 6, Page 21, otherwise they will show through and spoil the new surface. Smooth the surface with a sanding block, using pieces of successively finer abrasive paper until a medium smoothness is reached — a slight roughness gives the glue something to grip. After sanding, dust and then wipe with white spirit.

3. Mask the wooden surrounds with paper held in place by acid-free masking tape to prevent the paste seeping onto them. Then apply double strength wallpaper paste to the surface, using an old brush. Build up a few layers until it is gummy.

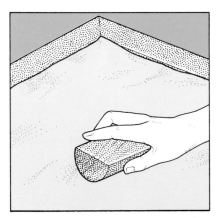

4. Cut the new piece of leather a little larger than the area to be covered. Position the leather on the surface. Then, starting from the middle and working towards the edges, smooth out wrinkles and puckers with a cork pad or rounded piece of softwood — even the heel of your hand. It is often helpful, especially with large pieces of leather, to put a piece of waxed paper or tracing paper between the leather and the glued surface. Gradually ease the paper out as you stick the leather in place. This technique ensures a smooth surface.

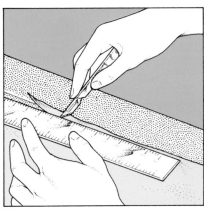

5. Once the leather is flat, let it dry for an hour. Then cut off the excess carefully with a scalpel or sharp knife with replaceable blades and a straight metal rule.

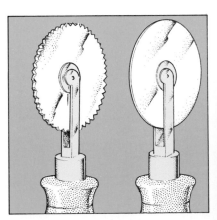

6. Run a brass embossing wheel that has been warmed to a hand-hot temperature along the edge of the leather to seal it to the surface. (If the wheel is too hot, the leather will shrivel.) Gold embossing gives a nice finish, but is a skilled job. However, if you want to try it, buy a roll of gold leaf. Feed out the gold leaf with one hand, rolling it in place with the embossing wheel held in the other hand. Rock the wheel from side to side to ensure that both edges of the leaf are sticking firmly, and move the wheel backwards and forwards so the leaf sticks firmly along its length.

STONE

All stone was originally, of course, part of the molten mass from which the earth was formed and from which, when it cooled, solid rock condensed. But much has happened since, and so geologists classify rocks as igneous, sedimentary and metamorphic. Igneous rocks are those formed by volcanic action; sedimentary are made by the deposition of materials such as pebbles, gravel, grit, sand and clay formed from other rocks, with perhaps organic material such as dead vegetation; and metamorphic rocks were formed by the change, or metamorphosis, of sedimentary rocks due to subsequent influences such as heat and pressure.

The most conspicuous property of volcanic rocks is their great hardness, and a high proportion of the material of most of them is silica, silicon dioxide, which turns up in all sorts of forms and is best known to us as sand. The most common volcanic rocks are basalt and granite. Basalt is chemically felspar, alumino-silicates of sodium and potassium; it is not much used by man as it splinters easily, however it but forms dramatic natural features. Granite, which comes in grey and red forms, has been used when great strength was needed as for lighthouses and breakwaters, and for domestic building in areas where it is the local stone. As it takes a high polish it was sometimes favoured by the Victorians for plinths and other features in buildings, and for tombstones, and in London granite horse-troughs were formerly common.

Another form of silica is obsidian, a glass occurring in volcanic slag. It is usually black in colour due to iron contamination, and was favoured by the Aztecs for knives and tools, and sometimes carved for ornaments. Flint is also an impure silica, and like obsidian was used by Stone-Age man for knives and arrow-heads; and knapped, or halved, flint-stones set in mortar are a characteristic and attractive building material in some parts of England.

Porphyry is a volcanic rock, usually red or purplish and dark olive-green in colour, with paler felspar or quartz inclusions. Porphyry can, like granite, be highly polished and has been used for pillars, table tops and ornaments. Jasper is another form of silica, from which Victorian "Scotch Pebble" is made; it is mostly red or brown or banded, sometimes with yellow or green tints. Still another form of silica is agate, which is a colour-banded chalcedony; cornelian, sardonyx, chrysoprase and onyx are variations of the same material. Such stones as these are found in cavities formed by gas in pumice, which is solidified lava.

Probably the most prized material of volcanic origin is jade, beloved of the Chinese, though jade is not found there. Until the early eighteenth century the Chinese used a form of jade called nephrite, found in Central Asia in pebble form, which ranges from dark "spinach" green to greenish white, sometimes with brown or rusty-coloured veins or patches. Especially desirable was the smooth, off-white kind called "mutton-fat". Later work is in "jadeite", from mines in Burma, brighter green and more glossy than nephrite. The intricately carved late nineteenth-century pieces are in jadeite. Nephrite is also found in North America and there are many modern copies in this material. It is also easy to confuse jade with chrysoprase, another volcanic material; serpentine, a mainly green magnesium silicate known in the west of Ireland as Connemara Marble; and soapstone, a natural mixture of magnesium and china clay also called steatite. Both serpentine and soapstone are soft materials.

A common unaltered sedimentary rock is coal, derived from compressed vegetation. In the form of black lignite, called jet, found on beaches in north-east England, it was popular for ornaments and mourning jewellery in Victorian times, and has recently had some revival in popularity.

The most usual types of stone, both for building and sculpture, are various types of limestone and sandstone. Both are metamorphic rocks formed by subjection to pressure. Limestone is mainly calcium carbonate, while sandstone is grains of quartz sand cemented together by iron oxide (red sandstone) or by lime in the form of calcite, or by a mixture, since pure white sandstone is rare.

Marble is a more or less pure calcium carbonate limestone which has been hardened by volcanic heat, and is found in many parts of the world. Uniform white marble like that of Carrara in north-west Italy, which has always been in demand by sculptors, is rare, most being coloured or veined by impurities. The Pentelic marble of which the Parthenon is built is a warm cream, and Roman mosaic was made of pieces of coloured marble about ½ in/ 1.75 cm square set in mortar. English rosewood marble is a veined dark brown colour and suggests rosewood as its name indicates.

Marble takes a high polish and was popular for purposes such as table tops, fireplaces, dairy shelves and the counters of food shops, in Georgian and Victorian times. It is now considered too costly for utilitarian uses but ornamental items such as lamps, vases and ashtrays of marble are still made in Italy and elsewhere. In fact the more ornamental kinds of marble have always been expensive and Italy, from the seventeenth century onward, exported a substitute called scagliola, which is made from coloured plaster and isinglass with inset marble chips.

Slate is another metamorphic stone consisting mainly of aluminium silicate and formed from clay and silt hardened by pressure. It is found in a variety of shades from dark grey, through pale grey to green and red.

A stone especially popular in ancient Egypt was alabaster, a form of gypsum (calcium sulphate) harder than that used for Plaster of Paris, but still very soft. It was used by carvers for making scarabs and figurines and also for sarcophagi. During the Middle Ages it was occasionally used for tomb figures and similar purposes where it was not exposed to the weather, as it is absorbent and must not be washed or allowed to get wet.

An interesting and attractive stone is Derbyshire blue-john, a variety of fluorspar (calcium fluoride) of mottled purple, blue and amethyst colour. From 1770 massive vases and other ornaments were made in this material and as it was very brittle it was sometimes strengthened with resin. The mines were substantially worked out in the nineteenth century and only small items such as costume jewellery and "eggs" are now made from it.

Cleaning and polishing marble

There are basically two kinds of marble: the fine, close-grained type used for statues and ornamental carvings, and the variegated type in which the limestone has become impregnated with mineral impurities, resulting in rich veining and subtle patterning.

White marble is found primarily in Italy, the finest and purest from the quarries around Carrara. However, other countries also produce good quality stone: in the USA quarries in the New England area and in England, at Purbeck, Dorset, are famous for their marble. Indian craftsmen working for the ever-resplendent Maharajahs were able to rely on considerable quantities of beautiful pale marbles from Rajputnan and Jablapur.

Variegated marble is formed by a combination of limestone minerals and silica; it is found in a huge variety of hues from dark forest green to palest blush pink and yellow. These more

1. Before beginning the cleaning process, remove the marble from the base in order to avoid water damage to wooden parts. If the marble object is small, it can be submerged in a plastic bowl or sink filled with the following solution: dissolve a cup of soap (not detergent) flakes in a gallon of water to which a few drops of 10 per cent ammonia have been added.

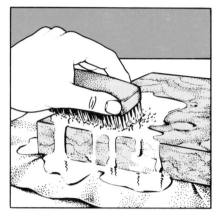

2. Position the slab of marble over a plastic sheet, or better still, keep it flat and allow a constant stream of water to run over the surface which is being cleaned. Start scrubbing with a bristle brush in one corner, working across the surface, rinsing and wiping up as you go, using clean white rags or white paper towels. (Do not use dyed rags or towel as the dye may come off on the marble.)

3. After the first washing, examine the piece for chips and stains – tabletops and mantlepieces often have stains caused by acidic substances such as fruit juices and wines, where the acid has eaten through the polish and dissolved the surface of the stone. If the damage is not deep, polishing should restore the surface. Use powdered chalk, pumice powder or tin oxide on a damp white cotton rag, rubbing the stained area in circles. When the surface feels smooth and the stain has vanished, rinse the powder off with clean water and dry thoroughly with white rags or paper towel.

REMOVING GREASE STAINS

1. These stains are caused by oily liquid seeping into the pores of the marble, without actually damaging it. In removing these, the idea is to draw out the grease. A series of poultices should do the trick: make a small quantity of paste, either of equal quantities of powdered kaolin and benzene or of potato flour starch and white spirit. Alternatively, dampen a piece of white blotting paper with acetone. If possible lay the marble flat at a comfortable working height.

2. Place the paste or the saturated paper over the stained area, and then cover this with a piece of plastic or tin foil, taped in place with acid-free tape, to keep the poultice from drying out too quickly.

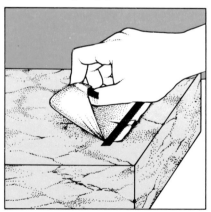

3. After about an hour, remove the cover and allow to evaporate. Then check the stain. If it has not disappeared, it may be necessary to repeat the process a few times using freshly mixed poultices.

unusual marbles are used primarily in large pieces where the patterning can be appreciated – such as on floors, walls, columns and tabletops; small bits are used for inlay while the tiniest pieces are set in mosaics.

Before beginning to work on marble, bear in mind that the following instructions for cleaning and waxing marble apply only to pieces of no great historical or monetary value. Also note that variegated marbles may be damaged by powerful stain removers, so be sure to test any of the following formulas recommended for white marbles on an inconspicuous spot. Do not, however, use the strong caustic solution in any case – this should only be applied to white marbles.

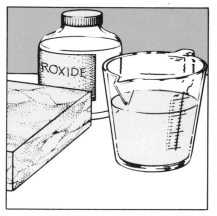

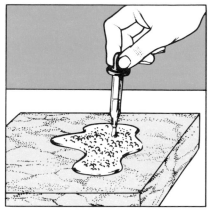

REMOVING STUBBORN STAINS FROM MARBLE

1. To remove deeper stains, the most effective treatment is a mixture of one-third 20-volume hydrogen peroxide with two-thirds water. Position the marble so that the stained area lies on a perfectly horizontal plane, propping up irregular pieces with lumps of clay if necessary.

2. Then pour a teaspoonful of solution over the stain, covering the entire area.

3. Immediately sprinkle a few drops of ammonia on top of the solution using an eye dropper. The peroxide will start to bubble. When the bubbling stops, rinse the area at once with clean water, repeating the rinse two or three times to make sure there is no residue of bleach. Repeat if necessary.

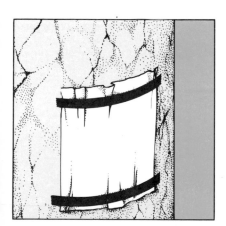

4. To remove stubborn stains from larger, vertical surfaces, make a poultice using a clean white cotton rag moistened with the peroxide solution as given above in Step 1. Tape it into place as before using acid-free masking tape. Alternatively, try any of the proprietary stain removers, providing they contain no acids, always testing their effect on the underside of a piece first.

CAUSTIC METHOD

5. If using the next method to remove bad stains, first make sure that any surrounding wood or metal is protected from the solution. Then, cut a bar of soap into chips and place in a saucepan. Add enough water to cover the chips and boil until the soap has completely dissolved. Pour this into a measuring vessel.

6. Make a note of the quantity of the liquid, then pour it into a clean bowl and put on a pair of rubber gloves.

Removing stubborn stains cont.

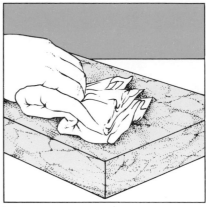

7. With great care, add the same measure of caustic potash, and the same of quicklime.

8. Paint this solution on the stained marble and leave for two or three days.

9. Then wipe with a clean rag or paper towel and rinse with water. Repeat if necessary, but after a few applications, pour the solution down the drain, rinsing the sink and drain at once with plenty of cold water. Destroy the rags or towels too.

Waxing marble

If the surface of marble needs its beautiful sheen restored, do not be tempted to use any of the proprietary furniture waxes. These tend to stain the stone, the solvents driving the tinted wax into the pores. Instead, use a mixture made up from two parts "Ketone N" synthetic resin, one part Cosmolloid wax, and a measure of white spirit.

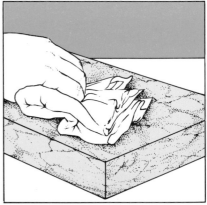

1. Use a double boiler with cooking oil in the lower vessel. Heat Ketone N and Cosmolloid in the top vessel until they melt into a uniform, honey-like liquid. When there are no more particles visible in this liquid, remove it from heat.

2. Gradually add white spirit, stirring all the time, until the mixture reaches the consistency of a loose paste. Let the mixture cool; it will go cloudy. Apply by brushing liberally onto marble.

3. Wipe off the surplus with a white cotton rag or paper towel that has been dampened slightly with white spirit. When dry, buff to a sheen using a clean, soft rag. (If you don't like the result, this wax can be removed by a wipe with white spirit.) Dust the area with white talcum powder when the surface is no longer tacky but not quite dry. This will fill any remaining pores with talc rather than letting them gradually become filled with grime. The surface can be buffed again for a higher shine.

Cleaning and restoring semi-precious stones

ALABASTER

Alabaster is very similar in appearance to fine marble, but it is much softer. Antique alabaster is a lime carbonate but most modern alabaster is a lime sulphate which is much more fragile, easily damaged and – especially important for the restorer to remember – soluble in water so never leave alabaster figures to soak in water, even if they are badly stained. Avoid alabaster ashtrays: it is very difficult to keep them in good condition because the black marks caused by stubbing out cigarettes or cigars will eventually penetrate the rather soft surface, leaving rough patches which are difficult to clean and repolish. The cleaning method is the same as for marble, except that the use of soap and water should be excluded. Use one of the vaporizing solvents – white spirit, benzene or lighter fluid. Apply with a clean, soft brush or rag and wipe dry immediately.

SOAPSTONE

Soapstone, also known as steatite, is the softest of all minerals, and frequently used for carvings. An ordinary steel knife will cut it fairly easily, and a piece of soapstone is far too soft to scratch glass. Try it and you will see a kind of chalk mark, like soap, on the glass surface, hence its popular name. Because of its extremely fragile surface, soapstone must be handled very carefully. Wash it gently using soapy water and a soft brush. Soapstone will not take a high polish and the surface will crumble away under rough abrasives, but gentle circular rubbing with one of the finer abrasives (jeweller's rouge, putty powder) will usually result in a pleasant sheen.

MOTHER-OF-PEARL

Several species of bivalves make a deposit of iridescent, nacreous material inside their shell and this can be detached in layers and used as mother-of-pearl, also sometimes referred to as nacre; it is the same material which forms around a foreign substance in the mollusc to make real pearls. Fine mother-of-pearl has the same light refraction and lustre. Individual pieces are mostly quite small, and almost always used as inlay or for small objects, such as buttons on men's shirts and children's dresses, and the handles of fruit knives and forks. Mother-of-pearl is not easy to repair, but since the chips seldom break, it is usually a question of replacing and/or reglueing them onto the background using a transparent cement. Thin pieces of abalone can be used to replace missing sections. Scratches sometimes mar the iridescent surface but unfortunately these will not polish out. Never use ammonia or any acid on mother-of-pearl. Mild soap and water should take off any dirt, and rubbing with a chamois will keep it glossy. Never let cutlery soak in water (it will loosen the glue) nor wash it in a dishwasher.

JADE: JADEITE AND NEPHRITE

The stone we know as jade is actually two slightly different minerals – jadeite and nephrite. Shades range from pure white to dark green. Jadeite has a very glossy look when polished, nephrite a somewhat oily, softer sheen. Jade is a hard composition usually carved and cut, like glass, on a wheel. It will also scratch a piece of glass and this fact is very useful these days because there are literally dozens of jade substitutes which are almost impossible to identify without scientific instruments. When properly polished, jade seldom needs more than a thorough wash with warm soapy water, aided by gentle scrubbing with a soft brush. Jade carvings should never be repolished by an amateur, although they can be well cleaned, but inexpensive jade beads or solid pebbles can be given a lovely glossy finish by by being tossed in the inexpensive rock tumblers now sold in most craft stores.

Sometimes other stones have been left to soak in aniline dye to imitate the more popular jade greens – a damp white rag rubbed firmly in the deeper parts of the carving will show traces of dye that have not been absorbed. Another kind of fake jade is made of glass. Note that pale tones are harder to imitate, and therefore not often copied by forgers.

JET

Jet is a kind of coal, which is very similar to an especially hard kind of anthracite but which can be cut and polished like stone. Unmounted jet can be cleaned with mild soapsuds and water, but be careful not to damage strings or clasps when scrubbing with a soft brush. A safer way to remove dirt is to pull out the inside of a few slices of soft white bread, crumble into a ball and then rub the crevices and corners of carved jet pieces. The crumbs will gradually absorb the dirt and grease and can then be brushed away with a soft toothbrush. This is particularly useful for mounted jet, where washing may loosen the cement, and for beads, where grease collects in the pierced holes and cannot be removed by washing without fraying the thread.

HORN AND TORTOISESHELL

Both horn and tortoiseshell are gelatinous substances; horn is a product of wild or domestic cattle, tortoiseshell is made from the back of the sea-turtle. Both substances can be shaped under heat and pressure; they are fairly flexible and, when cut into thin sheets, almost transparent. Cutting is done with knives or fine saws. Missing sections can be replaced by pieces cut to size from a sheet. Use a template as if you were replacing a bit of marquetry. Fine abrasive paper will smooth any rough edges. Broken items can be glued together with an epoxy resin but are unlikely to be of any practical use afterwards. To clean, use a very fine abrasive powder such as whiting or jeweller's rouge.

Assorted stones

CLEANING AND POLISHING

Although these various stones have different degress of hardness, in general they may all be treated alike, i.e. cleaned only with soap and water, avoiding bleaches or any acids which will eat through the surface. If properly polished, stains are unlikely; most dark marking, if not natural, is caused by dirt collecting in hidden cracks or tiny fissures – a good stiff toothbrush is the best for dislodging it. Small areas can be repolished with a fine abrasive such as jeweller's rouge, but be careful not to press down too hard unless the piece is carefully supported on a wad of soft modelling clay. This is particularly true of the fine parts of a carved figure or bowl. Single pieces can be smoothed and polished in a rock or pebble tumbler. Broken pieces can be repaired with the same glues and using the same procedures as for porcelain. Clean thoroughly and dry, then coat the broken areas with the transparent cement recommended for glass and china. Tape the pieces together with masking tape and let dry for around 24 hours. Remove the tape by dipping the object quickly in warm water and pulling it off carefully.

AVENTURINE: A feldspar rock containing flecks of other minerals which catch the light under the surface. Aventurine was always a favourite subject for glassmakers to copy. Don't confuse the true stone with the glass bowls and dishes popular during the Art Glass period, 1850–1920.

BASALT: Black, glossy rock mostly used for vases and memorial objects. Black basalt, a pottery imitation, has been made by Wedgwood since the 1770s in styles which reflect the classic Greek and Roman taste.

OBSIDIAN: Extremely hard black volcanic glass, used for ceremonial knives and ornaments, especially in South America. It takes a very high polish. It is not often imitated, but the usual substitute is black glass. This is one instance where the imitation has the same degree of hardness, since obsidian is only a naturally occurring glass.

MALACHITE, SERPENTINE: Both are minerals. Malachite contains copper and is always a deeply veined, marvellously rich green. Serpentine is silica-manganese and ranges from green to black. It is often used as a substitute for jade, since unlike malachite it is mottled rather than veined.

HEMATITE: Iron ore, dark red to blackish in colour, found and worked in small pieces.

QUARTZ: The generic name for silicas from crystalline deposits of all kinds: rock crystal, amethyst, onyx, cornelian and chalcedony are all varieties of quartz and share the same basic structure. The variation is the result of different impurities in the silica solution. Quartzes are often used as substitutes for more precious stones, and in their own right as finely carved ornaments or decorative inlays. Missing pieces can often be replaced with similarly marked quartz chips.

Cleaning amber, bone, coral and ivory

These semi-precious materials can be cleaned and polished with powdered chalk and white dentifrice, mixed in equal parts. Alternatively, the proprietary product Solvol Autosol (sold in motor accessory shops for cleaning chromium) can be used as it contains an ammonia and powder suspension which is non-abrasive. To rout dirt from crevices, use a toothbrush or cotton wool swabs and one of the above cleansers.

AMBER

Amber is a fossil resin, which can be pale yellow or the deepest brown. Translucent, glowing with light, it often contains plant or animal fossils which were trapped in the sticky, slowly hardening mass. Amber is quite soft and easily scratched, so it is usually simply carved and polished. Soap and water are the best cleaning agents, as amber dissolves easily in alcohol and most other common solvents – at one time amber was even used in furniture varnish together with linseed oil or turpentine. Amber can be lightly polished with a very fine abrasive, such as jeweller's rouge, but it must be done carefully by buffing. Finish with a soft cloth or chamois.

BONE

Bone, similar to ivory in appearance and treatment, is simply the cleaned and often-polished skeletal structure of any animal, fish or bird. Remember to handle bone very carefully, especially when wet; it is quite soft. It can be polished lightly like ivory, with jeweller's rouge and a soft cloth, but the surface is too fragile to take a really hard gloss.

CORAL

Natural branch coral is made of the skeletons of thousands of sea organisms which flourish in the warm waters of the Mediterranean and the Pacific Ocean. The most common is a deep pink shade. Coral was believed to have the power to ward off evil and so it has always been popular for children's pieces – tiny bracelets, armlets, teething rings and so forth. Finer pieces come in blush pink and white. It will take a high polish, but really needs cutting and polishing by an expert. However, it can be kept clean and free from dirt, which collects around the mountings and on the strings of beads. Clean these, like jet, with bread, or wash quickly in warm soapsuds. Never scrub any threaded beads – the hard edges of the stone will fray the string.

IVORY

Our own teeth contain material which is very similar to the ivory tusks which some large mammals carry. Most commercial ivory is made from elephants' tusks, although walrus ivory carvings are common among Eskimos and American Indians of the far north. Because of today's greater awareness of the need for wildlife protection, ivory is becoming progressively rarer. Ivory is often found as an inlay in furniture, as key-hole surrounds or as knobs on smaller pieces of furniture, and as handles for silver tea and coffee pots and for sets of cutlery. When ivory is mounted in this way, it is important to try and keep the furniture or metal polish from staining it. The texture of ivory is so close and smooth that the most finely detailed carvings can be made. Handle these very carefully, as old ivory is very brittle. This is one case where soap and water is not really recommended because ivory grows in layers and soaking may cause the layers to swell and separate. However, if the carving is really very dirty, make a lukewarm solution of mild soap with as little water as possible and brush quickly with a soft toothbrush. Rinse under clean water and dry immediately. For less drastic cleaning, a gentle wipe over with a soaped sponge and then a damp clean sponge should be enough. For adding lustre, ivory can be polished lightly with jeweller's rouge or a very fine abrasive powder. Rub gently in circles until the surface glows, then clean off excess powder with a soft rag. Ivory will yellow more quickly in the dark so don't lock it away. Fine ivory carvings are increasing in value every day so do not even try to repair them without the advice of an expert. Broken pieces can be carefully glued together using a clear-drying cement, but use only the minimum necessary.

Cleaning semi-precious inlays

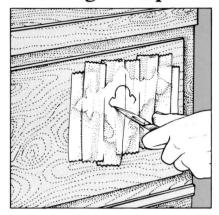 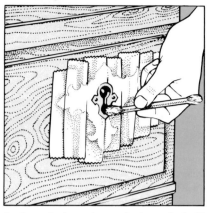 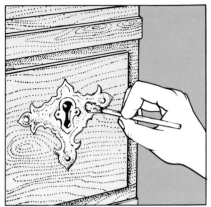

1. When ivory has been used as an inlay, such as surrounding the keyholes of fine furniture, it may be necessary to clean both the ivory and the metal (usually brass) around the hole itself. Begin with the metal, covering the entire area of ivory with acid-free masking tape cut to the exact shape using a knife with replaceable blades; try to apply only enough pressure to cut through the tape, avoiding scratching the ivory underneath.

2. Once the ivory is completely masked off, clean the metal surround using a proprietary cleaner, or follow the instructions given on the opposite page. If the area is very small, apply the cleaner with a cotton swab.

3. Finally, remove the masking tape from the ivoried area, and clean the ivory as suggested on the previous page, again using a cotton swab if necessary in order to prevent the ivory cleaner from damaging the surrounding wood. Rub with the grain or the ivory may be scratched. This method can be used for cleaning any semi-precious inlay.

Repairing semi-precious knife handles

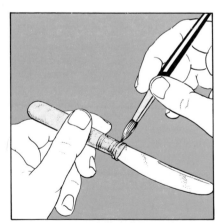 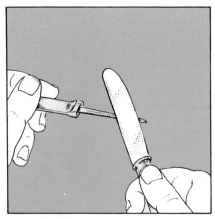 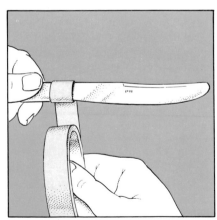

1. Loose cutlery handles can be repaired, but it is imperative to see that all of the old glue is removed first. Remove the handle completely, if possible – it may help to apply a glue solvent to the join using a pointed paintbrush. Follow the manufacturer's instructions regarding the time it will take to soften the old glue, then wiggle the knife from the blade very gently. Apply more solvent if necessary, never forcing either part at any time or further damage may be caused.

2. Clean off the old glue with the blunt edge of a knife, or with a gentle scrub using a small bottle brush dipped in solvent. Rinse with clear water unless advised otherwise by the solvent's manufacturer.

3. Finally, reapply a transparent cement recommended for metals and refit the blade into the handle. Hold the two parts together with acid-free tape until the glue has set.

PLASTICS

The history of plastics is a fascinating story of enthusiasm and endeavour, of genius and good fortune, in the hands of a mixed bunch of scientists and traditional "inventors" from a variety of backgrounds.

The plastics industry celebrated its centenary in 1962 — and it was at the Great Exhibition in Hyde Park, London, in 1862 that the product "Parkesine" was first displayed. In the early nineteenth century the chemical industry was just emerging from its academic chrysalis, and Alexander Parkes had already made his mark in metallurgy when he turned his attention to the industrial applications of a relatively new material, cellulose nitrate. This was first made in 1845 in Basle by a Swiss chemist, Schönbeim, and Parkes encountered it as "collodion" — a solution of the material in an ether/alcohol mixture. Parkesine was exhibited in 1862 as suitable for "medallions, hollow ware, buttons, combs, knife handles, and pens", and optimistically described as being "transparent or opaque", "of any degree of flexibility, waterproof, and maybe of the most brilliant colours". Parkes's inventive genius did not, however, extend to his business sense and the Parkesine Company, established in 1866 to exploit the new material, was in liquidation by 1868. It was Parkes's works manager, Daniel Spill, who established the Xylonite Company in 1869 to have another attempt at the commercial development of this new material. It is fairly rare to find any samples of Parkesine or Xylonite dating from this period, however, since the manufacturer was still troubled by returned articles that were shrinking excessively, curling and disintegrating!

Spill's company also foundered, and it was not until the British Xylonite Company was formed in 1877 that the product had any commercial success in Britain. Meanwhile in the United States, another inventor, an Illinois printer called John Hyatt, stimulated by a competition offering a cash prize for an alternative to ivory for billiard balls, had also started work on the manufacture of products derived from cellulose nitrate. He, too, was handicapped by the intractable nature of the material, and by its explosive flammability. He did, however, discover the solvent effect of camphor on cellulose nitrate. He noted the thermoplastic nature of the cellulose nitrate/camphor blend that enabled it to be moulded and shaped whilst warm, and Hyatt's invention of a "stuffing machine" to make rods, tubes, and dental plate blanks was the forerunner of today's plastics moulding machines. In 1872 the Celluloid Manufacturing Company was formed in Newark, New Jersey when Hyatt's Dental Plate Company changed its name.

In the closing years of the nineteenth century the plastics industry on both sides of the Atlantic continued to make progress, although it was not recognized by that title until the 1930s. The decision of the British Xylonite Company to manufacture collars and cuffs in the new material in 1885, in addition to combs, bangles and simple moulded items, ensured the company's growth from 29 employees in 1877 to 1160 in 1902.

The next group of plastics materials to be developed are now identified as "thermosetting" materials, since the effect of heat, although allowing moulding under pressure, is irreversible. They were first discovered by a Belgian chemist, Dr Leo Baekland, working in the United States, who was looking for an alternative to the natural material shellac. He studied the chemistry of the reaction between phenol and formaldehyde and produced a resinous substance he called Bakelite in 1907. In England an electrical engineer, James Swinburne, set up the Fireproof Celluloid Company and, working on the same reaction as Baekland, developed a process that was sufficiently viable for him to establish the Damard Lacquer Company in 1910. The subsequent development of the motor car stimulated demand for these materials which proved invaluable for moulded electrical insulating components and resinous binders for brake linings. At the same time the material Erinoid was being developed from casein and formaldehyde, and was commercially viable by 1914.

Materials based on cellulose nitrate were attractive, and the brand name was very soon to lose its distinction and become the generic celluloid, but both the manufacturing process and its application were hampered by its flammability, and many products were to be discovered in the hunt for a non-flammable alternative. Cellulose acetate was recognized at an early stage as an attractive material, but its manufacturing chemistry was not easy, and it was only the demand for a solution, or "dope", for proofing the fabric used on aircraft wings in World War I that got this product under way.

Many of the materials developed so far were dark, but in the 1920s the reaction between amines, such as urea, and formaldehyde was worked up to a commercial product with the introduction of "Beetle" urea-formaldehyde moulding powders in 1928. The improved moulding properties of these materials, and their light colours, made marbled mouldings possible. A few years later the development of accelerated moulding powders enabled the production of mouldings that often survive to the present. In 1935 melamine/formaldehyde resins were introduced to bring the plastics industry further in touch with consumers' needs.

The story of the plastics industry up to 1930 is largely the history of semi-synthetic materials — produced by reacting known materials, such as cellulose, in the form of cotton or paper, as the raw material. The modern polymer industry, responsible for all the materials now in use, is based on the work of a German scientist, Hermann Staudinger, in the 1920s, and of the American Wallace Carothers in the 1930s. The development of wholly synthetic macromolecules, or polymers, to produce polystyrene from styrene for example, was the product of academic excellence allied to commercial expediency, but it was due to the stimulus of World War II in Germany, Britain and the United States, that materials such as polyvinyl chloride (PVC), polyethylene, and polystyrene became commercially available.

All of these materials were developed with very little help from the business we know today as the petrochemical industry, but all are now firmly based on petrochemicals such as ethylene, styrene, vinyl chloride, and many more. The "traditional" cellulose-based materials still make their contribution, and the semi-synthetics are essential contributors, to the manufacture of semi-conductors for example, but mass-production has achieved what the pioneers could only dream of. Plastics are lighter, more colourful, and more versatile, but are still the tough and waterproof materials sought by Alexander Parkes when he described Parkesine as the product of 10 years' "development of the capabilities and application of this beautiful subject to the Arts".

Care and cleaning of plastics

Because the collecting of plastic "antiques" is relatively new, their care can pose many problems. The first is the identification of the plastic itself. In very general terms, the type of article provides a clue to the plastic from which it is made. But the diversity of plastics used in the 1920s and 1930s, and the short period that some were in production, pose problems even for the experts. In view of this, the notes on restoration and repair are for the simplest and most obvious damage. For anything more complicated or difficult, seek expert advice.

CELLULOSE NITRATE

This is better known under the trademarks Celluloid, Xylonite and Parkesine. Its early makers achieved many beautiful effects in imitation of tortoiseshell. It must not be stored in airtight containers—two of its major constituents, camphor and acids, are continually evaporating and if fumes cannot escape the surface may take on a jelly-like texture eventually leading to complete breakdown of the material.

In addition: avoid direct sunlight, which causes fading; avoid excessive moisture; keep in an even temperature—cellulose nitrate is extremely flammable! Do not display this plastic so that any other article rests on top of it—this may cause "leaching" of the plasticizer which, coupled with the fading caused by any direct light, will result in very uneven colorations.

Cellulose nitrate scratches fairly easily so surface dust should be removed with a soft cloth dampened with a solution of warm water and detergent. Rinse carefully and dry thoroughly with a clean soft cloth. Take particular care with hairbrushes, mirrors and the like, to avoid trapping water between the plastic and the wooden base. In any case avoid complete submersion, and never use abrasive cleansing powders or cleansers based on organic solvents.

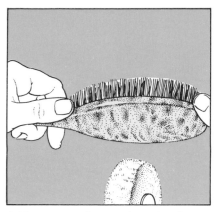

1. To remove surface scratches, mix soft soap and jeweller's rouge to a paste. Apply this to a rotary buffing wheel fitted with a lambswool cover. Once the small scratched area is improved, minimize the effect of buffing one area by buffing the entire piece with a clean lambswool cover. Incidentally, this will often release the camphor fumes which are so typical of celluloid and one of the prime clues in its identification.

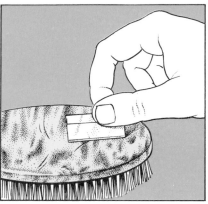

2. For deep scratches, use a process known as "radishing", recommended only to the most adept and on pieces of little value. With the flat edge of a single-edged razor, scrape and pare away the scratch; work from the middle and away from the scratch, tapering and feathering the "cuts". Then buff as before.

PHENOLICS

Popularly known as Bakelite and most often used for the manufacture of smoking accessories, as it is very heat resistant. Phenolics were the first true synthetic and are technically known as thermosets since they will not soften upon heating. Dust with a soft brush to remove surface dust, then clean with a soft cloth dampened with a solution of warm water and detergent. Rinse carefully and dry thoroughly. Avoid immersion as some of these plastics have limited resistance to moisture.

The surface gloss can be renovated and surface marks removed by buffing with a soft cloth dampened with a mild abrasive cleanser such as Brasso or a car-body renovating polish. Follow that by buffing with a good universal museum wax or a beeswax polish. Avoid aerosol polishes which may contain solvents damaging to one of the ingredients in these plastics. Also avoid storing with another piece of plastic, or displaying with another piece resting on top, for the same reasons as for cellulose nitrate.

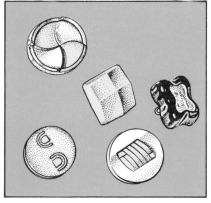

CASEIN

This is another semi-synthetic, derived from milk and is better known under such trademarks as Erinoid, Lactoid and Galalith. It was widely used in the production of buttons, knitting needles and ornamental novelties of all kinds. It has very poor moisture resistance and is sensitive to sunlight and humidity. Care for it as directed for cellulose nitrate but don't worry about keeping it well ventilated.

UREAS

Like phenolics, ureas are an early thermoset plastic. However, they are based on a water-white resin which enabled the manufacture of mouldings in light pale shades and with multi-hued mottled effects, characteristic of this type of plastic. Care and maintenance is similar to the phenolics, but special care should be taken to avoid excess moisture and humidity.

Repairing plastics

The relatively low value of articles made of plastic has discouraged the development of techniques for repair and restoration. However, as the early pieces acquire historical interest, it may be prudent to repair early plastic articles where possible, unless they are of value, in which case they should be taken to an expert.

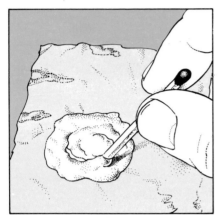 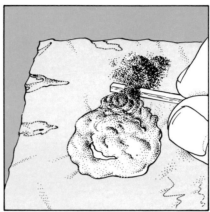 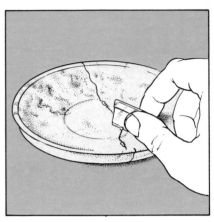

1. To join broken pieces, use a two-part epoxy adhesive. Avoid adhesives based on organic solvents, which may be harmful to the plastic. Squeeze out small amounts of the two adhesive components onto a piece of tin foil. Mix together using the end of a wooden matchstick or a toothpick until the two are thoroughly mixed.

2. Since most plastic articles are coloured in some way, it may be advisable to tint the adhesive using powdered pigments. Only a few particles of pigment will be necessary, unless you are trying to achieve a dark shade. Mix gradually using a clean matchstick or toothpick, aiming for an exact match.

3. Scrape away excess adhesive using gentle pressure on a single-edged razor.

TEXTILES

Textiles are fragile, so the first evidence that a community made them is always provided by spindle whorls—stones with a hole in the middle which were attached to a stick for the spinning of a fibre. The earliest known finds of textiles are fragments of clothing from burials, but there is a gap of several thousand years before there is any clear evidence of different textiles and the purposes for which they were made. Hangings, generally linen brocaded or patterned in wool, have been preserved in the dry sands of Egypt since the days of Tutankhamun, who ruled 1552–43 B.C.; ancient Chinese silks have been kept in the Japanese imperial collection of the Shōsō-in, and recovered at sites along the Silk Road from China to the west; coverlets and a hand-knotted carpet have been found in the tomb of a Scythian chief, buried in Central Asia in the fifth or fourth century B.C. Ancient statuary and literary references add a few details to our knowledge, but it is only from the Middle Ages onward that a coherent picture of the use of textiles in Europe can be built up.

Cloth hangings and tapestries survive from the late fourteenth century. The hangings were often woven strips of materials in contrasting shades sewn together, sometimes with further applied decoration. The tapestries used a limited range of dyed wools, and, later, costly gold and silver thread; their subjects were usually those likely to please their aristocratic or religious patrons—hunting, courtly love, allegories or lives of the saints. They were initially manufactured in the Netherlands, but in the seventeenth century important workshops were established in France (the Gobelins, followed by others) and elsewhere in Europe, even in England at Mortlake. Though their subjects changed with the times, tapestries gradually ceased to be fashionable wall coverings early in the eighteenth century, except in the grandest rooms of the very rich. Plain woven hangings in wool, silk or mixtures were current in the sixteenth to eighteenth centuries, and also hangings of wool or hemp with repeating patterns—an inexpensive substitute for tapestries. All were swept away in the course of the 1730s and 1740s in favour of wallpaper or even plain painted walls. The French factories continued to make imitations of traditional products in the nineteenth century, with new ideas and designs coming in only during this century; while tapestry-making in England saw a revival inspired by William Morris.

Bed curtains were a key feature of the fashionable interior from the sixteenth to the early nineteenth century. Even in earlier miniatures and panel paintings, beds are shown with curtains draped, looped up, or half open according to the scene. In cold castles and not much warmer houses they were practical to exclude draughts and keep in the sleeper's own warmth. The curtains could be quite simple fabrics or perhaps expensive Italian silk, further embroidered in silks. Linen and cotton (fustian) curtains embroidered in many shades of wool, often predominantly blue and pink with flowers and large trees reminiscent of imported Indian fabrics, are some of the most familiar survivals from the seventeenth century. (Now they are often tattered through long use and badly faded—the yellow has gone from the greens leaving them in shades of blue.) Different sets of curtains were used for summer and winter, invariably so in places with greater extremes of climate, such as the American colonies.

A surprising number of state beds survive from the seventeenth and eighteenth centuries, some finished in rich silks with matching linings, braids, fringes and tassels. Many simpler sets of printed cotton bed furniture from the 1770s to 1790s can be found in the United States. The British cotton manufacturers in Manchester, who sold their cottons worldwide, adapted their patterns to their customers, so these include such subjects as "The Apotheosis of Benjamin Franklin and George Washington" or "America at the Altar of Liberty". Bed curtains ceased to be so necessary as household heating improved in the course of the eighteenth century, and gradually became unfashionable though token draped bedheads continued for much longer. The coverlet, which originally matched or complemented the rest of the hangings, has however remained important to the present day.

Window curtains first came into use in the eighteenth century and their styles and materials quickly reflected fashion. Indeed, their correct drape was illustrated in engravings almost as often as dress fashions. The curtains would match the bed or walls; if these were covered in silk, then the window curtains would also be of silk. Printed linen, fustian and then cotton were, of course, more practical, and their production may have stimulated the use of window curtains. Inner curtains of fine net seem to be an innovation of the later eighteenth century—patterns came with the new power-driven jacquard looms of the 1840s—becoming ever more elaborate: ruched, draped and trimmed much like the outer curtains. Glazed block-printed chintzes were printed from the 1750s onward. As the range of shades increased so did their popularity for both dress and furnishing. During the eighteenth century, woven, printed and dyed cottons went into every possible domestic use. For perhaps the first time, the poorer classes could buy new and cheap materials for clothing and, possibly, furnishing. The rich bought elaborately printed and fashionable chintzes, and the manufacturers introduced patterns of block printed cottons with kaleidescopic speed to stimulate demand.

Throughout the nineteenth century window curtains were the focal point of interior decoration as bed curtains had been before them. Photographs from the 1870s and 1880s show pelmets, extra drapes, trimmings, tassels and curtain rods. Twentieth century taste, however, influenced by the arts movements of the later nineteenth century, has rebelled against such massive quantities of useless and often dusty textiles, with their overwhelming patterns, colours and textures. The fabrics, too, have changed. Silk ceased to be used for furnishing when the last cheap sources of raw silk disappeared after the First World War. Even wool and worsted became increasingly expensive. Man-made fibres became more important after the Second World War. Though central heating has lessened the need for heavy curtains in modern homes, heavy woollen curtains have remained in demand for older, draughtier houses.

The padded, stuffed upholstery known since the early seventeenth century would have been an unknown extravagance in earlier times. Until then, chairs and benches were simple structures of plain wood, but at last concessions were made to comfort. Rush and cane seating were introduced, and the upholstered chair with webbing, canvas and horsehair appears from the 1620s onwards. The general structure of upholstery has changed little since then, but the style of the chairs and their visible coverings have been modified by fashion. Up to the end of the nineteenth century, chairs, stools, and later, sofas, were always given loose covers for protection. The valuable chief covering would be revealed only on formal occasions. It might be embroidered in tent-stitch on canvas or with applied decoration on silk; or perhaps Italian silk damask, velvet, brocatelle, or plain silk; or perhaps hardwearing plain worsted. (Fashionable brocaded dress silks were seldom put on chairs except for state ceremonies; their presence today usually indicates an antique dealer's refurbishing.)

In the nineteenth century there were enormous variations in both the shapes of seat furniture and their covers, and the embroidery also changed markedly in character. Embroidered furnishings, like embroidered costume, had been extremely important in rich households from the sixteenth to the early eighteenth centuries, including everything from screens to bed curtains, and even wall coverings. Ladies embroidered exquisite cushions, though these were intended more for show than for use. A few nineteenth-century cushions also embroidered in raised work and beads come into the same category. Even then, every young girl of respectable family became a proficient needlewoman and spent many hours stitching. But the craze for "Berlin woolwork"—embroidery in thick, bright wools on a canvas already printed with a pattern (originally from Berlin)—killed the imagination of the domestic embroidress: these patterns were invariably executed in cross-stitch, quick and easy to do, and bright; but the style allowed for little variation.

The patterns and colouring of textiles, like their function, have followed the fashions of the day, but have been subject to restrictions in technology. Printed decoration was only used in European textiles from the late seventeenth century, when European studies in chemistry began to be applied successfully to the imitation of the textile printing and painting already known in India for many centuries. The shades were restricted by the dyestuffs available. Imported madder and indigo gave good reds and blues; browns were easy; but yellow was always more difficult and many greens have faded to blue over the years. Wool and silk take dyes well and consistently; cotton can be dyed but was not, at first, easy to print; linen did not accept any colour very happily. Hence the printed fustians of the eighteenth century have a speckled effect where the dye has taken on the cotton but failed to take on the linen in the mixture. Increasing understanding of dye technology greatly extended the range of shades available in the eighteenth and nineteenth centuries. Research culminated, unfortunately, in aniline dyes derived from coal tar, which produced colours that were bright, almost glowing in their intensity, the most notable being purple, pink and a virulent green. The dyes were, however, fast neither in water nor light, and nothing can be done to restore their vanished brilliance.

A second basic restriction upon textile design was the capacity of the loom. Table-linen and broadcloth looms were wide, but silks and fine worsteds were woven on narrow looms (the materials are from 18 – 22in/45 – 56cm wide before the mid-nineteenth century and often afterwards). Patterns had to be in proportion. The costs of production, in which raw material played a much greater part than labour, would also limit the imagination of the designer. Production itself was slow, 1½yd/1.4m a day of a patterned material was good progress before the power-driven jacquard looms were introduced in the mid-nineteenth century. The flying shuttle was never used in the silk industry because the silk itself was too delicate and precious; for the same reason only the more inexpensive silk handkerchiefs were printed. Embroidered textiles, on the other hand, are limited only by the time and materials available to the embroiderer. Professional workshops, from the Middle Ages to the nineteenth century, had to make money and so compete with both woven and, in due course, printed textiles. The domestic embroidress, however, could please herself.

Few old textiles of any type survive in pristine condition. Unlike many other materials, textiles can be totally ruined by light, water or just everyday use. Furnishing fabrics have suffered even more than dress materials for they are seldom kept out of sentiment. The silk in chair seats embroidered in silk and wool wears away from use before the wool, and so do areas embroidered in black wool because the black dyes used before the twentieth century had a destructive effect on the fabric. Rare well-preserved examples can astonish us with their workmanship; for the rest, only skilful conservation can bring back their vanished glory.

Opposite: Bentwood chair by Thonet with missing and damaged upholstery; the frame is weakened by nailheads and has a very worn varnished finish (see overleaf).

Preparing the frame and webbing

When choosing new fabric, buy a material of the right upholstery weight and consider a patterned fabric if the piece will get lots of of use — patterns are much better for disguising spots and wear than plain colours. The quantity of fabric required obviously depends on the size of the item to be upholstered, the width of the fabric chosen and whether it is plain or patterned, because allowance must be made for matching patterns. The style of upholstery will also affect the quantity of fabric required: there may be a skirt around the base of the piece and separate cushions. For an accurate estimate take all the dimensions of the piece that needs recovering and seek the assistance of the upholstery department of the nearest store.

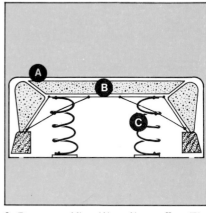

THE OLD COVERING

1. If the old upholstery fabric is beyond repair, first remove all visible tacks or staples with a screwdriver or blunt chisel and mallet and then carefully remove the stitches. Take the covering off piece by piece. This old covering is used as a pattern for the new, so remove it intact if possible! Turn the piece upside down and remove tacks and old covering from the underneath.

2. Turn right side up and remove tacks and/or stitches from the covering, first removing any loose cushions or buttons. Then continue in the order shown in the illustration.

3. Remove padding (A) and/or stuffing (B), making a note of the way the top covering is attached, the number of springs (C) and strips of webbing used and the height of the original padding. Dismantle only the materials that seem damaged, if the springs and webbing are still good leave them in place.

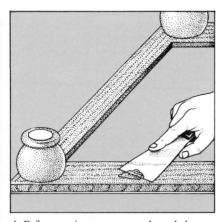

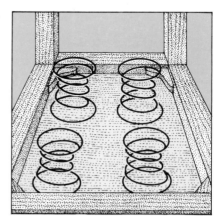

4. Before starting to renovate the upholstery, treat the wooden frame for woodworm (see Steps 1–6, Pages 22–3) and fill old tack holes with wood filler (see Steps 5–6, Page 21). If the springs are damaged, save them for matching with a new, non-rusting variety of the same size.

5. Assemble the following supplies. Choose upholstery fabric and thread. For stuffing, real horsehair is traditionally used, but it is difficult to find and very expensive. Instead use Algerian fiber (a palm grass), or curled hair (an animal mixture). Sometimes the old stuffing can be salvaged – hand-wash it in soapy water and rinse well; tease it out before reusing. Measure the lengths of webbing you have removed and buy twill webbing or upholsterer's rubber webbing. Buy a webbing stretcher or make one from a piece of wood 2in x 1in/5cm x 2.5cm x the width of the webbing. Strong twine made of flax and hemp is used for holding the stuffing in place, and for securing the springs.

Canvas, burlap or hessian is used to cover the springs, cut to the same size as the seat, plus 1in/2.5cm all around. Buy No. 3 carpet tacks for thin fabrics, No. 4 for heavier fabrics, No. 7 for webbing. Enough scrim, a gauzy material for covering the first layer of stuffing, is needed to cover the seat plus 6in/15cm all around. The second layer of stuffing is covered in unbleached cotton or calico, cut slightly larger. Wadding is used over the cotton.

Tools needed are various needles – darning, mattress, upholsterer's regulator or one thin knitting, half-circle (or spring) and sacking, and an upholsterer's tack hammer.

RENEWING THE WEBBING

6. The wooden frame of the piece should now be exposed, so the first step is to renew the webbing if necessary, as it is the basis for the rest of the upholstery. To fix the webbing turn the piece upside down on the work surface, preferably at table height.

Opposite: Bentwood chair by Thonet with newly upholstered back and seat and varnished frame —note that the piping has been used to conceal the damage done to the frame by the nailheads previously edging the upholstery (see previous page).

Preparing the webbing cont.

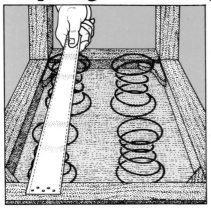

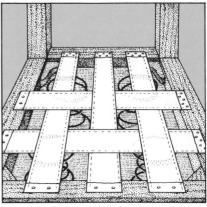

7. Use the webbing straight from the roll. Fold under ½–1in/1.3–2.5cm of webbing and place on the back rail so that the cut edge is up and ½in/13mm away from outer edge of the frame. Tack down with five tacks staggered in a "W" as shown. (Use finer tacks if the wood splits.)

8. It is best to use a webbing stretcher to get the webbing really taut. Brace the webbing along the length of the stretcher and lower stretcher and webbing across the frame. Use a cotton pad under the stretcher to prevent damage to the chair frame where the two come into contact.

9. Tack down with three tacks in a row, cut off webbing 1in/2.5cm from tack, fold over this cut end and tap in two more tacks between the first three to hold it in place. Attach the rest of the webbing in the same way, referring to your notes about the number of strips, the distance between each and the number of crossed-over strips. Try to ensure that the crossed-over webbing is above the springs.

The springs

Before putting new springs into an old chair, check the top of the seat rail. If there are tack holes along it, the chair was originally made without springs and those which have just been taken out were not part of the chair's design. Indeed, if there are many holes in the rail the springs were probably added to add life to the chair— webbing for seats with springs is usually attached to the bottom of the rail, not to the top.

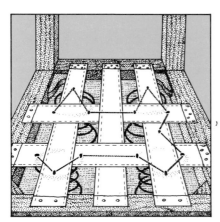

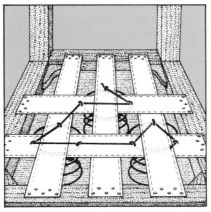

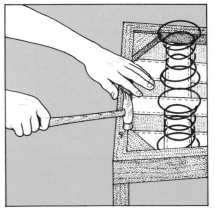

1. Sew each spring securely to the webbing with the half-circle needle and twine. Use a long length of twine and go from one spring to the next without cutting it.

2. Each spring is secured to the webbing in at least three places. Make a knot after each stitch and pull the twine taut. Seen from the underneath, three springs are arranged as shown in the illustration.

3. Turn the piece the right way up and align tacks on the frame with the rows of springs. Hammer tacks in half-way.

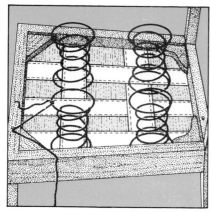
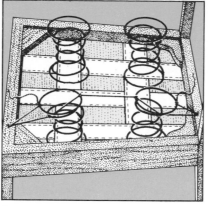
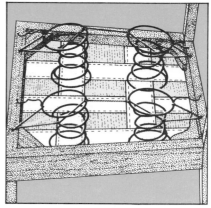

4. Cut enough twine (some people prefer a heavy type of cording) to go once around the frame. Tie it around the front of a front spring, leaving a tail 8in/20cm long. Wrap it around the tack and hammer the tack in to secure the twine. Take the main length of twine to the nearest spring at the back, knot it around the spring using a clove hitch knot, take it through the middle of the coil, and knot again at the front of the spring.

5. Move on to the other springs in the row and "lash" together in the same way, not pulling too tight, so that the distance between the top and bottom of each spring remains the same. When all the springs have been tied in, wrap the twine around the tack on the back rail and hammer the tack in. Repeat until all the springs in each row are lashed together, first one way, then the other.

6. To give a nicely domed shape take the 8in/20cm tail and tie the spring nearest each tack so that these springs tilt down slightly toward the frame.

The main stuffing

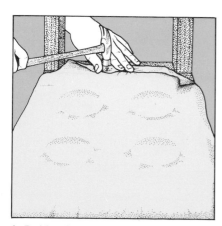
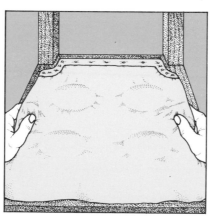
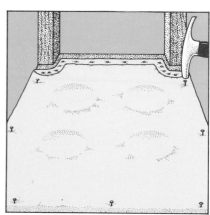

1. Position the canvas, hessian or burlap over the springs; fold over 1in/2.5cm on the back edge and tack this down on the back frame, spacing the tacks 1in/2.5cm apart. Fit it neatly around any back uprights or clip ¼in/7mm at a time to fit.

2. Pull this canvas straight to the front rail, keeping it taut, and tack it to the front rail with tacks half-way in through a single thickness of canvas.

3. Smooth it to the side rail and temporarily tack in place again.

The main stuffing cont.

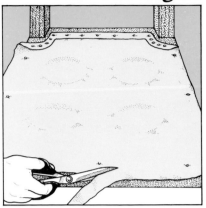

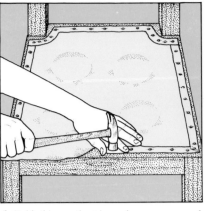

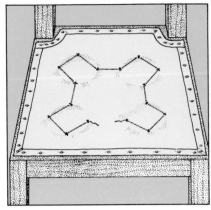

4. Look closely, and if the canvas lies smooth and straight, hammer the tacks in completely. Trim off excess canvas leaving 1-1½in/2.5-3.8cm.

5. Fold this neatly trimmed canvas up and over the first tacks and then secure with tacks spaced at 2in/5cm intervals.

6. Using the half-circle needle again, stitch the top of the springs to the canvas, again making a knot after each stitch.

The bridle ties

Bridle ties are fairly long back-stitched loops made about 3in/7.6cm from the edge of the chair. They are used to hold the stuffing in place.

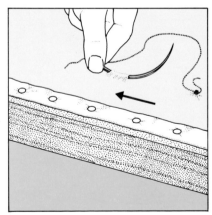

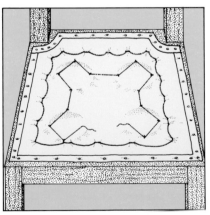

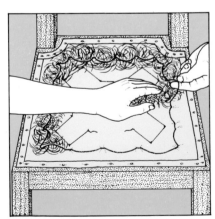

1. Thread the half-circle needle with enough twine to go around the chair one and a half times. Work about 3in/7.6cm from the chair's edge, taking back stitches approximately every 4in/10cm.

2. Stitch all round the chair, taking care not to pull the twine tight between stitches. Make sure that there is a 1in/2.6cm stitch at each corner. These back stitches are called bridle ties.

3. Take a handful of stuffing, tease it out, removing any lumps, and place it under the bridle ties between the rows. Then fill up any space between the rows, keeping the stuffing evenly distributed.

The scrim

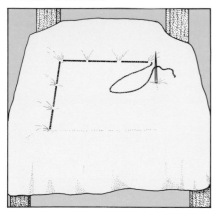 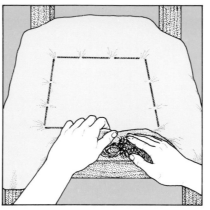 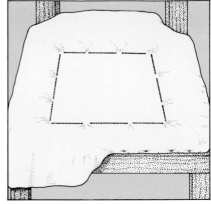

1. Place the scrim centrally over the stuffing and tap in tacks on each side to hold it in place. Thread a large-eyed double pointed needle, such as an upholsterer's needle, with 3ft/1m of twine and stitch through the scrim to the canvas, making the same rectangular or square shape about 3in/7.6cm from the edges of the seat. Pull the needle out between the webbing on the underside, leaving a 7in/18cm tail on top. Then push it back up, make a stitch about 3in/7.6cm long and go back down again. Pull twine tight so the scrim is pulled down. Do not catch the springs with the stitches.

2. Remove the temporary tacks on the chair frame and even out the stuffing underneath the scrim if necessary.

3. Add more stuffing under the scrim so that it protrudes slightly beyond the edge of the frame. Tuck the raw edge of scrim under the stuffing, and tack the folded edge to the chamfered edge of the frame – but don't pull this too tightly as there must be some "give" for the roll edge.

Stitching the edge

To make a firm edge, the stuffing must be pulled over and stitched alongside the frame. This technique is known as "blind stitching".

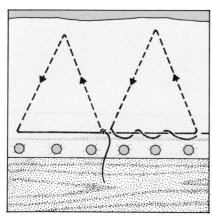 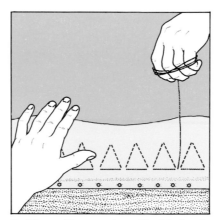 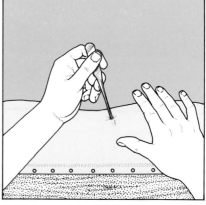

1. Thread the upholsterer's needle with 1yd/1m or so of twine and insert into the scrim just above the tacks and 1½in/3.8cm from the corner. Insert the needle at about 45° and pull the needle through on top about 2in/5cm from the edge, but stop before the eye is visible. Push the needle back into the stuffing again and down, making a V-shaped stitch or triangle in the stuffing. Knot the twine after this first stitch and begin the second blind stitch 2in/5cm along. Wrap the bottom thread to secure as shown.

2. After working around one side of the base in this manner put the needle into the middle of the top temporarily. Hold the stuffing edge and top with your left hand as shown, and pull on the twine with your right hand. Wrap the twine around your fingers or hand to get a good hold. You should feel the stuffing being pulled toward the edge.

3. Work around the chair in this manner, making the triangular blind stitches and then pulling the stuffing toward the edges. Knot the twine tightly when finished. Correct any unevenness you feel with the regulator or a long thin knitting needle by poking it through to the stuffing.

Top stitching

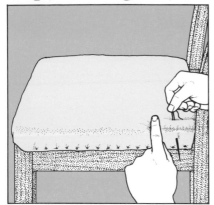

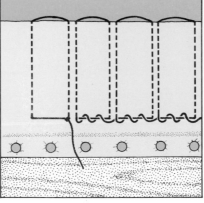

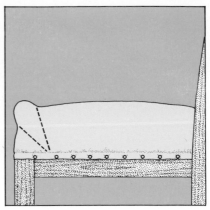

1. Top stitching is the second stage, similar to blind stitching, only the needle is drawn completely through on top of the stuffing so that a complete stitch can be made. Thread the upholsterer's needle with a long length of twine and start in a corner, placing the needle vertically into the scrim ½-1in/1.3-2.5cm above the blind stitching and pushing it through so that it emerges about 1in/2.5cm from the top edge.

2. Reinsert the needle 1in/2.5cm to the left of this point and push through so it comes out 1in/2.5cm to the left of the start. Wrap the twine around the needle to knot, and insert again 1in/2.5cm away toward the top, emerging so that the next top stitch forms a continuous line parallel to the chair edge.

3. In profile the effect of the stitching is as shown in the illustration.

The second stuffing

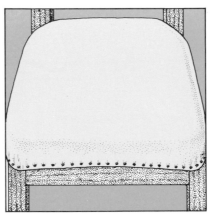

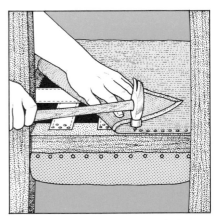

1. To begin the second stuffing make bridle ties on the scrim as before (see Steps 1-3, Page 132) about 2in/5cm from the edge. Fill the ties and the gaps between the rows of stitching with more stuffing.

2. Cover this with a piece of unbleached cotton cut to size. Tack it temporarily in place at the front, then the back and finally at the sides, spacing the tacks 2in/5cm apart. Smooth any bumps or sags by readjusting the stuffing before tacking the cotton firmly in place. Mitre corners to fit if necessary. Sink the tacks only after the cotton is smooth and the grain lies straight. The seat should look full and evenly stuffed and is ready for the final covering.

3. Turn the piece over and apply the bottom dust-cloth. Cut the cloth 1in/2.5cm larger than the bottom of the piece. Position, tacking lightly in place with a few tacks. Fold the excess under and tack down.

Top covering

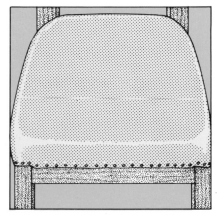

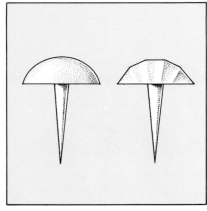

1. Cover the unbleached cotton with cotton wadding (sometimes called batting) to prevent the stuffing from working through. Again tack in place, spacing tacks ¾in/2cm apart. Cut a piece of the new upholstery fabric, using the original piece as a pattern. Keeping the grain straight, temporarily tack it in place through a single thickness, starting at the back. Mitre or pleat corners as necessary.

2. The tacks and raw edges can then be covered with gimp or braid which is glued in place with a latex adhesive, glueing 6in/15cm at a time. Do not apply too much glue or the excess will mark the gimp and upholstery fabric. Mitre the braid at the corners.

3. As an alternative, instead of glueing the gimp in place, use tacks with rounded brass heads to hold the gimp. This treatment is especially suited to leather-covered and heavier furniture styles.

Cleaning lace

You will need the following supplies for cleaning: purified water, liquid detergent, stainless steel pins, and acid-free tissue paper; for repairing: fine nylon net, bridal veil net and stainless steel pins.

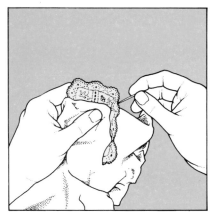

1. If the lace is mounted on another fabric, unpick it carefully before starting to clean or repair it.

2. To remove the dirt lay the lace on a sheet of clear polythene or plastic film in a flat tray or dish. Cover it with cold purified water and let the lace soak. Change the water frequently as it becomes dirty.

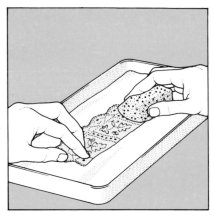

3. When the water no longer gets dirty pour it out, but leave the lace in the dish. Sponge the lace gently with a weak solution of mild liquid detergent and rinse several times with purified water.

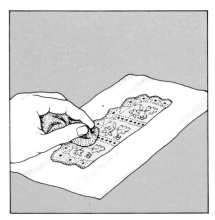

4. Lift the lace out of the dish, still supporting it with the sheet of polythene. Lay it on a flat surface, straighten it out gently and blot off the excess water with an absorbent towel. Dry it flat, away from direct heat.

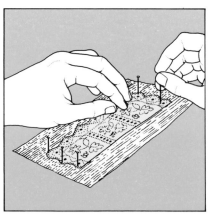

5. If the lace needs to be pinned to keep it lying flat and the pattern straight while it is drying, use stainless steel pins. Pin the lace carefully, taking care not to stretch it too much.

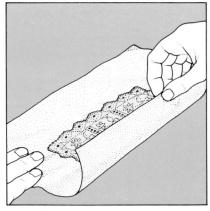

6. When dry, store in acid-free tissue paper. Do not use polythene bags, as these can attract dust and encourage moulds.

Repairing lace

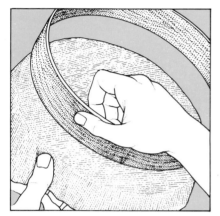

1. To repair the thicker laces, stretch a piece of firm fabric, such as canvas, in an embroidery frame.

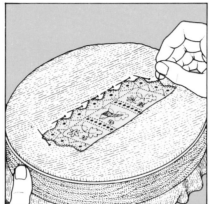

2. Pin the lace, right side up, onto the canvas. Ease the damaged areas very carefully into place, taking particular care that the pattern is straight.

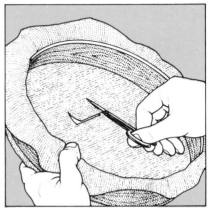

3. Cut the canvas away behind the damaged area.

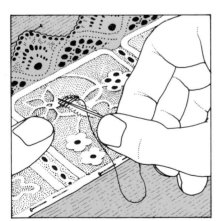

4. Repair the broken threads by laying a new thread, known as a "bar" across the hole, linking it to the stronger mesh of lace at each end with a slip knot. Lay as many threads across as is necessary to mend the hole.

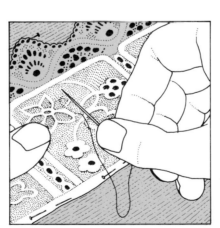

5. The edge of the tear can be caught down to the supporting threads with tiny stitches. Take care not to pull the threads too tight or they will distort the lace and may even tear it again. When the repair is completed, remove the lace from the canvas.

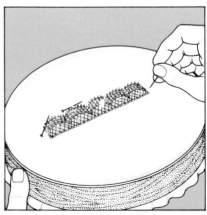

6. Repairing fine lace follows a similar technique, but uses finer materials. Instead of canvas, stretch a piece of fine net in a matching shade over an embroidery frame and pin the lace, right side up, to the net. If the lace cannot be removed, lay the net behind the lace and stitch it into the seams at each side. Repair the damaged area by sewing through to the net.

Repairing lace cont.

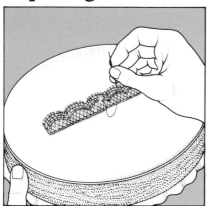
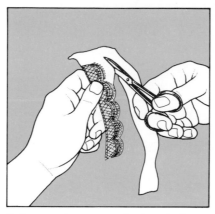
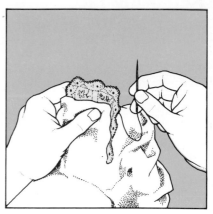

7. Stitch the lace to the net, using fine polyester threads pulled out of polyester fabric, and very small stitches. Work around the edge of the tear or hole.

8. Cut away the excess net, leaving only the net that is now sewn to and supporting the damaged area of lace.

9. If the lace was unpicked from a dress, sew it back with tiny stitches, using fine threads of the same fibre as the lace.

Care and cleaning of textiles

The best way to look after textiles is to ensure that they are clean before they are stored or displayed, that they are checked regularly for insect infestation, that they are protected from the harmful effects of strong light, both natural and artificial, and that they receive careful cleaning and maintenance as described in the following pages.

Before storing textiles ensure that the storage area, as well as the textile itself, is clean and free from pests. Never store textiles in plastic or polythene bags as these will attract dust and encourage the growth of mould. Cover textiles and upholstery with loose, light dust covers made from any slightly slippery, closely woven material which will not catch on the fabric underneath.

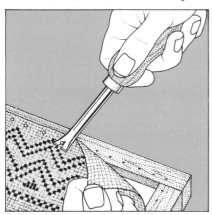

CLEANING SMALL TEXTILES

1. Remove the tapestry or embroidery from the wooden stretcher. If it is a seat cover, take care not to tear the fabric around the nails, which may have rusted into the frame. Unpick cushion covers carefully.

2. Lay the piece out flat and vacuum it carefully on both sides, following the directions in Steps 1 – 3, Page 140. Embroideries with sequins or beads should never be vacuumed in case the stitching has become weak and the sequins or beads are pulled off by the suction of the vacuum cleaner. Instead, dust gently with a very soft, small paintbrush.

3. Test all the colours with small swabs of cotton wool soaked with turpentine substitute to see if the dyes run. Try to find inconspicuous areas to do this. If the dyes run, do not try to clean the piece.

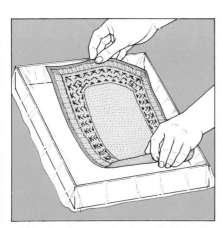

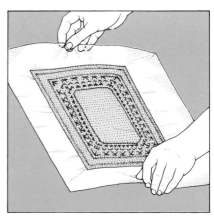

4. If the dyes do not run, lay the textile (right side up) flat on a piece of clear polythene or plastic film in a large flat try. (If the tray is plastic, first check that the solvent does not dissolve the plastic of the tray—even some photographic developing trays are not immune from the action of certain chemicals.)

5. Pour enough turpentine substitute into the tray to cover the textile. Rock the tray gently from side to side to agitate the solvent. Work out of doors or in a room with good ventilation. If the textile is very dirty and a great deal of dirt comes out, pour off the dirty solvent (it can be used to clean paintbrushes) and repeat the process. Do not skimp the amount of solvent you use, and never use a powder cleaner such as magnesium carbonate or fuller's earth.

6. When no more dirt comes out into the solvent, lift the textile out of the tray, supporting it on the sheet of plastic or polythene.

Cleaning small textiles cont.

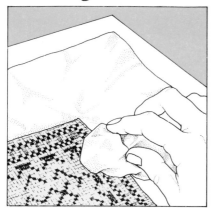

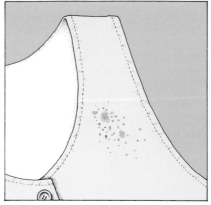

7. Lay the textile and supporting sheet down on a flat surface. Straighten the textile and blot off the excess solvent with a soft white cotton cloth.

8. Leave the textile, still on its supporting sheet, in a cold air flow for the solvent to evaporate. Using this technique there should be no need either to pin the textile in order to straighten it or to iron it. Ironing of old textiles should be kept to a minimum—try to avoid steam irons which can spit and stain. A gentle steaming with steam from a kettle is far more effective in getting rid of creases.

9. Textiles that have been attacked by mould will have been weakened not only in the area of its growth, but for quite some distance around. (The mould actually digests the textile to gain its nutrients.) The textile will also be impregnated with spores. If the textile is white, wash it in the same way as lace, (Steps 2 – 3, Page 136). If it is multi-coloured or an embroidered piece, it must be solvent cleaned, provided the colours are fast, as described in Steps 4-7.

Cleaning upholstery and large items

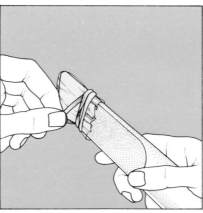

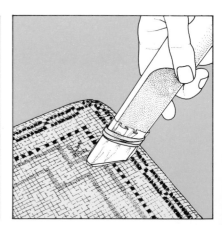

1. Remove drop-in chair seats and cushions. Release curtain tie-backs. If the fabric is in reasonable condition, brush it lightly with a large artists' paintbrush (a watercolour mop is ideal) to loosen the dirt.

2. Cover the nozzle of a small hand-held vacuum cleaner with a piece of soft nylon net held in place with a rubber band.

3. Hold the nozzle slightly above the surface of the fabric to remove the dirt. Make sure that any crevices in an upholstered item are thoroughly cleaned. But take great care when vacuuming any areas with weak stitching to ensure that no further damage is caused. Also take special care with fringing as this is easily torn by the suction of the vacuum cleaner.

Storing textiles

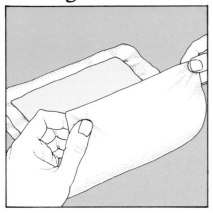

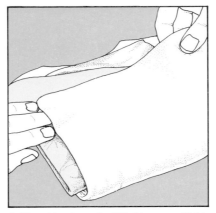

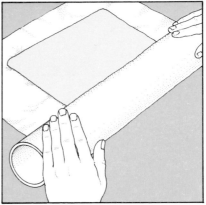

1. After cleaning, textiles must be carefully stored because irreversible damage can be caused by poor storage. Small textiles should be stored flat in a large box or drawer, each piece interleaved with acid-free tissue paper.

2. If an object has to be folded (try to avoid this wherever possible), pad every fold with rolls of acid-free tissue paper to prevent creases being formed, because the textile will eventually crack along them. For the same reason never pile too many objects on top of one another; they will be too heavy and crush those at the bottom. And never stack velvet or embroidered items one on top of another, because they will crush, however few there are.

3. Large textiles should be rolled around a stout cardboard tube. Lay the textile out flat, face down, on a sheet of acid-free tissue paper. Cover the tube with more acid-free tissue paper and roll up the textile carefully, smoothing out creases and keeping it as straight as possible. Then wrap it in cotton fabric (never plastic or polythene), kept in place with broad cotton tapes fastened with safety pins. Do not use string as this will eventually cut into the textile. Store the rolls horizontally and do not pile up too many on top of one another.

Repairing damaged textiles

The problem with repairing damaged textiles is that the entire fabric is as weak as the damaged area, so a darn will frequently cause more damage to the whole object. It is best to support the entire textile, stitching a fabric behind it which can be removed without damaging the object should it ever need to be more extensively conserved.

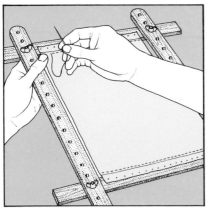

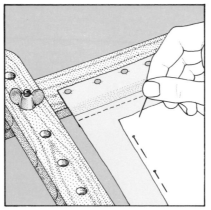

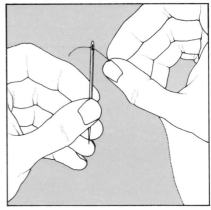

1. Take a piece of fabric larger than the whole object in a natural fibre, such as linen or cotton, with a similar texture to the textile being repaired. Preshrink the fabric by soaking it in hot water. (This also removes any dressing or loose dye.) If the right shade is not available, the backing material can be dyed to match the textile. When the backing material is completely dry, stitch fairly tautly to the carpet binding on a square embroidery frame (often called a slate frame), making sure that the warps run parallel with the sides of the frame.

2. Lay the textile on the backing fabric, taking care to match the direction of the warps. Pin or tack the textile to the backing material.

3. Thread a needle with polyester thread that tones with the area of the textile that is being repaired.

Repairing damaged textiles cont.

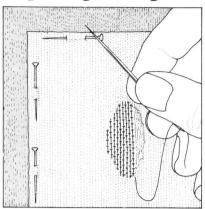

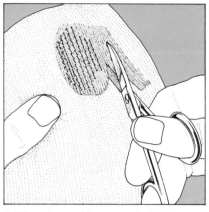

4. The next stage is to couch across the damaged area to attach the textile to the backing material. Thread a needle with polyester thread of the right shade. Bring the needle up in the stronger part of the textile and lay the thread longitudinally across the hole, bringing the needle down into the stronger part of the textile. Keep the thread parallel with the warps of both textile and backing. Secure the long threads by catching them down to the backing at regular intervals with small transverse stitches.

5. When the couching across the hole is complete, knot the final stitch at the back of the fabric and cut the thread. If the textile being mended only had one hole, cut the backing fabric away neatly and closely around the area of stitching. If the piece had many holes it is best to leave the backing material intact. But never, on any account, use the backing material as support for hanging the textile.

6. It is possible to repair both woven and embroidered textiles following this technique. It is not advisable to try and re-embroider the textile because not only is it almost impossible to match existing yarns and shades, but new yarns will fade differently to the original ones, which will continue to fade anyway. Furthermore, the action of re-embroidering an already weakened textile will cause further damage.

Never be tempted to use the "iron-on" backing materials available for hemming. They are almost impossible to remove if further work to the textile becomes necessary, thus increasing the risk of further damage. They also make a hard patch on the back of the textile and the heat of the iron often pulls the adhesive through the fabric, forming a very obvious stain.

Care and cleaning of costumes

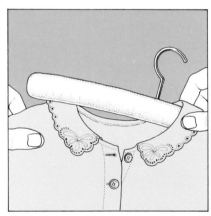

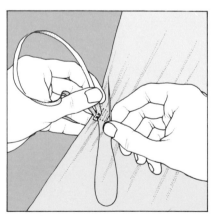

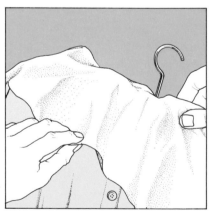

1. Careful treatment is the most important rule to observe when caring for costumes. Never hang anything from thin wire hangers, always use padded, shaped ones.

2. Carefully sew extra tapes on the waist seams of dresses so that these, too, can hang from the clothes hanger and take some of the weight off the garments' shoulders.

3. Never store anything in polythene or plastic bags as these attract dust and can encourage the growth of mould. Use cotton, nylon or polyester dust covers. Store beaded items flat, because of their weight, in acid-free tissue paper.

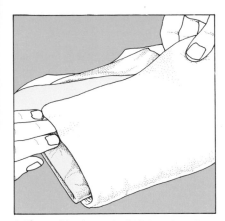

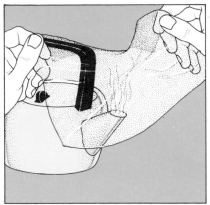

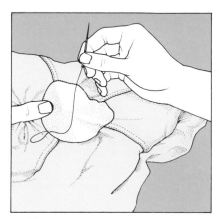

4. If something has to be folded, pad the folds with rolls of acid-free tissue paper to prevent creases forming which will eventually become cracks.

5. Avoid ironing old costumes. Instead use steam from a kettle to remove creases. Net, chiffon and satin respond particularly well to this treatment, but never let the article become damp from the steam and never steam fur, because the skin will go hard.

6. If the costume is to be worn, sew dress-shields into the armholes and wear a cotton slip, because old textiles can be damaged by the chemicals in modern deodorants and anti-perspirants.

Cleaning costume

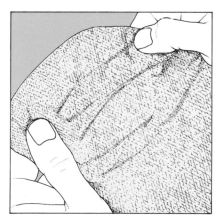

COTTON COSTUME

1. Before starting to clean cotton fabrics, test that the material is strong enough to take it by pulling the fabric diagonally. If the fabric seems firm it can be cleaned by being boiled.

Put ½ cup/0.2 litre of soap powder or liquid detergent and ½ cup/0.2 litre of washing soda into a large saucepan or similar container. Fill with water, put in the garment and bring to the boil. The container must be large enough for the garment to move around. Stir occasionally.

2. Keep the saucepan topped up with water, because otherwise the garment will reabsorb the dirt as the water evaporates. The heavier the cotton the longer it will take to whiten, but check every ten minutes or so and test the material by pulling it in opposite directions to make sure that it has not deteriorated. (If the garment is very dirty, change the water several times.)

OTHER COSTUME

Silk-satin and man-made rayon satin can be washed in warm soapy water. The water should not be too hot or the colours will fade. For the same reason do not leave prints to soak. If in doubt, have the article dry cleaned—although no old costume should go in a cleaning machine that rotates.

Do not use powder cleaners on fur or feathers. The particles will be trapped there and will eventually cause damage. Instead seek the advice of a textile expert if the costume is valuable, or of a specialist dry cleaners if it is to be worn for fun.

Beaded dresses should never be washed or cleaned at home. Some old sequins will dissolve in water. Some modern types dissolve in dry cleaning solvents. "Pearls" can be made of wax, hollow glass or plastic and any of these materials is easily damaged. Take the garment to a specialist. Check carefully for loose beads and sew them back on. If there is a long loose thread, sew it firmly into the back of the fabric. Dress-shields must be sewn into the armholes if the dress is to be worn, because the chemicals in modern deodorants will damage beads and sequins.

Restoring patent leather

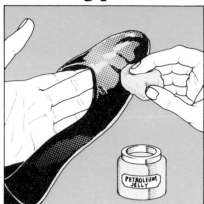

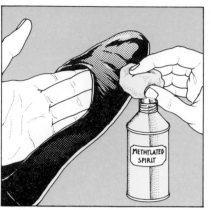

1. Patent leather finishes are made in two ways. The modern method is to bond a flexible vinyl or plastic layer onto an inner layer of fabric. This should be cleaned with proprietary vinyl upholstery cleaner/polisher obtainable from car accessory shops. The older technique was to layer tinted shellac varnish onto fabric. This material is brittle and is liable to crack. Keep it clean and polished with a petroleum jelly such as Vasilene.

2. Patent leather made from shellac varnish can be damaged by heat, which softens it, causing the leather to distort. If a piece is distorted it can be restored to its correct shape by wiping the entire surface with a swab of cotton wool moistened in methylated spirits (denatured alcohol). This softens the patent finish and allows the distortions to be gently eased out. But this must be done with great care, otherwise the finish will gradually dissolve, and thinly covered areas may even become bald.

3. When the distortions have been removed, pack the object tightly with screwed-up tissue paper. Allow it to dry and then polish with petroleum jelly.

Opposite: Cleaned and restored carpet showing only essential repairs, such as the oversewing of frayed edges (for close-up, see overleaf) the removal of weft threads and the trimming of the fringes.

CARPETS AND RUGS

Ordinary woven fabric is made up of warp threads which run the length of the fabric, and weft threads which run across it, and a pattern is created on the surface of the fabric by using different coloured threads and interlacing them in different ways. In carpet terms, this is a flat weave. A knotted pile carpet is made by using usually uncoloured warp and weft threads, and by tying knots to the warp threads in coloured materials which are cut off short. Only the ends of these knots are visible when the carpet is finished, the pattern being created by the arrangement and colours of the knots, and the warp and weft threads being concealed by them. Carpets may, of course, also be made in other ways, such as crochet, knitting, or embroidery, and a kelim, for instance, has an exposed weft. According to the quality of the carpet, there may be 16 to 500 knots to 1 in/2.5 cm square.

There are two kinds of knots in general use, the Turkish or Ghiordes and the Persian or Senneh (see Steps 5 and 6, Page 152); they are usually tied around two adjacent warps only, though sometimes more. Two other knots are also sometimes used: the Spanish, which is looped around two alternate warps so that the ends are brought out either side, and the Jufti, which is tied around four warps. The geographical names of these knots are more or less arbitrary.

The carpet loom is usually arranged so that the warps are vertical; they may run round rollers at the top and bottom so that the working level may be kept opposite the weaver, who sits at the bottom of the warps with the thread for the knots in his (or more usually her)left hand and a short knife in the right. The thread is fed with the left hand, tied with the fingers of both hands, and cut with the right. The weavers achieve great dexterity so that they may tie over 100 knots per minute and the knots are cut with great uniformity so that an even pile is formed without further treatment (though in Chinese and some other rugs the pile is trimmed or shaved after completion). After a row of knots has been completed, the weft and knots are compacted by beating with a comb-like instrument. Nomads use a horizontal loom which can be dismantled when they move; this is not nearly so convenient for the weaver, and also limits the size of rug which can be made.

The most usual material for the threads and pile is wool, but silk has sometimes been used for high quality Chinese, Persian and Ottoman court rugs; cotton is also found, especially in India and Central Asia, while coarse Indian rugs may use jute as weft material.

In most villages of the Orient there was a dyer, often Jewish, who kept his art a secret. Until the middle of the nineteenth century natural dyes were used exclusively — cochineal, madder, indigo, berries, bark, plants, fruit and fungi. They could be mixed to produce intermediate colours and most antique rugs have six to twelve different colours. Different wools and different water supplies produce different shades with the same dye. Natural colours are remarkably fast; they may fade slightly but in general old rugs are of surprising brilliance though not hard in colour, and

Opposite: "Before" (above) and "after" (below) of the edge of the carpet on the previous page, showing the effect of the oversewing to prevent further damage.

noticeably faded rugs will generally have been produced after the introduction of aniline dyes in the 1850s.

It is not known for certain where knotted pile rugs were first produced, but modern scholarship considers that the technique probably originated in Mongolia and came westward to the Middle East with migrating tribes. Ancient writers refer to weaving, and it is certain that various forms of flat weaving were well known, but the earliest known knotted pile carpet is a large, well-preserved fragment discovered in Siberia and datable to the fifth century B.C. Fragments of pile carpets found in Persia can be dated to the first half of the third century A.D. Fragments of true knotted carpets tied with the Spanish knot have been found in Egypt and reliably ascribed to the fifth century A.D. There is documentary evidence that pile knotting was established in Persia and Turkey by the beginning of the Christian era. With the rise and spread of Islam from the seventh century onward, carpet weaving is documented by Arab writers. In surviving carpets, the date is often woven into the design.

The spread of pile carpets over Europe was due variously to the presence of the Moors in Spain, the Crusades from the eleventh to the thirteenth centuries, the travels of Marco Polo during the second half of the thirteenth century, and the Venetian trade with the East from the thirteenth century onward. Oriental carpets appear fairly frequently in European painting from about 1350, usually set under the throne of the Virgin or in some similar context, and it appears that they may have been too prized to be put to secular use. Later they were used as table coverings and as altar cloths, but by 1600 a distinction was drawn between floor carpets and table carpets. Some carpets of this early period incorporate European coats of arms and were clearly woven to order in Turkey from designs supplied from Europe.

The oldest European pile rugs were produced in Spain; production started there in the twelfth century and was highly developed by the thirteenth. The single warp knot used in Spain could not have come directly from Turkey or Persia but was probably brought from Egypt by Coptic weavers. Many early Spanish carpets, and illustrations of them, can be dated by the armorial devices incorporated. The quality of Spanish carpets declined after the expulsion of the Moors in the sixteenth century, and the industry tended to copy imported Turkish, and later Western European, originals.

Carpet weaving also developed in Poland and Romania. Poland was an important market for Turkish and Persian wares, including carpets, and pile carpet weaving started there in the seventeenth century, the Poles developing their own style, more naturalistic than the Islamic. There are also examples of knotted rugs from Italy showing Oriental influence dating from the same period. Oriental rugs reached the Baltic by the fifteenth century, and pile rugs were made in Sweden by the seventeenth century using the Turkish knot but also showing Spanish influence because they had more than one weft thread between each row of knots.

In 1601 Henri IV of France appointed a Commission to start new industries. One result was the establishment in the Louvre of a workshop under Royal Licence to make carpets "à la façon de

Perse et du Levant". In 1627, Dupont, the founder of this workshop, started further workshops in a former soap factory and from this time the name Savonnerie was applied to the carpets. The carpets produced were of excellent quality and the designs rapidly lost all oriental influence and became distinctively European. The output of the Savonnerie factories was always largely, and at times, exclusively, reserved for the furnishing of royal palaces. In 1662 the then owners of the Savonnerie brought a property outside Paris belonging to the brothers Gobelin and started a tapestry workshop there; the designs of the Savonnerie were always controlled by an artist, who from this time came from the Gobelins, so that tapestry and carpet designs became linked.

Colbert had granted a Patent for a tapestry workshop at Aubusson in 1665, and in 1743 a carpet factory was established there for making thick pile carpets on vertical looms, samples being sent from Paris to be copied. Short pile carpets were also made on horizontal looms using the tapestry technique. The first productions were direct copies of Turkey carpets. The later designs were much simpler than those of the Savonnerie and the carpets directed more to the prosperous bourgeoisie. Due to competition from cheap carpets made on English power looms, and later from copies of French carpets made in India, production in Aubusson ceased after the war of 1870, however.

In England it is clear from the account books of great houses that rushes were often strewn on the floor until as late as the beginning of the seventeenth century, and a German traveller, Paul Hentzer, said that he saw hay on the floor of the Queen's presence-chamber in Greenwich Palace in 1598. However, the earliest English pile carpet known, which belongs to the Earl of Verulam, shows the initials of Queen Elizabeth and the date 1570; the pattern is completely English in style and the warp is of hemp, so that the evidence that it was made in England is very strong. Other English carpets of the late sixteenth century are known, but the art declined owing to competition from carpets imported from Turkey, Persia and India after the establishment of the East India Company. However, the craft was revived by the influx of Huguenot artisans from France and especially by one Parisot who in 1750 obtained the patronage of the Duke of Cumberland and who by 1753 was employing a hundred weavers. However, in 1753 he failed, apparently owing to the high prices asked, and was bought out by a Swiss named Passavant who moved the factory to Exeter where it prospered. But in 1754 Thomas Whitty, a woollen cloth weaver of Axminster in Devon, who had been inspired by a large Turkish carpet imported by an acquaintance, and had visited Parisot's factory, established the manufacture of pile carpets at Axminster using the Ghiordes knot. From 1756 the Royal Society of Arts offered an annual prize for Turkey carpets made in England, and this was divided between Whitty and another in each of the three succeeding years.

One of these others was Thomas Moore, who established his factory at Moorfields in London; he was a friend of Robert Adam the architect, who designed the carpets for the great houses which he built, and had them made by Moore. After Adam died in 1792 Moore's factory collapsed, but Whitty's Axminster factory continued to prosper in the hands of his sons and grandson; the firm made three huge carpets for George IV for the Brighton Pavilion

in 1820. But in 1828 the factory burned down and the firm never recovered; in 1836 it was bought by a Mr Blackmore and moved to Wilton.

A carpet factory had been started at Wilton in the middle of the eighteenth century by the Earl of Pembroke making carpets with a looped pile, the loops being afterwards cut. Carpet weaving had also been established at Kidderminster, which became and remained a great carpet-making centre. Power was applied to weaving in the last quarter of the eighteenth century and machine carpet weaving was more easily adapted to making looped rather than knotted pile. The process was facilitated in 1825 by the invention of the Jacquard mechanism, in which the loops were raised over wires; a Brussels carpet usually has nine wires to 1in/2.5cm, and a Wilton ten. In 1839 "Chenille Axminsters" were patented; these had a separately woven pile with tufts inserted to form the pattern, which was afterwards attached by hand to a linen or jute base. This saved money on wool but made a poorer carpet as the pile could come adrift from the base. (The terms Axminster, Wilton and Brussels no longer have any geographical significance but are merely generic terms for European knotted, cut looped pile and uncut looped pile carpets.)

However, it was in the United States that the machine was first applied intensively to carpet production due largely to the invention of a Brussels power loom by Erasmus Bigelow, which was brought to England by Crossleys of Halifax. In the 1870s the moquette or Royal Axminster loom was developed by Alexander Smith & Son of Yonkers, New York, and in the 1890s the Crompton Knowles spool Axminster loom was introduced.

It is doubtful if carpet weaving in China started much before the end of the seventeenth century; it does not seem to have been a highly regarded craft, and in any case China has no wool and regarded wool fabrics as uncouth, so that the earliest Chinese carpets are of silk. But a factory was established in 1262 in the Mongol city of Karakoram to supply carpets to the Chinese court, and the Mongol invasion of China and the establishment of their Yüan dynasty in the fourteenth century no doubt promoted their use. The Chinese mainly used floor coverings of reed and other vegetable matting, and where carpets are shown in early Chinese paintings they are of Mongol design. When the Chinese began to make carpets their designs were seldom purely decorative; all the motifs have an exact symbolic meaning and were often selected to be appropriate to the circumstances of the person who had ordered the carpet. Modern Chinese carpets are woven for export from imported wool and are often "washed" with acids to give a silky appearance; they are also usually copies of European designs.

Apart from the main streams of commercial carpet production already described there have of course always been sources of rugs in small quantities. During the last half of the nineteenth century and the first half of the twentieth, there were many individual craftsmen and small workshops weaving Arts & Crafts, Art Nouveau and Art Deco designs, especially in England, France and Germany. In North America rugs were woven by the Pueblo and Navajo Indians after the introduction of sheep by the Spaniards in the sixteenth century, and in the nineteenth century there was a considerable cottage industry among European settlers, making yarn-sewn, shirred and hooked rugs.

Cleaning carpets and rugs

It is particularly important to keep carpets and rugs clean and in good condition, since grime, dirt and stains can destroy even the heaviest pile, if they are left for long enough. Unwrapped rugs stored in an unventilated place provide perfect conditions for moths to feed during the warm summer months. Double-sided and braided rugs should be turned often to avoid uneven wear.

All fine rugs should be repaired by experts, and this is particularly true of woven rugs—so make sure your rug is correctly valued before you begin to tinker with it. However, tears and fraying should be stopped at once, even if really "invisible" repairs must wait until you become an expert yourself or can afford to pay one.

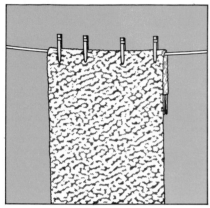

1. If the rug is encrusted with the accumulated deposits of years of hard use, and grey with dirt and dust, begin renovation outdoors, if possible. Put up a very strong clothes line, sufficiently high to let you whack the dirt out of the backing and pile. The rug should hang freely with as small a turnover as possible, to allow beating from the back; never beat the pile as it drives the dirt back into the knots. Hooked or knitted rugs should not be beaten at all. For very fragile rugs see Step 5 for further instructions.

2. An old-fashioned carpet beater is still the best tool for the job. They are still made in the Middle East, and it may be possible to find one in an ethnic store which imports traditional basket-work. A possible alternative is a shag rug comb, or rake, which can be used with the tines pointing away from the back of the carpet, or even a plastic garden rake (the kind with splayed-out tines used for gathering leaves).

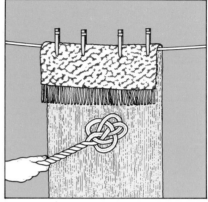

3. Choose a dry day with not too much wind. Wear old clothes and a scarf. It's amazing how much dust, dried-up debris and dead insects can accumulate in a neglected carpet. Ordinary woven carpets, even valuable Oriental rugs, can be beaten quite vigorously. Even if all the dirt doesn't fall out, it will be considerably loosened, and easier to remove; but be much more gentle with embroidered and knotted rugs and be particularly careful not to catch stitches on the back if you are using a rake. When dust has stopped rising, pull the rug over the line so that the other end hangs free, and beat from the back.

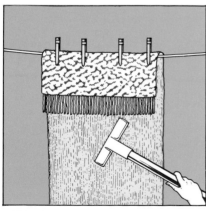

4. Never leave a rug hanging outside overnight—dew or sudden showers may dampen the fabric, which will take days to dry out. After beating, vacuum the rug, while it is still hanging free, if possible. Use the curtain cleaning hose attachment of the vacuum cleaner.

5. Start working at the back as before, using medium suction for heavy canvas or light for finer backings. After the back is finished, work on the front. Try to keep the nozzle or roller always moving in the direction of the pile. Working the other way will enable the base to be reached, but it may dislodge threads and leave the surface ragged and tangled. Flat embroidered carpets have no pile, of course, so work up and down along the length of the stitches with very light suction. If the rug is very fragile, or cannot be taken outside, spread a thick layer of brown paper on the floor and lay the rug face or pile down. Do not use newspaper—the ink may be absorbed by the fibres. An old sheet will do, but obviously it will have to be washed afterwards. Hit the back gently with the beater, shaking the whole rug from time to time to let the dirt fall out onto the paper. When finished, wrap up the paper carefully and throw it away. Vacuum the back carefully, using light or medium suction; for very dirty rugs, a nozzle may be better than the wide brush since it can get into corners and seams; but do not use the nozzle on knitted or crocheted rugs as the wool will be pulled out of the stitch surface.

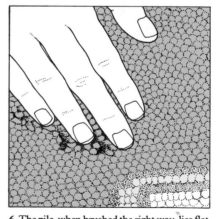

6. The pile, when brushed the right way, lies flat and even, covering the backing, and in Oriental rugs it will have a glossy sheen. Brushing the wrong way will leave threads untidy with patches of backing showing in long-haired rugs, and make the pile look dark and rough in short pile ones.

Cleaning carpets and rugs cont.

7. Knitted, crocheted and fine hooked rugs must always be handled very carefully. Look for pulled threads or loose stitches and mark the position of any damaged areas by basting around the spot with bright contrasting yarn – leave a long tail

REMOVING STAINS

8. The following pages give instructions for cleaning and repairing the various types of carpet and rug. After repairs have been done, all the carpet will need is gentle care and maintenance.

If something is spilt on a domestic carpet, providing the colours do not run, lift it immediately, if possible, put plenty of newspaper underneath, and thoroughly soak the area with soda water. Then, blot it up with towels, and allow to dry naturally, raised off the floor if possible. Never daub the stain to try to dry it off. If the spillage has been on a valuable carpet or rug do not let it dry out and seek specialist advice at once.

Paint stains can be removed by flooding the area in the same way with white spirit BS245 (Stoddard's Solvent). Dry in cool air. (Prevention is, of course, better than cure, and if the carpet cannot be removed when a room is being decorated, it should be covered with a thick layer of acid-free tissue paper and then with a dust sheet.)

Never clean an old carpet or rug with any of the proprietary cleaning solvents, because these leave sticky deposits that ultimately attract dirt. Powder cleaners must also be avoided as the particles remain trapped in the carpet's fibres and will also eventually cause damage. Industrial steam-cleaning machines should never be used. The cleaning action is far too rough for old carpets and may cause the carpet to shrink.

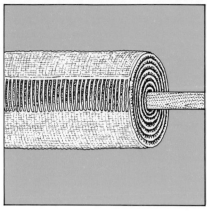

9. To store rugs, keep them flat, enveloped in brown paper and plastic sheet (remembering never to store a rug in plastic unless it's bone dry). Rugs too big to lie flat can be rolled around a light pole, with the pile inside, lying in the right direction as in Step 6. It's usually suggested that fine hooked rugs be rolled pile out – but sound, sturdy examples will be safe either way.

Repairing braided and rag rugs

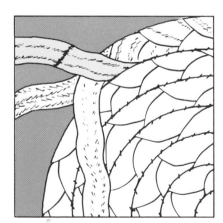

1. Old braided (coiled) rugs can suffer from two main problems: the outer length of braid wears away, or the lacing between the braided strands may come undone and break off. If the wear is very bad, consider replacing the worn strip with a new one. Match the predominant shades as closely as possible, using a similar fabric. Unpick the outside braid, cut away the worn parts, then sew on new strips. Try to stagger the cuts so the change is gradual and unobtrusive.

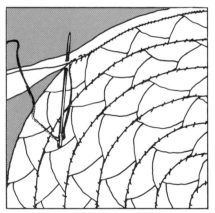

2. Rebraid, following the original pattern as far as possible – most rugs are braided with three strips. Work as much as needed, lace together and tuck the ends under. After repairing protect the outer edge with a strip of bias binding in a complementary shade. Lacing can easily be replaced, using an upholstery needle and matching thread. Follow the pattern on the rest of the rug.

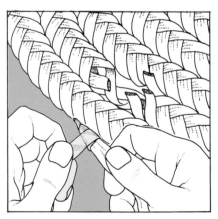

3. Most rag rugs are made by a braiding process. The rags are cleaned and joined into continuous lengths, then braided and laced together in the usual way in straight strips, rather than circular coils. Care and repair are the same as for braided rugs above. Some rag rugs are strips of fabric woven on coarse fabric or canvas. To replace worn bits, unpick the damaged area, find a matching fabric and restitch, using a rug needle. If the rags are too thick even for that, make a "needle" by wrapping clear adhesive tape around the end of a piece of rag until it makes a point.

Repairing crocheted and knitted rugs

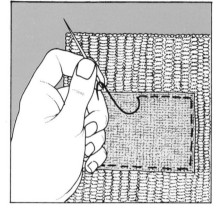

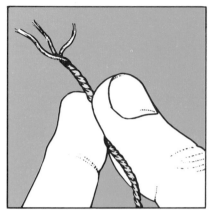

1. If the rug was worked as a single piece it may require some skill to repeat or replace a pattern, but it can be done. Before attempting it, though, see if the effect can be simulated by darning with a needle and matching type of thread. First, baste a canvas patch big enough to cover the affected part onto the back with a good margin to spare. This will keep the area flat while you work. Choose a shade of yarn as close as possible to the base shade of the rug.

2. Then, splice a loose end from the top of the damaged area to the new matching yarn. To do this, unravel a small part of each end into its separate plys.

3. Next, snip each ply a different length and twist them together. Each join should be at a different length so that the splice does not have a single weak point.

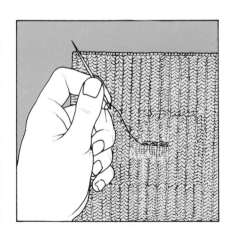

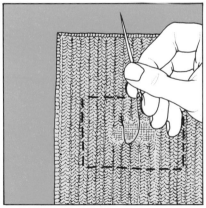

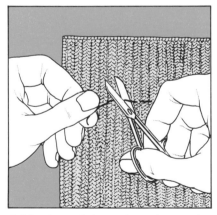

4. Thread a needle onto the new yarn and, starting at the top, stitch back and forth across the damaged area. To start each crossing, place the needle about ¼in/6mm away from the damaged area; and as you cross do not darn through the temporary backing. Then weave vertically until the hole is darned.

5. Be sure to catch all the damaged threads. To incorporate another shade, work on top of the first darning. To simulate an irregular texture, use a suitable thread worked into the base darning to create the effect of tufts.

6. After the repair is complete, snip away the basting stitches from the patch and remove it. Remember that all repaired rugs need very careful handling.

Repairing flat embroidered rugs

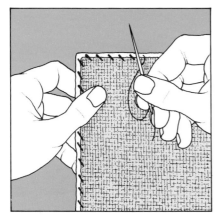

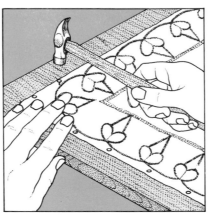

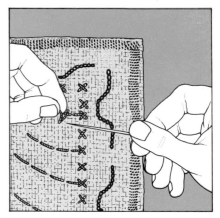

1. Most large flat embroidered rugs were worked in squares and put together much like a chess board, so look carefully to see if the joining was badly done, or the seams have been damaged – a beautiful room-sized carpet can fall apart into little mats! If there's any sign of weakness, sew a backing onto the entire piece. Use strong open-weave burlap or hessian, trimmed and machine-hemmed to the right size. Slipstitch to the outside edge of the rug.

2. Small embroidered rugs can be gently cleaned with carpet cleaning fluid, or washed with the foam of soap suds, but they may need blocking afterwards to retain their correct size. Measure before cleaning, rinse with a moist sponge, and tack down to the right shape on a wooden board.

3. If the stitching has worn away, unpick the damaged area, keeping the edges irregular. Tuck the ends of the yarn through stitches on the back to keep them from coming undone. Match the yarn as closely as possible to the original shade.

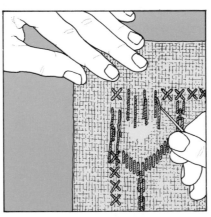

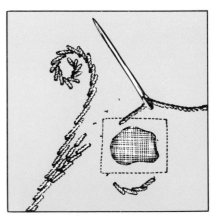

4. Rework the damaged area in the same stitch. If a large section of a repeated motif is missing, mark the pattern with embroidery markers while removing the old threads so that the design is clear for re-sewing. (These markers are sold in most craft stores; do not use ordinary felt tips as they will run and stain the wool.) Otherwise, copy the pattern from an undamaged place onto tracing paper and re-work the bare canvas in matching yarns.

5. If the canvas itself is damaged, unpick the stitches around the hole or tear, going at least 1in/2.5cm in every direction. Let the unpicked threads hang down from the back.

6. Cut a new piece of canvas slightly larger than the damaged area, aligning the holes if possible. (If the original canvas seems an odd size, use fine petit-point canvas – it has so many holes that some will align with the original.) With embroidered side up, thread the old yarn through an embroidery needle through both thicknesses of canvas. Work all around the area, making sure the patch lies flat. There will probably not be enough old yarn to cover the patch completely, but match shades as closely as possible. Do not pull the thread too tight or the rug will not lie flat.

Repairing hooked rugs

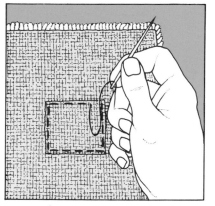
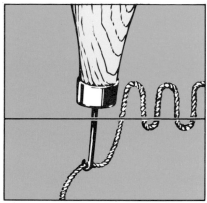

1. Hooked rugs need very careful handling. Dirt can be removed by vacuuming from the pile side, but only when the rug is flat on the ground, and using the lightest suction. Before embarking on any more serious cleaning, test all the different fabrics for fastness — the printed patterns were generally bought by the yard, but many plain shades were dyed at home and will run easily. Use a mild soap solution with plenty of cool suds, and work with these suds only. Gently brush a sponge over the surface, but be very careful not to soak the backing. Vacuum gently when thoroughly dry.

2. Hooked rugs are fairly easy to repair since the worn or damaged stitches can usually be pulled out without difficulty. Occasional stitches around the damaged area should also be removed, so that the repair will blend in more naturally. When purchasing new fabric try to match the texture as well as the shade. Cut a patch of new backing material larger than the damaged area, and baste to the original backing.

3. Turn face side up and hook through both old and new backing. The easiest tool to use is an old-fashioned hooker, which pushes through the fabric from above and catches a loop guided by the hand underneath. Pull through to the correct height to match the other pile, and release. Push through a little way along the line, keeping spaces and loop heights the same as the original. When repairing badly worn edges, undo the braid binding, and pull out stitches evenly all the way around until you reach sound work. Turn under the backing and re-bind with fresh braid.

Cleaning and repairing woven rugs

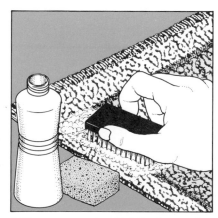
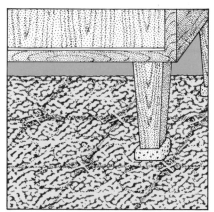
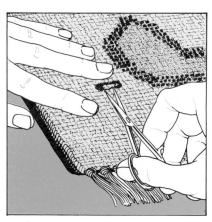

1. Woven rugs are generally the hardest-wearing rugs of all and so do not need especially careful treatment unless they are valuable antiques or badly damaged. Clean with a good carpet cleaning liquid (follow the manufacturer's instructions carefully) poured on a sponge and brushed over the nap, in the direction of the pile. Don't use too much liquid or it will soak the backing. Shampoo vigorously, using a fairly stiff brush or a special carpet shampooer.

2. Early Oriental rugs and other woven carpets were made with vegetable dyes, but almost all modern dyes are aniline. If there is a chance the piece may be old, check for fastness before shampooing. It may be worth having it cleaned professionally. Short pile rugs remain damp for a deceptively long time, so do not brush or vacuum until they are absolutely dry. It is best not to replace furniture until the carpet is bone dry in case it makes permanent marks, but if the furniture has to be put back, place a thick pad of foam rubber under the legs of each object.

3. The most common repairs necessary are re-stitching torn fringes and edges, and reweaving small damaged spots, often caused by cigarette burns. To reweave the latter cut away the blackened pile, and examine the mark. You may find that once the dark scorch has gone, the shorter pile is scarcely noticeable, but if the burn is very deep, use tiny pointed scissors to cut the knots which tie each loop.

Repairing woven rugs cont.

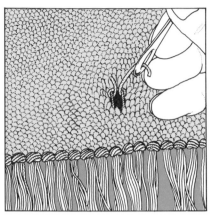

4. Look carefully at an existing knot to see what kind it is. For repairing short pile rugs use pre-cut yarn strands; for long pile cut the skein to the appropriate length. Use a needle threaded with matching yarn to make tiny new stitches; knot and cut off at the same height.

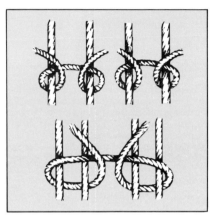

5. One of the two basic knots in Oriental carpets is the Ghiordes or Turkish knot.

6. The second is the Senneh or Persian knot. Variations of these are used for all woven rugs.

7. Repairing Oriental woven rugs is not a job for the amateur, however enthusiastic. Trying to match the yarns is almost impossible, and the skill needed to reproduce some of the beautiful, complex patterns comes only with years of experience.

8. The only repair it is really safe for the amateur to undertake is to prevent a frayed edge from deteriorating.

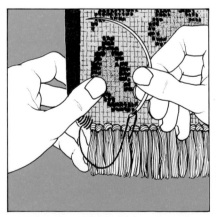

9. Choose yarn in a shade as close to the background as possible. Thread an upholsterer's needle with a length of thread and oversew the worn edge. Take care not to start a stitch too close to the damaged edge as this will soon cause pulling and increase the damage.

Removing stains : general advice

Never try to remove a stain from an old or valuable textile without first seeking expert advice. This is *the* golden rule, not least because the wrong treatment may damage the fabric and dramatically reduce its value. The stain removal hints given on the following pages, therefore, apply to relatively ordinary, everyday fabrics, not to treasured heirlooms.

Should disaster strike and the worst happen, refer first to the relevant section on textiles in this book. If no appropriate treatment is detailed there, look for the treatment below, according to the type of stain to be treated. All stains should be treated as quickly as possible, fresh stains are much easier to remove than those that have set and dried. Always try cool water first and enzyme detergents on washable material. Never iron over a stain.

GREASY STAINS

When trying to remove a greasy stain just saturate the area with liquid detergent and then launder. A cleaning fluid can also be used before or after laundering. Sponge non-washable fabrics with a cleaning fluid, allowing it to dry between applications perhaps with the aid of an absorbent fabric placed underneath.

NON-GREASY STAINS

To remove non-greasy stains from washable fabrics sponge immediately with cool water, then later soak in cold water for 30 minutes or overnight. On non-washables try cool water, followed by diluted white spirit (2:1). For combination stains (greasy and non-greasy mixtures) like soup, treat the stain first as a non-greasy one, using cool water and liquid detergent and then treat any remains with a cleaning fluid. A bleach can sometimes be employed for all kinds of stains but test on an inconspicuous area first if possible; the reactions of bleach with certain textiles is uncertain.

Stain removal chart

Adhesive tape	*Sponge with cleaning fluid.*
Alcohol	On washable fabrics: *stretch over a glass bowl and tighten with a rubber band or string; sprinkle with salt and pour boiling water over it from about 18 inches (45cm).* On non-washables: *sponge with spirits diluted with two parts water for acetate.*
Blood	On washables: *rub or soak with cold water and then wash with detergent in warm water.* On old stains: *put a few drops of diluted ammonia on the spot and then wash as usual.* On non-washables: *sponge with cold water, followed by a small amount of hydrogen peroxide.* Blood stains set by heat: *on cottons and linens use a warm solution of trisodium phosphate.* On carpets: *mix an absorbent with water into a paste; spread on, brush off when dry; repeat if needed.*
Candlewax	*Scrape away as much a possible with a blunt knife, place area between paper towels and press with a warm iron. Sponge any traces left with cleaning fluid.*
Chewing gum	*Rub with a piece of ice to harden, then scrape off with blunt knife; otherwise, saturate area with cleaning fluid, even if material is non-washable.*
Chocolate	On washables: *dab or soak with cold water for at least 30 minutes, then rub undiluted liquid detergent into spot and rinse. Let dry and sponge with cleaning fluid.* On non-washables: *sponge stain with cool water, then liquid detergent; if required, sponge with white spirits, diluted with two parts water for acetate; rinse with cold water.*
Coffee and tea	On washables: *stretch stained area over bowl, fasten with rubber band and pour hot water over stained area from a distance of about 18 inches (45cm); then wash in usual manner.* On non-washables: *wipe with damp sponge; shake an absorbent onto spot, allow to dry and brush off.*
Cosmetics and crayons	On washables: *apply liquid detergent and rinse; repeat.* On non-washables: *sponge with cleaning fluid; repeat.*

Removing stains cont.

Eggs	*Scrape off with blunt knife and sponge with cold water; if non-washable, let dry after sponging, and sponge with cleaning fluid.*
Fruit	*Sponge immediately with cold water; do not use soap and water initially.* On washables: *after sponging with cold water, pour on boiling water from a height of 18 inches (45cm).* On non-washables: *apply glycerine gently; dab with vinegar (but not on acetates), and rinse.*
Glue (household and model airplane)	*Sponge with acetone except on materials damaged by acetone; on these use amyl acetate.*
Grass	*Treat with methylated spirits (on acetate dilute with two parts water). Then use liquid detergent on washables followed by a rinse. You may then apply a mild sodium perborate bleach or hydrogen peroxide.*
Gravy	On washables: *soak in cold water and wash; follow this by sponging with cleaning fluid.* On non-washables: *sponge with cold water, then cleaning fluid.*
Ink (ballpoint)	*On acetate, Arnel, Dynel and Verel, use amyl acetate.* *On other fabrics, sponge with acetone.*
Ink (India)	*Sponge immediately with cold water and wash with liquid detergent then soak in 4 tablespoons of ammonia diluted in one quart of water.* On non-washables: *force cold water through the stain and sponge with ammonia (1 tablespoon to one cup water); rinse. Work in liquid detergent and rinse again.*
Iodine	On washables: *dampen with water, place in sun, on a radiator, or in steam from the kettle; also try soaking in cold water and then washing.* On non-washables: *sponge with white spirit (diluted with two parts water for acetate). On fabrics not damaged by water, mix 1 tablespoon sodium thiosulphate crystals in 1 pint (½ litre) water and sponge the spot; rinse well.*
Iron rust	On washables: *use bleach; or lemon juice squeezed onto cottons and linens and then held in front of kettle to gather or catch the steam usually works. Afterwards rinse and repeat. Strong fabrics may be boiled in a solution of 4 tablespoons cream of tartar to 1 pint (½ litre) water. Boil until spot is gone and then rinse.*
Metallic stains (brass, copper, tin)	*Never use a bleach. Apply white vinegar, lemon juice or acetic acid and then rinse with cold water.*
Mildew	*Keep moisture out of closets by airing in humid weather. Sun and para crystals are the best preventatives. Use soap and water.*
Milk, cream	On washables: *launder as usual.* On non-washables: *wipe with damp sponge; shake on an absorbent, let dry and brush off residue.*
Mustard	On washables: *rub on liquid detergent and rinse. If stain persists after repeated applications, use sodium perborate bleach.* On non-washables: *sponge with solution of 2 parts water to 1 part spirits.*
Nail polish	*Never use nail polish remover on acetate or triacetate. Use a blunt knife to scrape it off these fabrics. For fabrics that cannot stand acetone, use amyl acetate.*
Oil, heavy grease	*Treat with eucalyptus oil.*
Paint (oil based)	*Follow the instructions for nail polish.*

Paint (water based)	*If still wet, sponge with water immediately. If dry, scrape with your nail.*
Pencil	*Try a soft eraser initially; rub detergent onto area and rinse. If stain is stubborn, use a few drops of diluted ammonia and then add detergent.*
Perspiration	*Use enzyme detergents on new stains; if yellow stain remains, use sodium perborate or hydrogen peroxide. If these methods are unsuccessful, send garment to the dry cleaners.*
Scorch	*Sponge with hydrogen peroxide and rinse. Nearly impossible to remove from silk and wool. Try brushing spots on thick wool with a very fine sandpaper.*
Shoe polish	*First try same procedure as for cosmetics. Next, sponge with spirits (diluted with 2 parts water for acetate). Alternatively, sponge with cleaning fluid.*
Soft drinks	*Sponge at once with cold water.*
Tar	*Scrape off what you can first; sponge with carbon tetrachloride.*
Urine, vomit, mucus	On washables: *soak with enzyme pre-soak and wash, using a bleach.* On non-washables: *sponge with mild detergent; rinse. Also try a solution of ¼ cup white vinegar in 1 cup water. If colour changes, neutralize with ammonia (1 tablespoon to 1 cup water).*
Water	*Hold water stained articles in the steam of a boiling kettle until the material is damp, shaking frequently. Press with a warm iron. If rayons, silks or delicate fabrics have been stained with sprinkled water, dip gently in warm water. Gently squeeze out the excess water and roll in a towel. Iron while damp. Modern leathers, particularly those used for shoes, can be treated for the stains water leaves if they get wet. Sponge gently with cotton wool soaked in water, gradually working out from the stain until all the shoe is soaked. Then pad it firmly with disposable baby nappies and allow it to dry naturally.*
Wax	*Scrape off what you can. Place stained area between two paper towels and press with a lukewarm iron. Repeat with fresh towels. Finally, sponge with cleaning fluid.*
Wine	*Soak immediately with Perrier, soda or any other sparkling mineral water. Swab the water up with a clean, absorbent cloth.*

POTTERY AND PORCELAIN

Billions of years ago, as the earth's crust cooled, extreme temperatures, wind, storms, ice floes and heavy rain all took their toll of the surface rock. Over thousands of millions of years the different rocks broke up into smaller and smaller particles, and the surface became covered with a deep layer of soil—pure sand, solid clay, and every possible mixture in between. The first settled communities found lumps of different muddy clays, mixed with stones and debris, but elastic and cohesive enough to retain the footprint of an animal. Perhaps after a long dry spell a hunter realized that the same footprint was still there, but by now perfectly retained within a hardened crust.

This may have been the beginning of pottery. Clays are dug out of the earth, dissolved in water to wash away the impurities, then drained, pounded and kneaded until they are smooth and malleable. Clays vary in mineral content, and this determines the texture and tint of the finished pot body, which can be anything from pure white through grey, buff and yellow to the reddish terracotta colours.

Clay may be shaped by various methods—by modelling or building by hand, by casting in moulds, or on a potter's wheel. It can be decorated at this early stage by inlaid, incised or applied ornament, or with slip (thinned-down clay which can, for example, be trailed over the object). The article dries hard, and must then be baked to increase its strength. After the first baking, or firing, the piece is said to be at the biscuit stage. Earthenware is fired at 1652–2224°F/900–1200°C, and at the biscuit stage is still porous. To make it waterproof it must be sealed with a glaze—a hard, glassy coating—and refired.

Glazes are commonly composed of silica, borax and fluxes such as soda, potash, lime and lead. The most commonly and generally used glaze on both earthenware and soft-paste porcelain is a lead glaze. Certain hues that can withstand high temperatures can be painted on before glazing, or can be mixed with the glaze itself, in the form of metal oxides. These are blue (cobalt), purple (manganese), green (copper) and yellow (iron or antimony), and are the hues found on the earliest ceramics. They vary according to the temperatures reached and the effects on them of the other ingredients. A complete range of hues is obtained only by using those that cannot withstand these high temperatures, and which are therefore painted on over the glaze and refired at a low temperature. These are enamel colours, which were not extensively used on Western ceramics until the eighteenth century, although they were introduced on Chinese porcelain in the mid-fifteenth century.

Earthenware vessels have been made throughout the world for centuries. Outstanding among the more sophisticated European types was Italian maiolica. It was made from the fifteenth century, inspired by the Hispano-Moresque wares brought from Valencia, in Spain, via the island of Majorca, whence the Italian name for this pottery arose. Originally the work of Moorish craftsmen, the Spanish pieces had a tin glaze with a lustrous finish achieved by the use of silver and copper oxides. The early Italian pieces, which were generally drug-jars and dishes for apothecaries and hospitals, copied the tin glaze (which gives an opaque white ground), the basic shapes and some of the decorative motifs of the Spanish wares, but not the lustre. This was finally achieved in the early sixteenth century by Deruta and Gubbio, the only two of the many Italian maiolica factories to succeed with this technique. Every factory developed its own styles of decoration. After the mid sixteenth century, however, demand fell and standards declined.

Tin-glazed earthenware made in France from the early sixteenth century is termed faïence. Early examples are very similar to Italian maiolica. The factory at Rouen also made tiles for walls and floors, and with time the French factories developed their own styles. The late seventeenth century brought a demand for large dinner services and grand vases, and the trade continued throughout the eighteenth century.

Delft, near Rotterdam, was the principal producer of Dutch tin-glazed wares. Dutch potters took many of their shapes, and the distinctive blue-and-white decoration, from Chinese porcelain, although other styles and colours were also used. Motifs, however, included tulips and windmills! Similar wares made in England and America until the eighteenth century were often called "delftware".

Trade dwindled for all these products as the lighter, porcelain-type wares became increasingly available. True, or hard-paste porcelain, which is prized for its glossy sheen and translucency, was made using kaolin (china clay, which has a highly refractory white body) and petuntse (china stone, a felspar) in China from the T'ang dynasty (618–906). It is fired at a very high temperature (up to 2854°F/1400°C), and becomes a hard, completely vitrified body, impervious to liquid. The Ming dynasty (1368–1644) is the best-known period for porcelain production in China. It was Ming porcelain that came to Europe, from the sixteenth century onwards, and the quality of the material and its varied, many-coloured decoration astonished the West, which had nothing comparable. Japanese porcelain followed, and also became very popular. Japanese wares were made at Arita specifically for export, and sent from the port of Imari; this latter name is often used for Arita porcelain. A distinctive style was "brocaded Imari", which had elaborate decoration in underglaze blue, with red and gold over the glaze. Even more popular was the style introduced by the potter Kakiemon, and carried on by others, which appeared on pieces imported from the late seventeenth century. The decoration, which was delicately executed and pleasingly off-centre, was of birds, bamboo, flowers and other naturalistic subjects and figures, painted in bright enamel colours on a milky-white ground.

Attempts were made to imitate the Oriental substance, but until the eighteenth century Europe produced only the type known as "soft-paste", or artificial, porcelain. This was composed of kaolin and glass constituents with various experimental additions, such as soapstone, but lacked the vital ingredient of china stone, and could not be fired at the necessary temperature to vitrify the material. The first kind of soft-paste porcelain was made in Florence at the Medici factory in 1575, but production ceased within 12 years and only about 50 pieces are known from this source. A hundred years went by before the French factories of Rouen and St Cloud devised a better type, and subsequently further factories in France, Italy and England began production of their own versions.

A very hard, heavy earthenware—stoneware—was made in Germany from the late Middle Ages, and refined over the years. This ware is fired at a high temperature—even up to 2854°F/1400°C—and vitrifies, and is therefore impervious to liquid. It is so hard that it can even be carved or cut and polished. The German potters made quantities of stoneware pots and tankards, many of which had an "orange-peel" surface, caused by salt thrown into the kiln during firing. Then, with cargoes of tea from China in the seventeenth century, came some hard, fine, red stoneware teapots, of a kind not seen before. These provided further inspiration to European potters in their attempts to make true porcelain.

It was at the Meissen factory in Germany that the first true porcelain was made in Europe, after much experimentation with refining stoneware. The name of Meissen became synonymous with beautiful, fine-quality porcelain with a hard, pure white body, and the best-known of its products were figurines, followed by little boxes for trinkets, patches and snuff, and tea and coffee services. At the beginning, the craftsmen employed at the factory were confined there in order that the secret of the true porcelain be kept; but some did manage to escape. Two found their way to Du Paquier's factory in Vienna, and under their auspices this factory was the second producer of hard-paste porcelain in 1718; its products reached a high standard of craftsmanship and decoration. From the 1740s many further factories started up for the production of porcelain, across Germany and elsewhere. All hard-paste porcelain has a felspathic glaze: china stone and lime are the main ingredients. Hard-paste is glossy, very slippery and cold to the touch; whereas soft-paste is slightly soapy, more clinging and not so cold.

In the second half of the century there was further progress in ceramic techniques. The Sèvres factory in France became renowned for its fine soft-paste ware. Stringent regulations laid down by the king to govern the production of porcelain ensured that, from 1756 to 1766, the best French workmanship and all technical advances in the medium were carried out at Sèvres, which in 1769 began also to make hard-paste. Clear enamel floral and other decoration, in a variety of colours, and gilding were part of the distinctive ornamentation of the finest Sèvres pieces, and later work included biscuit statuary. In England the Chelsea factory was executing elaborately modelled and decorated figures in soft-paste, and Derby, Worcester and others were famous for fine dinner-services. The English "bone-china" is a basis of hard-paste porcelain with added bone-ash (ox-bones were the usual source). Bow, in 1749, was probably the first factory to include this ingredient. Spode improved the formula and by the early nineteenth century bone china was a standard product of most English factories. The bone ash gives extra strength to the piece, and makes a slightly creamier, less transparent body. England did not make hard-paste wares in any quantity; the only factories to do so were Plymouth, Bristol and New Hall, towards the end of the eighteenth century. In America, the factories of Bonin and Morris in the 1770s, and Tucker and Hulme, and Fenton, in the nineteenth century, all made porcelain, some of it hard-paste, but floods of imports swamped the market.

The factory of Josiah Wedgwood in England was innovative and influential. Among other wares resulting from experimental work

were three types of stoneware: basalt (black, dense, unglazed), red stoneware, and the famous jasperware (white or coloured), which had white relief decoration in the classical mode. Wedgwood blue was the most commonly used ground colour for this last type. Wedgwood exported his wares in quantity, and started mass-production methods. He added bone china to his repertoire in the early 1800s.

In the nineteenth century, Staffordshire became the centre of the pottery industry in Britain, and mass production took over. Transfer printing, introduced in the previous century and later improved, meant cheap and colourful tableware for all. In this process, copper plates are engraved with a design and paint applied; the design is then transferred to the ceramic body (either under or over the glaze) with a gelatine "bat" or with tissue paper. Monochrome decoration—obviously the cheapest—became very common. In the 1830s the process was further refined and elaborate colour printing was done from that time. Many of these transfer-printed wares were exported, particularly to America. Favourite decorative elements were landscapes, buildings, portraits and scenes of rural life.

The nineteenth century brought many revivals and imitations of earlier styles—and many clever forgeries. A new substance was Parian ware. A dense, unglazed porcelain body with the appearance of white marble, this was used by Minton, Copeland and others for statuettes, urns and similar ornamental pieces from the 1840s; some later pieces had a coloured ground with white or gilt relief decoration, and some were slightly glazed to enable them to be wiped clean.

William De Morgan breathed the fresh air of the Arts and Crafts movement into the pottery industry in the 1870s. Avoiding the then current obsession with elaborate pastiche and idiosyncratic technical showpieces, he used ancient classical, Renaissance and Islamic designs and colours, and, to a great extent, lustre decoration. The new wave of art potters in the following decades steered modern ceramics into a generally "cleaner" look, including both geometric and naturalistic designs, and incorporating certain Japanese and other influences. Similar activities were taking place in Europe, and also in America, centred on Cincinnati and later Ohio, New Orleans, Boston and elsewhere. A highly popular domestic stoneware for everyday use was Dedham ware, produced in Massachusetts from 1895.

There were by now two distinct branches of the domestic ceramics industry: the mass-produced wares, available in abundance for the vast majority market; and the products of the artist potters who worked in their own studios making individual pieces for those with a desire for originality.

Cleaning and repairing pottery

Broken glazed pottery will show two distinct layers: the porous body (usually white or off-white) and a glaze (a thin, sometimes shiny, layer of colour on top of the body), as clearly shown in the photograph facing page 161. These two distinct layers distinguish it from porcelain or stoneware.

When a pottery object breaks, be sure to keep as many of the pieces as possible, including the smallest bits. Wrap each in a soft clean rag or tissue paper until you are ready to begin the glueing

process. However, do not store dirty pieces. Always clean each piece as directed below before storing.

Assemble the following supplies: cotton swabs, paper towels, acetone or cellulose paint thinner, abrasive cleanser (optional), soft toothbrush, baby bottle sterilizing fluid, powdered pigments, matchstick or toothpick applicator, masking tape, single-edged razor blade, needle file and garnet paper and a slow-setting, two-part glue such as 24-hour Araldite.

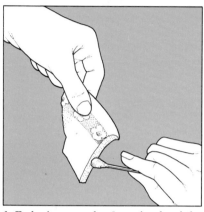

1. Each piece must be clean, rinsed and dry before it can be glued. First, wash around the broken edges of each piece with soapy water, using a cotton swab as applicator for small areas or a white paper towel for larger surfaces. Avoid unnecessary soaking—if water gets through the body and seeps under the glaze, it will take longer for the piece to dry and will hold up the glueing process. If soap and water fail to remove the dirt, wipe each surface with acetone or cellulose paint thinner. As a last resort, scrub each piece with abrasive cleanser using a soft toothbrush. Rinse and dry thoroughly.

2. If the pieces are clean but still appear grimy or if the surface cracks are filled with dirt (especially noticeable on white china), then the piece will have to be bleached. Under no account use a proprietary household bleach. It will remove years of grime but may take away the glaze and any painted decoration as well. Instead place the object in a solution of three parts water to one part baby bottle sterilizing fluid in a vessel large enough to cover the pieces completely.

3. Before beginning to apply the glue, arrange the pieces on a sheet of clean paper so you can see how they might fit together and also to check whether a large chunk or piece is missing. By stacking and fitting the pieces together logically, you will be able to work out the best order in which to stick them together so that a piece is not left out when it comes to the actual glueing. When practising the fitting and stacking, use the force of gravity to help you, letting each piece rest on the one below it. If a piece is missing see Step 9 for filling instructions.

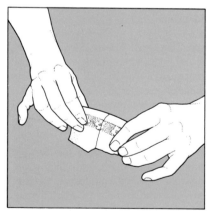

4. It may make sense to glue lots of smaller pieces together to make two or three larger pieces, facilitating the final glueing process. However, the actual glueing must be done all at once, so you can adjust the work before the glue sets. Use a slow-setting, two-part glue such as 24-hour Araldite; only use a rapid setting glue when the piece is critical to the whole assemblage. Use your fingers to feel if the various pieces have been properly aligned.

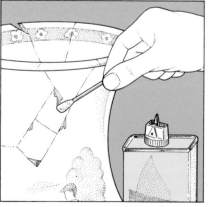

5. Swab away excess glue while it is still wet, using lighter fluid or acetone on a cotton swab.

6. If the pottery is white, add a few particles of titanium white powdered pigment to tint the glue once it is mixed. If the glaze or body is a dark shade, such as terracotta, then the appropriate shade of powdered pigment must be added.

If a missing piece of pottery has to be replaced, you will also need: tracing paper, a palette knife, talcum powder, an emery board or pointed typewriter eraser, a modelling clay such as plasticine, carbonless carbon paper, proprietary china paints and metallic paints (optional).

7. Use a wooden matchstick or toothpick to apply the glue, coating both edges to be stuck. Press them gently together. Proceed with the glueing process, either working from the base upwards, or making larger bits from the smaller pieces. To hold the glued pieces together, use strips of masking tape torn in appropriate lengths and applied at right angles to the break.

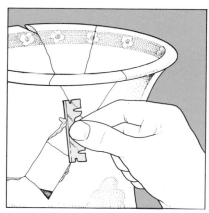

8. Leave the glued object to dry for at least 24 hours at room temperature. Shave off any excess glue with a single-edged razor blade, using a very light touch. Avoid scraping off any of the painted decoration—gold and silver accents are especially vulnerable.

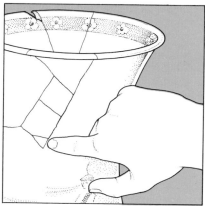

9. Sometimes when arranging the pieces prior to glueing or while actually glueing, you will discover that a small piece is missing *or* will not fit in. In this instance, the missing piece can be replaced by making a filler as follows: mix some two-part glue, tinting it to match the glaze, (as described in Step 4), and blending it with talc until it acquires the consistency of clay. (Do not use Plaster of Paris which is not waterproof.) Using a palette knife or your fingers, force the filler into place, carefully attempting to follow the contours of the surrounding area. Leave to set. When set, rub to exact shape with needle file and garnet paper.

10. If the missing piece is larger, such as the hand of a figurine or the rim of a dish, take a simple mould by laying high-quality modelling clay such as plasticine on an equivalent perfect part. Push the wad of clay gently around the perfect area, forcing it into small contours until an impression has been taken. Carefully transfer this "mould" to the broken or damaged area.

11. Apply a line of tinted two-part glue along all the broken edges. Holding the mould in place with one hand, use the other hand to lay the filler (as described in Step 9) into the mould using a palette knife and/or your fingers. (If the mould tends to fall away or you need both hands to apply the filler, hold the mould in place with masking tape.) Once the mould is filled, leave it in place and allow the filler to set until hard.

12. When the filler is absolutely dry, remove the mould and smooth the surface of the new piece with very fine garnet paper. An emery board or pointed typewriter eraser is useful for smoothing smaller, or highly detailed areas. Do not go over onto the surrounding area or the glaze will be scratched.

Cleaning and repairing pottery cont.

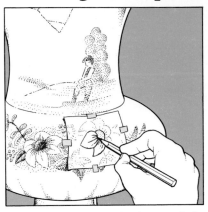

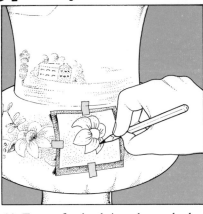

13. The filler may be painted to match the background using proprietary china paints. Follow the pattern as best you can, taking a trace if necessary from an undamaged area.

14. To transfer the design, place carbonless carbon paper between the tracing paper and the filled area, and run a pencil over the tracing. To touch up silver or gold use the best possible metallic paints.

REPAIRING PORCELAIN

It is generally not advisable to repair any valuable porcelain, leaving restoration on these pieces to an expert. However, if the repair is simple, or to a non-valuable piece, follow the instructions below.

To the restorer, the most important difference between pottery and porcelain is that the glaze on porcelain does not show up as a separate layer along the break. Instead, any break will expose a smooth, glassy, non-porous texture all the way through, as in the photograph facing page 161 In practical terms, this means that it is possible to clean a piece of porcelain very thoroughly without worrying about water saturation, and to glue immediately after cleaning.

Follow the glueing instructions for pottery as given on the previous pages, having first tinted the filler and fitted the pieces as accurately as possible. Once the glue has completely dried, it may be necessary to touch up the painted decoration and/or disguise damage. Use slightly translucent acrylic paints, which have the appearance of glazed enamel and are designed for china painting. Follow the design as closely as possible, tracing the details, even the brush-strokes, as suggested in Steps 13-14, but do not attempt to paint in the background shade, it will never match.

Repairing hairline cracks

1. Clean the area round the crack by following directions in Step 1, Page 158. Mix and tint two-part adhesive as directed in Step 4, ready to apply. Then, place the object in an oven set at the lowest possible temperature, i.e. 225°F/110°C until it is hand hot. The crack will open slightly and will suck the glue into the body.

2. As soon as the piece comes from the oven, force the glue into the crack using your fingers or a palette knife, so that the crack absorbs as much of the glue mixture as possible.

3. When the crack will take no more, remove any excess with a soft cloth or by gently scraping with a single-edged razor blade, taking care not to remove any of the painted decoration on the surrounding area. Let the object cool.

Opposite: "Before" (above) and "after" (below) of a porcelain exportware bowl with gilt decoration. The photo shows the characteristic feature of porcelain, i.e. no demarcation between the body and the glaze, as opposed to pottery (see overleaf).

METALS

We all know what a metal is — or do we? There is in fact a scientific definition of a metal which prescribes what physical and chemical properties it must have, and there are over sixty metals known, though one at least — scandium — has never been isolated, its properties having been deduced from its compounds. Some metals are very rare indeed, and some do not occur in nature but are the result of nuclear reactions.

It is supposed that the first metals known to man were those which occur in nature as the free metal: these are gold, silver and copper, which were known in the later Stone Age, prior to 4000 B.C. Gold and silver are both very soft, too soft to be used as tools or weapons, but were appreciated for their rarity and beauty and used as ornaments. Jewellery techniques were well advanced by 2500 B.C. and the metals could by then be obtained by smelting oxide ores. Silver and lead often occurred together (and there is in fact always a small proportion of silver in a primarily lead ore) and were separated in a clay or bone-ash vessel called a cupel; air was blown over the molten alloy to oxidize the lead, which was partly skimmed off and partly absorbed into the cupel, leaving the silver. The lead could afterwards be recovered. Silver is still obtained by alloying with lead and subsequent cupellation. Silver and gold also occurred together, giving rise to a gold/silver alloy called electrum. However, the world's main silver-bearing deposits are in Central and South America and it was the Spanish Conquest which made silver freely available in Europe.

In modern times both gold and silver are deliberately alloyed to make them less soft. Gold is alloyed with copper or silver to make red and white gold respectively. The "fineness" of gold is denoted by the number of parts of gold in 24 parts of the metal, so that 18-carat gold, for instance, has 18 parts of gold in 24. The sterling standard for silver has been 92.5 per cent silver since about 1300 A.D., the balance of 7.5 per cent being copper. A higher standard, the Britannia standard, was compulsory for silver plate from 1697 to 1720 to prevent silversmiths melting down silver coin, and is still occasionally used. Silver has also important industrial uses; it is the best conductor of electricity known, and considerable quantities are used in photography.

It has been compulsory for English gold and silver plate to be submitted to an Assay Office for testing and marking since the early fourteenth century; in 1363 a maker's mark was added, and in 1478 a date letter. Makers' marks before the middle of the seventeenth century are not identifiable, however, owing to the loss of records in the Great Fire of London in 1666. Both English and French silver prior to the end of the seventeenth century is rare. Much English silver was melted down during the Civil War, and French silver went to sustain the wars of Louis XIV. An inexpensive booklet giving Assay Office marks and date letters for English and Irish silver and gold since the middle of the sixteenth century may be obtained from almost any dealer in old silver and from some bookshops. It also gives Sheffield Plate marks. Most countries have some system of marking silver plate but none is so complete or so systematic as the English, and the identification of marks on Continental silver is a matter for the specialist.

In dealers' and auctioneers' jargon "silver (or gold) plate" means that the article is made wholly of the precious metal, but "plated" means that it is made of a base metal with a coating of the precious metal; usually the article will be electro-plated. However Sheffield Plate is fabricated from metal sheet consisting of a sandwich of copper between two sheets of silver. The process was invented in 1742 by Thomas Bolsover of Sheffield, the metals being fused together by heat and then rolled out into sheet form. The design has to be contrived to conceal the cut edges where the copper would show. Manufacture of Sheffield Plate continued until about 1860. The silver layers were much thinner than the copper core but much thicker than in the case of electro-plate. If the silver is worn away, as it may be by much cleaning, then of course the copper shows through. From about 1840 the core might be nickel-silver, which is whitish, instead of copper. Sheffield Plate makers' marks had to be registered at the Sheffield Assay Office and are consequently on record. Sheffield Plate is prized by collectors.

A patent for electro-plating was taken out in 1840 by G. R. Elkington of Birmingham. In electro-plating the silver or other metal is deposited on the finished article of base metal, as opposed to the Sheffield Plate method of fabrication from plated sheet. In electro-plating the coating of precious metal can be, and often is, extremely thin so that it wears through very quickly. Early electro plate was sometimes on copper, in which case there is the possibility of confusion with Sheffield Plate, but usually it is on whitish metal. Usually, also, it is stamped with marks vaguely resembling silver marks. A mark such as "Something [brand name] Plate" will certainly be electro-plate. Common marks are EPNS and EPBM which mean Electro-Plate on Nickel-Silver and Electro-Plate on Britannia Metal respectively. Nickel-silver, also known as German silver, has nothing to do with silver but is an alloy of nickel, copper and zinc. Britannia Metal was invented in the 1790s and is an alloy of tin, antimony and copper.

Copper occurs as a free metal in many parts of the world. It is often very pure and in large masses. It is very soft, but can be hardened by hammering to make tools. It was also the first metal to be extracted from ores, in the Middle East about 4000 B.C., and probably also the first to be cast, about 500 years later. It has since been used throughout history to make a wide range of ornaments and domestic utensils. As it is slightly poisonous when in contact with some foodstuffs, the interior surface of copper cooking vessels is usually given a coating of tin. Modern copper vessels can be distinguished from older ones by the fact that they are made of machine-rolled sheet of uniform thickness, whereas the old coppersmiths always made the bottom thicker than the rest. Uniform hammer marks are also a sign of modern manufacture. Copper is used extensively in industry, as it is the second best conductor of electricity, after silver.

Copper is the principal constituent of many useful alloys, the oldest of which is bronze, an alloy of copper and tin probably first produced by accident from a mixed ore. Bronze was known in Sumer by 3000 B.C. and it was soon discovered that the most generally useful bronze contained 10–12 per cent of tin. Over the ages various formulations of bronze have widely extended its range of uses, encouraged by its properties of suitability for casting, and its hardness, strength, sonority, brilliance, colour and patina. Bronze vessels were decorated by the Greeks and Etruscans as early as 300 B.C. with *champlevé* enamels. In this art, which is still practised, hollows were excavated or cast in the bronze and filled with coloured enamels to make a smooth surface.

The other principal alloy of copper is brass, which is an alloy with zinc. This was also probably discovered by accident during the making of bronze, by the unintentional smelting of naturally occurring mixed copper and zinc ore. It appeared about 1000 B.C., but its usefulness was not appreciated until the Romans made use of it for coinage. To some extent this may have been due to the fact that metal zinc was not known until it was isolated by Paracelsus in the sixteenth century; in the meantime it was an unknown impurity in the ore. A commercially economic way of extracting it was not discovered until the early nineteenth century. The principal deposits of zinc ore in Europe were near Dinant in Belgium, so that from the Middle Ages brassware was known as *dinanderie*, and most English brassware was made from imported brass until the late 1700s. Some was made from sheets made by hammering, and was called latten. Old ornamental brassware is now much collected. Brass was cast more often than copper, and often items such as candlesticks are made in sections joined by screw threads. In the case of old work, these are obviously hand-formed.

English brass was much improved after 1781 when James Emerson patented a golden-toned brass. Other brass products are ormolu, which is golden brass cast into mounts for furniture, clocks etc. in the eighteenth and nineteenth centuries, and is gilded with pure gold; and pinchbeck, so named after its eighteenth-century inventor, which was a golden brass claimed to resist tarnishing and used for cheap jewellery, in which it imitated gold.

Iron does not occur in nature in the free state, except for small quantities derived from meteorites, and the smelting of iron ores dates from about 1300 B.C. It appears to have been the Hittites, living in a district to the south of the Black Sea, who originated the reduction of iron oxides by smelting the ore with charcoal. The result was a spongy mass which had to be heated and hammered repeatedly to produce wrought iron. The hardness of iron depends on the carbon content. This is very low in wrought iron, which in consequence, although malleable and ductile, is too soft to use as weapons and tools. It could be hardened by prolonged heating in charcoal, however. From the sixth century A.D., Britain became an important iron-making region since iron ore was plentiful. The industry underwent further and sudden expansion after the invention about 1700 by Abraham Darby of a method of smelting using coke from coal, instead of charcoal. In modern practice the ore is reduced with coke in a blast furnace, and the iron run off into channels and solidified into "pigs" which may be remelted to make articles of cast iron. In this, however, the carbon is not dissolved or uniformly distributed, but is in the form of discrete inclusions of irregular shape, which makes cast iron very brittle. Consequently eighteenth- and nineteenth-century structures of cast iron such as the frames of machinery, bridges, and beams, had to be very massive. Not until 1946 was it discovered that the addition of magnesium to the iron would cause the inclusions to assume a spherical form, with improvement in the physical properties of the iron casting.

A great advance, therefore, was the introduction in the middle of the last century of the Bessemer process for making steel. In this, air is blown through molten iron to oxidize the carbon, and then a correct amount of an alloy of iron, manganese and carbon is added to produce steel of the required quality.

Wrought iron, however, had properties not possessed by steel. It is extremely rust-resistant, and could be welded by heating and hammering. Beautiful gates, railings, balconies and other ornamental ironwork could be made by skilled craftsmen. Today wrought iron is no longer produced commercially in Britain, and there are few craftsmen, so that the production of new wrought ironwork and the repair of old is almost prohibitively expensive. The "wrought iron" gate offered commercially is made of mild steel strip joined by gas or electric welding.

Tin is a silvery-white corrosion-resistant metal taking a high polish, and domestic ware was made from it from the sixteenth century to the nineteenth. Tin workers were controlled by the Pewterers' Company and by 1800 were more numerous than the pewterers, as pewter was increasingly replaced for domestic use by cheap earthenware. Tin articles are sometimes marked "English Block Tin". Tinplate is sheet iron or steel dipped into molten tin to coat it with a thin layer of tin. It has been in demand since the invention of food canning in the late eighteenth century, although the Romans were the first to line food containers with tin.

Pewter is an alloy mainly of tin, but its composition is rather indeterminate; the additives may be bismuth, antimony and copper. Pewterers have been organized into guilds in England and France since Saxon times, but pewter made before the seventeenth century is very rare. It is extremely soft and soon became damaged or worn, and it was customary to have it melted down and remade by travelling pewterers. The Pewterers' Company was established in 1348 and had strict rules regarding the composition of different quality wares. Makers' marks, or "touches", were struck on many articles, both in Britain and on the Continent, but they are not Assayers' marks and had no legal sanction, and consequently are not systematically recorded. A late Victorian vogue for pewter has resulted in a large quantity of modern work, including many reproductions and outright fakes.

Cleaning iron and tin

The worst enemy of iron is rust which, in time, can completely destroy a large piece and, even after a short time, may leave the surface pitted and flaky. So the first and most important task is to get rid of every trace of rust. Although soap and water will do this, it is best to use one of the proprietary brands of rust remover based on phosphoric acid, having first checked that it will not corrode the metal under the rust. Always follow the manufacturer's instructions very carefully. A wire brush, steel wool, abrasive paper and silicone

wax are also required, blacklead and paints are optional finishes.

Tin may be cleaned in the same way as iron. It is, however, much thinner and lighter than iron, so clean it carefully—use wire brushes carefully and do not use coarse grades of abrasive paper. If the tin has a painted exterior and most of the paint has come off, remove the rest with fine abrasive paper. On the other hand, if there are remnants of a hand-painted motif, see Steps 1 – 3, Page 74, for notes on restoration.

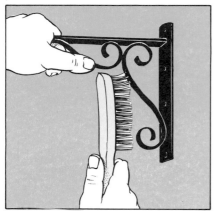

1. To remove any loose deposits of dirt or flaking rust scrub chinks and crevices with a wire brush and flat surfaces with fine steel wool pads or silicone carbide abrasive paper.

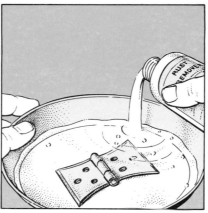

2. If there are any places too deep or too curved for the brush to reach, use a phosphoric rust remover such as Jenolite and follow the manufacturer's instructions for small objects. If the object has an engraved surface which might be damaged by rubbing, put it in a plastic container and cover with rust remover. Some rust removers may etch into the surface of the metal, so check first that it is safe to use on the object to be cleaned.

3. After thoroughly cleaning the piece, rinse it well in clean water. Dry immediately, because if the piece remains damp or is exposed to dampish air, even for a short time, the rust may start forming again. It is particularly important to bear this in mind when using iron cooking utensils.

FINISHING IRON

4. When the object is completely free of rust and any repairs that are needed have been done (see Steps 1 – 3, Page 168), the ironwork is ready for finishing. If the object is going to be handled frequently, polish with a little silicone furniture wax or a specialist conservation wax. Do this regularly to keep the piece looking good.

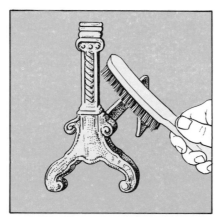

5. Firedogs, irons and tongs kept in a fireplace which is used regularly will seldom get rusty, but they will accumulate layers of soot and wood ash. To remove this scour regularly with a wire brush or coarse steel wool. They are best left in their natural finish, although they can be blackleaded with a proprietary brand of blacklead, which is also excellent for all iron objects kept indoors. Never use ordinary paints on any fireplace or kitchen equipment; use paint made especially for iron objects.

6. Other objects, for example locks and keys, can be painted the traditional black or white, sometimes highlighted with a little high quality gilt paint. First remove all rust, wash, dry and paint with one or two coats of a good anti-corrosion primer for steel, which is usually a red oxide (deep burnt red) shade. Then paint with two or three topcoats. Be sure to apply the paint thinly, otherwise it will accumulate in decorative curves and make the design look thick and clumsy.

Cleaning copper, brass, pewter and bronze

Copper often acquires a lovely patina from years of polishing, so do not destroy this by using harsh abrasives. Copper sheeting was often used for wall plaques, candle sconces etc, and was decorated with repoussé work which was hammered out from the back. This can easily be dented by too much pressure with steel wool or a brush. Remember that certain foods affect copper so that some of the metal may dissolve and poison the contents. All cooking utensils made of copper must therefore be lined with tin.

To clean copper, assemble the following tools and supplies: proprietary copper cleaner (or make your own from iron oxide, pumice and oleic acid), nailbrush, toothbrush, shaving brush, and metal lacquer (optional).

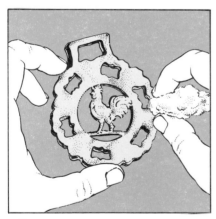

1. Copper does not rust, but it does become green from a deposit called verdigris. To remove this use a proprietary cleaner applied with a natural bristle nailbrush or toothbrush. Never use either steel wool or nylon as these will scratch the copper. For parts not badly affected by verdigris use a proprietary brand of copper cleaner.

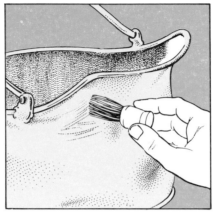

2. It is also possible to make an effective copper cleaner at home. Take 1oz/30g of iron oxide, 3oz/85g of ground pumice stone (pumice powder) and gradually add enough oleic acid to form a paste. Apply this to the copper with a pad of soft cotton fabric or a shaving brush, taking care not to scratch the surface. Wipe off with a clean dry cloth.

3. Copper can also be lacquered with a special clear gloss lacquer for metals. This prevents tarnishing, but can only be used on articles not used for preparing or cooking food.

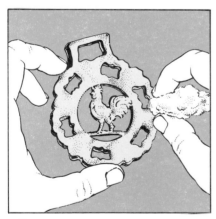

BRASS

4. Although old brass often has a dark sheen, it can also become dirty or tarnished. Sometimes, too, if a piece has been varnished the old varnish will have worn away, leaving a dull film over the piece. Remove this film with a cotton wool swab moistened with acetone and then wash the piece carefully in mild soap and water or water and household ammonia.

5. Any underlying corrosion will show up once the film is removed and can be removed by rubbing hard with a good proprietary brass polish. Badly tarnished pieces will require real effort.

6. If a small piece is badly corroded put it in a container of water containing a cup of white vinegar and a rounded tablespoonful of salt. Bring to the boil and boil for several hours—the dirtier the piece the longer it will need—remembering to top the water up from time to time. This treatment is not suitable for pieces with delicate inlays or that incorporate other materials.

7. The best and easiest way to polish brass is to use a good metal polish, following the maker's instructions carefully. Leave the darker crevices, as they contrast well with the gleam of the polished parts. After polishing the piece give it a final wash with soap and water to remove any acid deposits. Then polish it with a clean, dry soft cloth.

8. Brass that is not used for cooking or near the fire should be protected with transparent metal lacquer. This comes in both liquid and spray form. Be careful when applying it that the lacquer does not accumulate in thick, ugly deposits.

It is best to have large pieces, such as beds and lamps, professionally lacquered. It is extremely difficult to get a thin even coating all over a large piece. Lacquered brass will keep its bright appearance with regular dusting and the occasional rinse in warm water and mild soapsuds.

BRONZE

Bronze, looked after with care, ages beautifully, acquiring a deep glowing patina. It is also possible to achieve this effect deliberately by a process called patination, so a good patina is not always a reliable indicator of the age of a bronze object. But patina, whether the result of age or artifice, should never be removed. Clean the object with soap and water, rinse well and dry very thoroughly with a soft cloth.

PEWTER

Like copper, pewter does not rust and old pewter has a lovely lead-grey patina. Do not try to remove this as it will immediately reduce the value of the piece. Instead, restrict cleaning to washing with soap and water and a soft brush. Modern pewter, which contains no lead and is silvery in appearance, can be cleaned with silver polish.

Cleaning ormolu

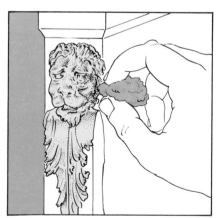

1. The first step when cleaning ormolu is to remove all trace of old varnish or lacquer with swabs of cotton wool or rag wrung out in acetone. This usually dulls the surface considerably, but will not affect the final appearance. When cleaning porcelain vases or lamps mounted in ormolu, take care not to get the acetone into the joints, because these are often reinforced with acetone-soluble glue.

2. Then scrub with soap and water or water and a little ammonia. Ormolu must be scrubbed because dirt accumulates easily in its highly textured surface, but always use a pure bristle nail or toothbrush as nylon is too scratchy.

3. Rinse well when all traces of dirt have disappeared and dry thoroughly with a clean, dry, lint-free cloth. Polishing is not advisable—it will merely highlight the shadows and rough surfaces which give ormolu its distinctive appearance.

Cleaning silver and chrome

Old or neglected silver acquires a heavy, ugly tarnish that can be very difficult to remove. But patience, a good proprietary silver cleaner based on thioglycolic acid and a silver brush will, in the end, work wonders. The method of cleaning given below also works well for silver plate and Britannia metal.

1. Wash the silver gently in very warm soapy water. Then rinse thoroughly in clean warm water. Dry with a clean cloth.

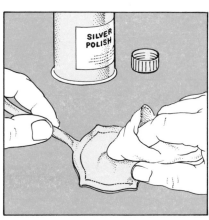

2. Apply the polish, a little at a time, with a cloth. Rub quite firmly backwards and forwards, not in a circle.

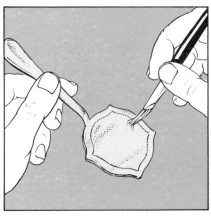

3. Use a special silver brush to get into any parts that are not otherwise easily accessible. But do remember that many patterns are intended to have some tarnishing in the recesses, as this serves to give the contrast of shadows to the brighter polished areas.

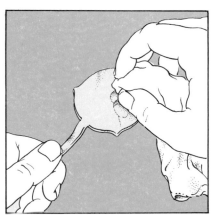

4. Rub with a clean cloth to remove all traces of the polish. The silver should now be clean and bright. Wash it again and dry it well.

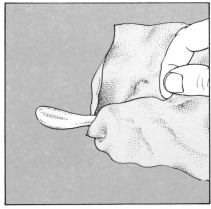

5. Silver responds to being used, so if possible do not shut it away. If you have to store it, wrap it in one of the cloths made by manufacturers of silvercare products that are specially designed for wrapping silver that is being stored.

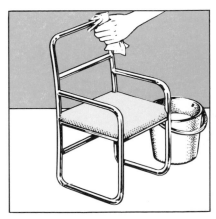

CHROME

Chrome plating is easy to clean with a damp cloth. Follow this by rubbing briskly with a dry one. Never use any kind of abrasive, they will mark the finish indelibly. If the chrome is very dirty use soap and water or else a small amount of fine liquid or cream silver polish on particularly dirty patches. Never leave salt on chrome, as it will corrode the plate very badly. And the only treatment for badly scratched chrome is to have it professionally replated.

Repairing metalwork

The golden rule to observe when considering the repair of any metal article is: take it to a specialist for advice before doing anything to it yourself. If the piece is old and valuable an ill-advised repair will immediately reduce its value substantially. If the piece has only sentimental value and is not worth the expense of professional restoration, buy some really junky pieces and practise repairing these before starting on an old favourite.

Soldering is a fairly simple means of repairing metal objects. It is a way of joining or seaming two pieces of metal, or repairing small holes or gaps. Practise on pieces of scrap metal or worthless damaged pieces to learn how much solder is required and the length of time that the heat must be applied.

Solder comes in three grades: easy, medium and hard. Easy solder melts at the lowest temperature and gives a good joint, but is not particularly strong. Medium is slightly stronger and melts at a higher temperature. Hard solder melts at the highest temperature and it is also the strongest. The three grades are primarily intended to enable successive solderings on a single piece without melting the previous joint. In such cases start with the hard solder, make the next joint with the medium and finally use the easy.

Flux is used in conjunction with the solder. It prevents oxides from forming under heat, and helps the solder melt more easily. It is painted on the joint before soldering.

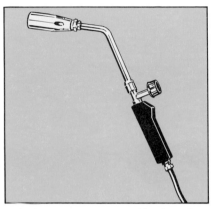

1. It is best to use a propane gas blow-lamp that is small enough to handle easily both to make working with it easier and to avoid damaging surrounding areas. Never use a torch with inflammable liquids or fabrics lying nearby. Keep a small fire extinguisher handy in case of accidents.

The type of solder and flux used varies according to the different types of metal. For silver, brass, copper, nickel and stainless steel use silver solder and flux such as Easiflo; for gold, use gold solder, and flux as for silver; and for cast iron, use special brazing rods and brazing flux, such as BOC Saffire flux.

2. Before starting to solder, it is essential to prepare the piece properly. Clean it thoroughly, following the instructions for the different metals given on pages 164 – 6. Smooth out any dents as described in Steps 1 – 2, Page 160. If the repair is to a seam that has opened, gently hammer the sides down until they lie flat together.

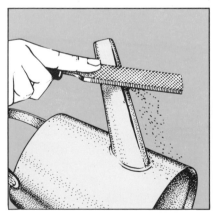

3. Rub the edges to be soldered lightly with a file or abrasive paper to give the solder a grip.

4. Paint the seam with the flux, covering the entire area that is to be soldered.

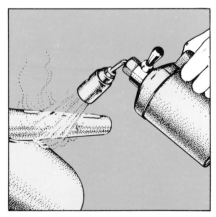

5. Put several small panels of solder on the seam, and apply the flame, first heating the whole piece and then moving it to and fro along the seam. When the solder melts it will run towards the flame, a characteristic which, with experience, can be used to encourage the melted solder to flow evenly along the entire joint.

Repairing iron and brass

Wrought iron corrodes more easily than cast iron. The metal was worked when hot, so it is fairly malleable and comparatively easy to repair. But even so, it is best to go to a workshop that specializes in restoration. Old wrought iron was made with simple tools and on an open fire, so the modern electric and acetylene torches for welding and riveting leave different marks on the metal. They should not, therefore, be used on any wrought iron, old or new, that has been made in the traditional way. Before doing any

repairs, remove all traces of rust to ensure that the metal is strong enough to be repaired. If it is not, the whole part must be removed and replaced—a task for the expert. Brass is a very hard alloy and therefore difficult for the amateur to repair. There are foundries that specialize in the repair of brass.

1. A few simple repairs to iron objects can be done at home. For example, spikes and ornaments that have been pushed out of position can be hammered gently back into place.

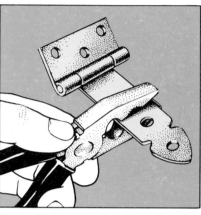

2. When working on small or delicate pieces, it is best to hold them in a vice or a pair of pliers. It will be easier to keep the piece in place if this is done.

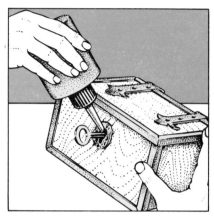

3. One of the commonest problems with iron objects is keys jammed in locks. This is particularly common on old wooden boxes bound with iron straps and secured with massive iron locks and keys. When this happens never try to force the key. Instead, put some easing oil, such as WD40, into the keyhole. Wait as directed by the instructions, then try to turn the key again. If it seems to move a little put in some more of the oil, wait, and so on. Eventually the key will move. Any more serious problems must be dealt with by an expert in old locks.

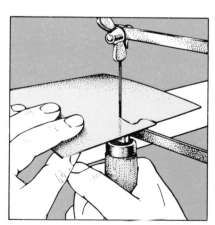

4. To replace broken bits of Boulle-work or other brass inlays of simple design have sheet brass cut to match, or cut it to shape with a piercing saw.

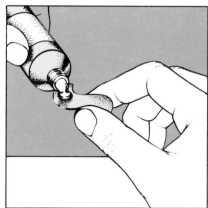

5. Smooth the edges with abrasive paper. Polish with brass polish and glue into place with a general purpose glue. This requires care as the surfaces to be glued are often small, so do not apply too much glue to begin with. It is easier to add a little more than to clean up after applying too much.

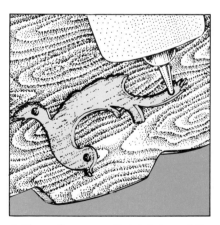

6. Pieces of more complicated design and the larger pieces are often held in place with tiny brass screws. If the screws are loose, put adhesive into the screw holes and reinsert the screws.

Repairing copper and pewter

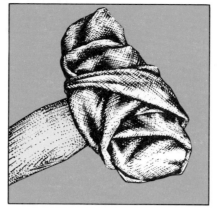

1. Old copper and pewter items are often badly dented. To repair these some sort of appropriately rounded shape is necessary. It is possible to buy a silversmith's shape in heavy wood, but this is only sensible if many repairs are to be done. Otherwise get a block of any hardwood about 1ft/30cm long and 6 – 9in/15 – 25cm square. Turn it on end and plane away the edges to make a rounded pillar. For extra solidity, screw the block down onto an old table top. A smaller piece about 3in/7.6cm square is good for small items.

2. Slip the piece to be repaired over the rounded piece of wood, holding it so that the dented or damaged part rests on the top. With a ball or soft-face hammer, hit the piece repeatedly with very light blows, gradually working the metal back into its original shape. Use many light blows, not a few heavy ones. It is always a help if the piece is warmed first. To prevent damage to the surface of the piece, wrap strips of cotton rag around the head of the hammer.

3. Holes in kettles and pots can be patched with slugs which expand with heat to make a water-proof seal. Unfortunately they will never match the shade of the original piece, so it is again best to have repairs done professionally.

Repairing silver and silver plate

Silver is a soft, malleable metal and so responds to all metalworking techniques. However, it is a precious metal and good silverware is valuable, and really should be repaired by a silversmith. Home repairs should be restricted to careful straightening of feet, finials and other unobtrusive parts. Use wooden mallets, hammers and shapes made especially for such work and *never* handle the material roughly.

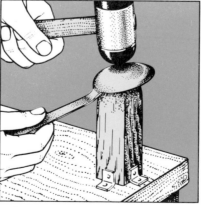

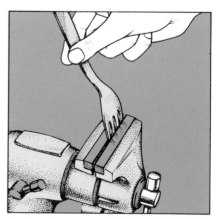

1. Wooden shapes (see Step 1, above) are a great help for dented spouts and sides. If very thin spouts, such as those on tea and coffee pots, have been dented, a piece of dowel, or even a pencil, can be inserted to act as a cushion for the hammering. Move the silver constantly while hammering, so that each blow is on a slightly different area. Check frequently to make sure that the basic shape is not being distorted.

2. Spoon bowls can be hammered very gently back into shape, again using a rounded wooden shape.

3. The easiest way to straighten forks is to put the pronged end into a vice. Then gently clamp it until the prongs line up correctly.

Repairing silver and silver plate cont.

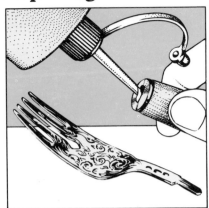

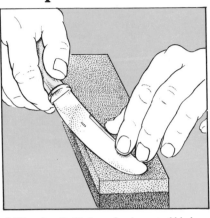

4. Handles which snap off knives and forks can generally be soldered on, but remember that cast silver, like cast iron, is more brittle than the wrought metal. Epoxy-resin instant bonding glues are useful when a knife or fork has come away from a handle made in a different material. Put the glue in the handle socket and re-embed the tang of the other part back into it. Spoons must be straightened very carefully, if they have been bent before the metal will be very weak at the bent part.

5. Silver-handled knives often have steel blades. These, and other steel knife blades, can be sharpened by rubbing them at a constant angle over an oilstone which has been lubricated with a drop of oil. This should not, however, be attempted on plated knife blades!

6. Silver plate and Sheffield plate should be treated in exactly the same way as silver, except the repairs are more difficult because the base metal will show through a bad join. If the surface silver on silver plate items has worn thin, have it professionally replated by a craftsman using the electrolysis method. *Never* have Sheffield plate replated as this will ruin both its patina and its value.

Restoring metal furniture

Whether you have a Victorian cast iron garden bench or an austere-lined tubular chair formed from steel tubing in the 1930s, the problem of removing rust and restoring the painted finish is the same. The following steps assume that the piece is in good condition, with no parts missing or hanging loose. If the latter is the case take the article to a metal restorer, who will use a welding process to form new pieces—repairs of this sort must not be attempted by an amateur who may inadvertently reduce the value of the article.

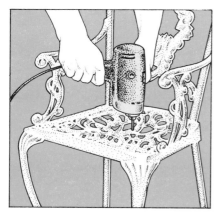

1. Should two pieces simply need to be joined, use a hand or power drill fitted with a bit suitable for metal. If the bit shows a tendency to over heat while drilling, lubricate and cool it with a few drops of oil. Use a rivet to join the pieces.

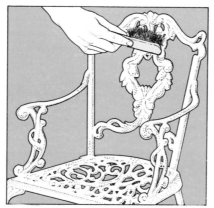

2. If the article has been in damp conditions, there will be signs of rust. To remove the loose particles, use a stiff wire brush, taking particular care with the corners and crevices—it is very important that all the rust is removed. If the rust is very bad, flake it off using an old, blunt knife or chisel, then treat it with paraffin as below.

3. To remove stubborn rust, apply a proprietary rust remover, or soften the rust by applying paraffin on a cloth. Soak the area with the paraffin for a few days if possible. When completely clean, rub the article with emery paper or emery powder to provide a "tooth" for the primer.

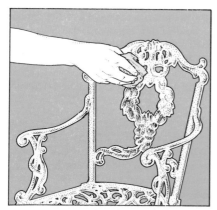

4. If the piece has had the paint removed, and you intend to keep it in its unpainted state, it will be necessary to seal the metal. Seal the surface from the action of the oxygen in the air by coating the article with a proprietary metal polish, a thick application of petroleum jelly or mineral oil (for articles to be used indoors) or make polish as follows: mix 2oz/57g rottenstone, 1oz/28g soft soap and enough oxalic acid to make a thick cream. Apply three coats, allowing the polish to dry for 24 hours between coats.

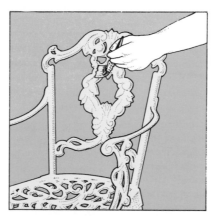

5. After all traces of rust are removed, paint the entire article with a rust-preventive paint. These usually come in a deep red shade, but a white universal primer is also acceptable. Aerosol application is not recommended as so much is wasted during application. If applying the preventer with a paintbrush, be sure to get into all the crevices and not to overload the brush.

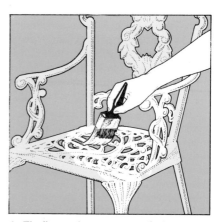

6. Finally, apply two coats of gloss paint, designed to be used over the rust preventer, and specially formulated to be used outdoors to provide the maximum protection. Sand between coats with a fine emery paper and dust thoroughly before applying the next coat.

JEWELLERY

From earliest times, and in even the most primitive societies, human beings have adorned themselves with "jewellery", in the sense of wearing decorative articles which serve no apparent useful purpose. The desire to make and wear jewellery springs from many motives: superstitious belief in the magical protective powers of a talisman, identification with a religious creed, the decoration of the body to enhance sexual attractiveness, the display of wealth and power or simply an innate creative urge to exploit the beauty of natural materials.

The history of jewellery is mainly the history of developing techniques dictated by the special properties of the raw materials available. The skills of gold- and silversmiths, gem cutters, lapidaries and enamellists have existed and remained virtually unchanged for thousands of years. It is only in the last hundred years or so that machine processes have replaced traditional handwork to any great extent and even today much of the finest jewellery is either wholly hand-made by individual craftspeople or hand-finished to a degree of perfection which machines still can not achieve.

The greatest change in the appearance of jewellery between the Renaissance and the end of the seventeenth century was in the way that precious stones were set and displayed. Goldwork and enamel dominated Renaissance jewellery design, but with the voyages of discovery and the expansion of trade with distant countries in the sixteenth and seventeenth centuries, precious stones began to arrive in Europe in increasing quantities. Faced with the challenge of displaying them to their best advantage, jewellers evolved increasingly sophisticated techniques of cutting and setting. During the seventeenth century the rose cut was evolved; this was one of the earliest styles of facet cutting, in which the base is flat and the upper surface is faceted. At first 16, then 24 and finally 36 facets were the norm. It was superseded by the brilliant cut, with 33 facets above the "girdle" of the stone and 25 below; this is still the most widely used cut. Initially, flat backed stones had been set against a metal foil to reflect the light, but with the development of facet cutting, settings were reduced to expose the maximum area of the stone and open backs were used to obtain brilliant effects from light refracted within the stone.

During the eighteenth century the style and standard of fashionable jewellery was set by the French court. Popular styles followed fashions in dress rather than current taste in other artistic fields, often reflecting decorative touches originally executed in other materials, such as bows, ribbons and lace. The finest work, using precious stones such as diamonds, sapphires, rubies and pearls, was only accessible to the richest patrons, but its influence reached a wider public, stimulating a demand for less expensive jewellery among the middle classes. The eighteenth century saw the creation of what today would be called costume jewellery: very attractive crystal and paste necklaces, brooches and ear-rings were made and are now highly prized for their workmanship and wearability rather than their intrinsic value.

Other semi-precious stones, such as garnets, amethysts, topaz, citrines and opals, increased in popularity from the beginning of the nineteenth century, and there was a revival of interest in hardstones – jasper, agates, cornelians and others – either simply polished and set in gold or carved or engraved as cameos or intaglios. Fine steel and marquisite, filigree, seed pearl and fine wrought or cast-iron Berlin work were other popular materials until the middle of the century. Jet, which today seems particularly typical of the Victorian period, became extremely fashionable after Queen Victoria adopted mourning on the death of Prince Albert in 1861. The Industrial Revolution brought about major changes in manufacturing processes and made possible the mass production of cheap jewellery in lower priced materials such as pinchbeck (an alloy of copper and zinc), and rolled gold (thin sheet gold fused to base metal and rolled out into sheets or wire).

Historic revivals were another important influence on Victorian jewellery design. Archaeological, medieval and Renaissance styles were all very popular and were thought by writers on aesthetics to be a preferable alternative to the vulgar displays of wealth of the *nouveaux riches*, whom they considered to be interested only in the value of the jewellery they acquired. The quest for more interesting and less ostentatious styles encouraged the artists connected with the Arts and Crafts Movement in England and the Art Nouveau style in France to produce some wonderfully elegant and delicate pieces.

In the United States English influences prevailed in the eighteenth century, but the French Revolution caused a reaction in favour of all things French and there was little native innovation. The famous French firm of Boucheron supplied many wealthy American clients and its jewellery was sold in the New York shop opened in 1837 by Charles Lewis Tiffany, although for much of the century a somewhat puritanical attitude toward the expenditure of large sums of money on personal adornment prevailed. With increasing prosperity towards the end of the century, however, the situation changed so dramatically that rich American industrialists and entrepreneurs became the main customers of the famous European jewellery houses. Cartier, Boucheron and Van Cleef and Arpels all opened their own shops in New York and America's most famous designer, Louis Comfort Tiffany, son of Charles, turned increasingly from designing glass to the production of the stylish and original Art Nouveau jewellery for which he is equally famous.

The design and production of jewellery in the twentieth century has been subject to conflicting influences. Increasing mechanization brought about the proliferation of cast settings, often of poorer quality and less durable than the hand-made settings of the Victorian period. The discovery of platinum and the mining of diamonds in much larger quantities, mainly in South Africa, also affected design. Though the finest gem stones will always be rare and vastly expensive, the price of, for example, a simple diamond engagement ring has decreased immensely in real terms to become an item almost anyone can afford. Dissatisfaction with the unimaginative design of much mass-produced jewellery has brought about a reaction, however, and there is today a remarkable revival in original hand-crafted one-off designs making imaginative use of new and unexpected materials such as plastic and paper, which are as much works of art as the masterpieces of the past.

Cleaning jewellery

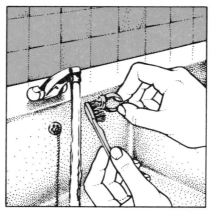

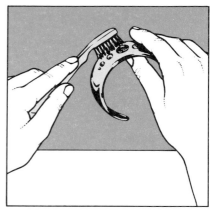

1. Use warm soapy water to clean gold jewellery or chains, dipping the piece gently in and out. However, if it looks a little dull, put it in fresh liquid silver cleaner to remove the sulphur oxide deposits.

2. Wash in cold, then warm, running water. Dry carefully using a soft cotton cloth or tissue. Take particular care when washing stones such as pearls and turquoise, as these are cemented into their settings and liquid can melt the glue. Also, if stones have a foil backing, the moisture can get behind the stones and spoil their appearance. To avoid this, always dry both settings and stones quickly.

3. Jewellery can also be cleaned with a brush. Choose an old toothbrush, soften the bristles with hot water and then rub the article very gently with soap and water or jewellery cleaner. If the piece is badly clogged with grimy deposits, use the bristles first to force out the dust and then apply a small dab of toothpaste to the brush and scrub the grimy area again. Rinse and dry thoroughly.

Repairing chains

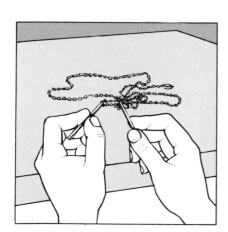

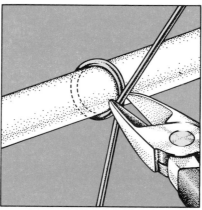

1. Chains, whether of valuable metal or the costume variety, frequently get into knots. Lay out the chain on a flat surface and tease out the knots using a sewing needle in each hand. Never tug at the chains, as this will either tighten the knots or damage the links, and could well do both.

2. If the chain is broken, a temporary repair can be made with yellow or white thread by stitching the links together. However, to replace a link use matching wire and wrap it around a knitting needle of the appropriate size to form a link. Cut the wire. For very fine chains use a toothpick.

3. Slide the wire, which now forms the new link, off the needle. Thread it onto the links where the break is, and close the link as shown in the illustration.

Repairs to costume jewellery

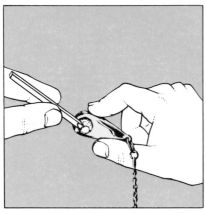

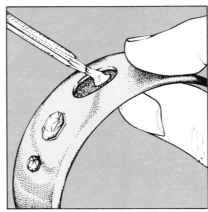

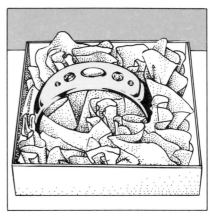

1. Resin cement is excellent for repairing costume jewellery, but it is best to use a slow-drying variety which will allow plenty of time to make any adjustments in the repair that might be necessary. When cementing stones back into a setting, clean away any dirt or loose bits of old glue with a clean, soft brush, such as a lipstick brush, or some cotton wool held in tweezers.

2. Apply the cement with the tip of a matchstick. If the area to be glued is very small or difficult to reach, first shape the tip of the matchstick to a point with a sharp knife.

3. While the cement is drying, prop up the piece in a "nest" of tissue paper to support it and keep the repair in place. Do not be afraid to apply more glue than strictly necessary, as this will give the repair extra strength, but make sure that the excess will be on a side that does not show.

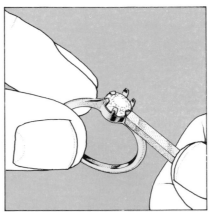

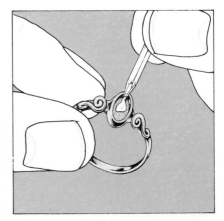

4. Frequently stones with closed-in settings are backed by shiny foil. To replace these, use foil in an appropriate shade from good quality sweets or, of course, shiny foil bought from a stationer or art supply store.

5. Stones fall out of claw settings because the tips of the claws have broken off or become worn. Never try to replace stones that have fallen out of these settings in good antique jewellery. Instead, take the pieces to an experienced restorer. But for costume jewellery replace the stone, if possible, putting a dab of glue on the underside. Then, bend the claws gently back over the stone. But take care, because they may have been weakened where they were bent.

6. If flat bottomed stones, such as pearls, garnets, turquoise or opals have fallen from good antique jewellery, it is possible to make a temporary repair. Gently clean the little spike or box that holds them in place with a brush as described above. Apply a small amount of a soft polyvinyl acetate adhesive and gently press the stone back in position. You must use a soft adhesive, so that the jeweller will eventually be able to remove the stone and do a proper repair.

Repairs to brooches

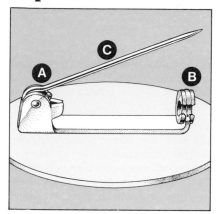

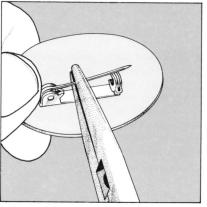

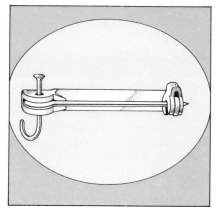

1. Pins have three parts: a joint (A), a stop (B), and a shaft (C).

2. Pins frequently become bent. To tighten or straighten a pin, use a small pair of pliers or strong tweezers and hold the pin tightly by the joint. Bend the pin very gently with your fingers so that the pin just springs into the catch. Remember that the metal will crack if bent backwards and forwards.

3. If the joint pin has fallen out, it is possible to make a temporary repair with a straight, stainless steel pin. Push it through the hole in the joint, and bend the back end so that it does not fall out.

Repairs to necklaces

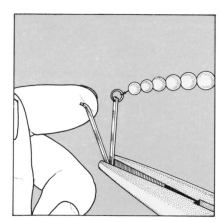

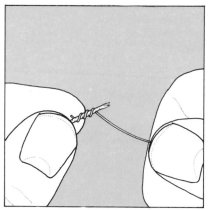

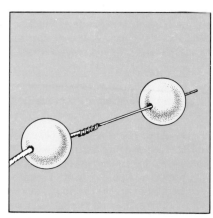

1. When the snap fastening of a necklace is not holding properly, it is usually because the half snap has become bent. To tighten a snap, hold the end of the snap with a pair of pliers and slightly bend the snap upwards. Do not overdo this, as a snap that is too tight is as bad as one that is too loose.

2. The best material to use for restringing pearls or beads is stranded silk embroidery floss. Choose the appropriate shade and separate into strands. If the silk is too thick, strip the strands into finer thread. Bind some fine fuse wire tightly around the end to form a needle.

3. Then, with 6in/15cm or so of the silk hanging free, depending on the length of the necklace that needs restringing, thread the "needle" through the beads.

PAPER

It is almost impossible to establish the exact date when paper was invented, but it has probably been in use for about two thousand years. Archaeological evidence exists to show that the Chinese were making paper by the second century B.C., but the secret of its manufacture was not known in Europe until the eleventh or twelfth century. The earliest methods of making records were carving them on stone or stamping on clay bricks; the first "books" in anything approaching the modern sense were the papyrus rolls of the ancient Egyptians, who discovered how to make a useful writing material by cutting strips from the stem of the papyrus reed. These were laid on a board with other strips laid over them cross-wise, then soaked in water, pressed together and dried in the sun. When the resulting sheet had been well polished it made a fairly good writing surface. It could not be folded well but it would roll up, and there were large libraries of books in rolls.

Papyrus was the chief writing material used by the Greeks and Romans, but it was gradually replaced by the early Middle Ages by parchment, made from the skin of sheep, and vellum, very fine calfskin. All these materials were costly and time-consuming to produce, however, compared with the "real" paper of the Chinese, which could be produced in relatively large quantities from natural materials—rags or wood—available in virtually unlimited supply.

The technique of making paper was known to the Arabs by about the year 800 A.D. and spread through north Africa into Spain, where the Moors established the first paper-making plant in the eleventh century. From Spain paper spread all over Europe and by the year 1400 was in common use, though parchment had still not been replaced completely. Paper-making in England dates from the fifteenth century; the colophon to Wynkyn de Worde's *De Proprietatibus Rerum* mentions the paper mill of John Tate at Stevenage in Hertfordshire. Thus by the time printing began with the invention of movable type by Gutenberg in about the middle of the fifteenth century, paper could be manufactured in sufficient quantity to meet the suddenly increased demand.

The paper made in China was soft and absorbent, suitable for brushwork and wood-block printing on one side only. In Europe, by contrast, the demand was for a harder, less porous surface that could be used for pen work on both sides.

The old process of making paper was first to boil clean cotton and linen rags and then beat the resulting mixture into a pulp. The pulp was diluted to a creamy consistency in big vats, into which flat wire trays were dipped. A wooden frame round the tray kept the pulp from running over the sides. The trays were shaken so that excess water drained off through the mesh, leaving a deposit of fine, felt-like fibres which were compressed into a smooth layer and then left to dry. After this they were sized with good quality gelatine to provide a smooth surface and make the paper less absorbent.

In essence, all paper is still made by this principle today, but only the highest quality drawing and writing paper is now made by hand. The paper-making machine was invented by a Frenchman, Louis Robert, in 1798; with some improvements, the machine was introduced into England by Henry Fourdrinier, giving a new impetus to the industry. Little paper is now made from rags or linen; nearly all paper for general use, from newsprint to books and packaging materials, comes from wood pulp. The quality of the paper depends on the degree of chemical refining to which it is subjected.

Because of its fragile nature, paper is susceptible to various types of damage which can result in premature ageing, brittleness, discoloration and eventual disintegration. It is therefore very important to store paper, whether works of art or books, in suitable conditions. The atmosphere should be well-ventilated and dry, as paper absorbs damp very easily, causing it to swell and also encouraging the growth of mould. Hanging a work on paper on even a slightly damp wall can cause serious damage which may not be noticed until it is too late to reverse it. On the other hand, excessively dry and over-heated conditions are bad because they can cause the paper to contract and crack. Works on paper should never be placed too close to a radiator or other source of heat, nor in direct sunlight, which may accelerate chemical changes and contribute to the fading of the image. Frames should be kept in good repair, with backing panels well sealed so that dust and dirt cannot accumulate under the glass on the surface of the image. Unframed works are best kept flat in drawers, separated by sheets of acid-free tissue paper. They should be handled carefully and the top surface touched as little as possible.

Although paper is one of the most fragile and easily destroyed of all materials, much of our history has been recorded on it and it has been the medium for many of our finest works of art. Given the right treatment it can survive for centuries so it is worthwhile to try and ensure that works on paper are given the treatment they merit so that they can continue to give pleasure to succeeding generations.

Opposite: A badly-stained print by Alphonse Legros (1837-1911) in need of cleaning and bleaching (see overleaf).

Restoration of works of art on paper

Restoration of works on paper is a delicate and complicated process, and amateurs should not attempt it on items of any great value. Only the more stable types of works on paper, such as engravings, etchings and pencil drawings, will not be adversely affected by immersion in water; watercolours and certain types of print must never get wet. If in doubt, take it to a professional.

Assemble the following supplies: shallow vessel such as a photographic tray, large enough to hold the print lying flat; measuring vessel, clean white blotting paper, soft erasers or erasing granules (as used by architects), round-ended scalpel, soft camel hair brush, two clean sheets of thick glass, sponge, atomizer sprayer, teaspoon, cotton wool swabs and paper towels. Specialist supplies are: support sheets large enough to hold the print, made from a non-woven, non-stretch fabric, such as polyester; Japanese paper or lens cleaning tissue, silicone release paper, light magnesium carbonate, hydrogen peroxide, soda water and de-ionized water.

REMOVING PAPER BACKING

1. Before beginning the restoration process, it may be necessary to remove one or more backing sheets from the work. However, it is important to remove the paper from the work, not the work from the paper. Fill a photographic tray three-quarters full of cold water and place a support sheet on the bottom of the tray. Float the work face upwards in the water until the adhesive begins to soften.

2. Gripping the support sheet on both ends, lift the print from the water and turn it over together with the support sheet, laying it face down on a clean sheet of white blotting paper.

3. Carefully lift away the support sheet and gently remove the backing paper from the print, beginning at one corner, using a rounded scalpel to lift off stubborn bits of backing paper. When all backing layers have been removed, any residual adhesive can be taken up with a damp sponge or cotton wool swabs.

4. If there are still some small bits of backing paper attached, lay the work face down on a sheet of glass and sponge the back of the work with warm water, allowing the moisture to penetrate so the paper can be "dragged" away or picked up with the scalpel. Clean off residual adhesive with cotton wool swabs.

REMOVING CARDBOARD BACKING

5. Lay the work face down on a clean sheet of glass and sponge the cardboard backing with plenty of warm water; leave for a few minutes until the board becomes softened. Use the rounded scalpel to remove the card, peeling off one layer at a time by inserting the blade between the layers.

6. When there is only a thin layer of backing card left, great care must be taken not to pierce the print—it is advisable to remove the last layer by scraping it off with a rounded scalpel or rubbing it gently away with a finger. Finally, the print can be immersed in a photographic tray three-quarters full of water, and gently brushed with a soft camel hair brush in order to remove the remaining adhesive.

Opposite: The print by Alphonse Legros after it has been dry cleaned, washed and bleached (see previous page).

Dry cleaning

1. First, use a soft camel hair brush to dust the print in order to remove loose dirt and dust. Then proceed to the following treatment. Dry cleaning will remove surface dirt and even the powdery remains of mould deposits. It is a good idea to try it before the immersion method below. Bear in mind that dry cleaning is abrasive; it should be done with great care, never tried on wet or damp paper, and never used on the front of a pencil drawing.

2. Lay the print face down on a clean sheet of glass and disperse the particles of a granular eraser over the work, using a finger to rub the cleanser gently over the surface with a circular motion. Then remove the dirty particles by dusting with a soft camel hair brush.

3. Where dirt is deeply ingrained, a second rubbing with a soft eraser is recommended. Also rub the edges of the print and clean the front of the print in the same way, making sure that any signatures and/ or edition numbers are not affected.

Immersion method of stain removal

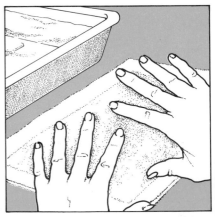

1. To remove most stains, including yellowed areas and residues of adhesive, a print may be washed in water. First, prepare a shallow bath using a clean photographic tray or similar shallow vessel large enough to hold the print. Cut a support sheet slightly larger than the print, and spread several sheets of white blotting paper on a flat surface nearby. Place the support sheet on the bottom of the tray, fill the tray three-quarters full of cold de-ionized water, and float the print face upwards.

2. Leave for approximately two hours. Then, using the support sheet, raise the print slowly out of the water and lay it carefully on the clean blotting paper. (Always use the support sheet because wet paper tears very easily.)

3. Next, place the print in a bath of fairly hot water, following the same process as before. Once the print is lying on the blotting paper, cover it with another sheet of blotting paper, and press lightly all over the surface to remove excess water.

Bleaching

Paper is often yellowed or stained by age, or covered with rusty brown spots called fox marks, which are probably due to the presence of iron. The immersion method will already have reduced the density of the foxing, but the paper will also need bleaching before the foxing disappears. However, bleaching paper does entail a certain risk; discoloration and/or damage to the paper itself may result if any traces of the bleaching solution are left behind.

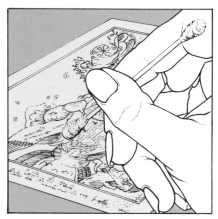

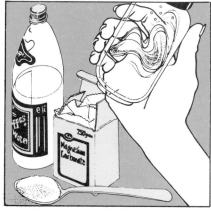

1. After the print has been washed so that no more discoloured material comes out of the paper, it should be dried and examined in order to determine whether local or overall bleaching is necessary.

2. First, test for pigment stability to make sure that the shades will not discolour or fade. Dip a cotton wool swab in the bleaching solution, moisten a small area of the print where it is tinted, and leave to dry. Repeat the process, then decide if there is any serious loss of colour. If not, bleaching can be carried out.

3. The print must be de-acidified before—and after—bleaching, to remove acids that might damage the print. Prepare the de-acidification solution by mixing 2 tbsp/30ml light magnesium carbonate with 2 pt/1 litre soda water; the magnesium carbonate becomes magnesium bicarbonate. Shake well and leave to stand for a few minutes or until a white powder appears on the bottom of the mixing vessel.

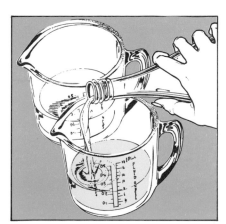

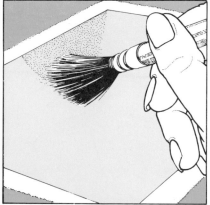

4. Carefully pour out the carbonated water into a measuring jug and then mix it with an equal amount of tap water.

5. Lay the print face down on a sheet of clean white blotting paper and brush the de-acidifying solution over the back using a soft camel hair brush. Leave to dry. Alternatively, the solution can be sprayed on evenly using an atomizer.

6. Make the bleaching solution from two parts magnesium carbonate and one part hydrogen peroxide; stir well. Pour into a photographic tray and, using the support sheet, lower the print into the bleaching solution. Immerse it until the desired improvement is obtained, and only until the stains become faint.

Bleaching cont.

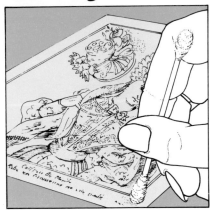

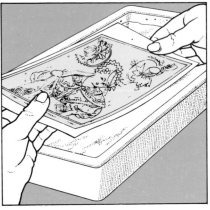

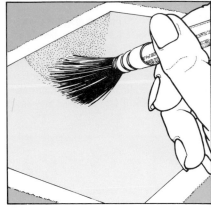

7. With the support sheet, slowly lift the print out of the bleaching solution and place it on a sheet of clean white blotting paper. Dip a cotton wool swab into the de-acidifying solution and moisten a small area of the paper, near the corner, to check that the paper does not turn slightly blue or pink.

8. If discoloration does take place, just rinse the print in clean water, changing the water three or four times as necessary. Use the support sheet to lift the print in and out of the bath. The re-rinsing is very important to prevent traces of chemicals from causing the paper to deteriorate.

9. If no discoloration has taken place, the paper can be de-acidified as directed in Step 5.

Drying

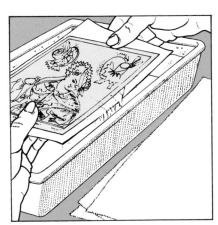

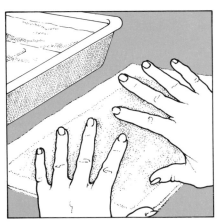

1. Relax the paper by floating it face up in water for a few minutes with the support sheet underneath. Place four to five sheets of blotting paper on a sheet of glass, and, holding the support fabric at the corners, lift the print out of the bath and put it on the stack of blotting paper, face down.

2. Remove the support sheet, and cover the print with another sheet of blotting paper for a moment, pressing it lightly to remove excess moisture. Remove this dampened sheet of blotting paper.

3. Cover the print with a clean sheet of glass and place weights such as books on top of the glass. Check the print for dryness every 24 hours, and change the blotting paper at the same time to avoid the possibility of mildew forming. After four or five days the print should be completely dry, but bear in mind that the drying time depends on the temperature and humidity in the room.

Repairing paper

Works on paper will often have tears, holes, creases and/or missing corners. Most of these can be repaired by the amateur using flour paste and a strong paper such as lens cleaning tissue or Japanese paper. The latter is preferable, as it comes in a wide variety of tones and thicknesses. Before attempting to repair physical damage to a print, clean it as directed on page 178. Then, assemble the following supplies: blotting paper, photographic tray, flour, paste brush, pointed sable brush, atomizer sprayer, strong paper, silicone release paper, pointed tweezers, paper knife or teaspoon, pumice, de-ionized water, two sheets of thick glass.

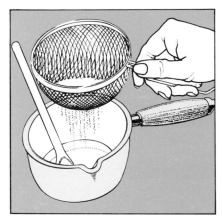

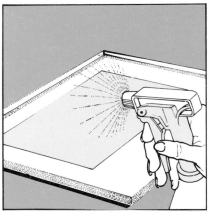

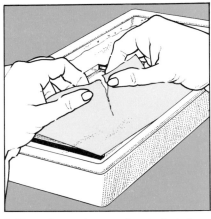

1. Make flour paste by mixing ⅜oz/10g wheat flour with 4fl oz/100ml de-ionized water, sieving the flour into cold water. Stir, then bring the flour and water to the boil, stirring constantly. Let it simmer for 15 minutes, then leave to cool. The consistency should be creamy; store in the refrigerator, where it will keep for about a week. If a large amount of restoration is planned, keep small amounts of the paste in little jars to prevent contamination.

2. To remove creases, lay the print on a sheet of clean glass, spray it with de-ionized water, then cover the print with blotting paper. Press the blotting paper lightly in order to remove excess moisture. Leave it to dry slowly on the glass; the slight contraction of the paper on the glass will eliminate most creases and folds.

3. To repair tears, immerse the print in shallow water, face down on a plate glass support. While it is still submerged, carefully align the torn pieces into the correct position, then very slowly lift the glass support and print out the water.

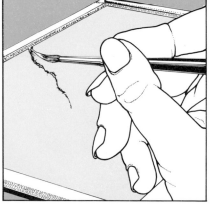

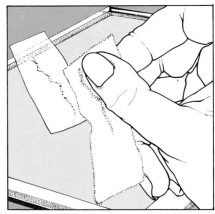

4. Remove the excess water by pressing a sheet of clean blotting paper over the print, removing it when any excess has been absorbed, then leave the print to dry a little. When it is half dry, tap along the torn edges with the back of a teaspoon in order to "weld" the fibres of the two pieces of paper together.

5. Next, apply a little paste along the tear using the paste brush, then cover the join with a torn piece or strip of silicone release paper, and a piece of blotting paper. Press along the join with a finger for about 15 minutes, exerting a little pressure.

6. After the blotting paper has absorbed some moisture from the paste, it can be removed. Leave the print to dry in a well ventilated place.

Repairing paper cont.

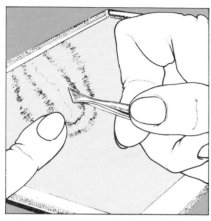

7. Large tears may have a tendency to break apart, and therefore an extra layer of Japanese paper or lens cleaning tissue may be needed as a reinforcement. Make the outer layer larger and the other closer to the outline of the tear.

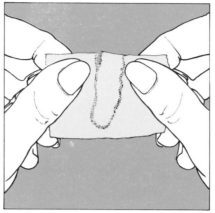

8. While the print is drying out, holes and missing corners can be repaired with Japanese paper, by matching the tone, thickness and texture of the original as closely as possible. To make the patch to cover the hole, mark the desired shape with a dampened pointed brush, then pull the surrounding paper away from the shape giving the patch torn edges which will merge more imperceptibly with the original paper surface.

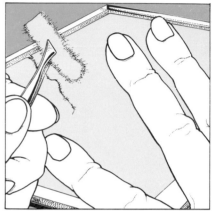

9. Apply flour paste around the edge of the tear, then position the patch over the tear, using the tweezers. If necessary, draw the two sides of the tear together with the other hand.

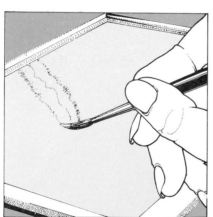

10. Next apply paste to the top of the patch and position a second patch on the top of the first. Remove any excess paste.

11. Finally, cover the patch with silicone release paper followed by a layer of clean blotting paper. Over this, place a piece of thick glass evenly weighted down with books. Leave to dry.

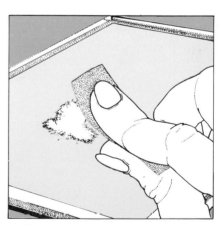

12. To repair a hole or missing area in a print, again use Japanese paper of similar tone, thickness and texture to the original. Begin by rubbing the edges of the hole and the replacement paper with a very fine abrasive paper. Prepare the patch as above in Step 8, position and paste as above, then cover with silicone release paper. Dry under a weighted piece of glass. When completely dry, the patched area can be gently rubbed with a block of fine pumice or a dusting of pumice powder.

Suppliers' Index

Many of the materials mentioned in this section are available by mail order; please enquire from individual manufacturers and suppliers.

TOOLS AND SUPPLIES

ABRASIVE TOOLS LTD
Abrium Works, Colne Road,
Twickenham, Middx.
Files and abrasive implements.

BEAVER ENGINEERING
Greenhills Road, Taliaght, Co. Dublin,
Eire.
Bosch power tools.

BLACK & DECKER LTD
Cannon Lane, Maidenhead, Berks.
Power tools.

BOSTIK LTD
Consumer Products Division,
Ulverscroft Road, Leicester, Leics.
Manufacturers of woodworking adhesive.

CEKA WORKS LTD
Pwllheli, Gwynedd, N. Wales.
Power tool accessories, rasps.

**CIBA GEIGY PLASTICS AND
ADDITIVES CO**
Duxford, Cambridge, Cambs.
*Manufacturers of Araldite two-part epoxy
resin adhesive.*

**GRAHAM OXLEY TRADE TOOLS
LTD**
London Works, Bridge Street,
Sheffield, S. Yorks.
*Manufacturers of carpenter's and cabinet-
maker's tools, with large selection of chisels,
gouges and gauges.*

RABONE CHESTERMAN LTD
Whitmore Street, Birmingham,
W. Midlands.
Hand tools, measuring devices.

STANLEY TOOLS LTD
Woodside, Sheffield, S. Yorks.
General hand tools.

STERLING RONCRAFT
Chapeltown, Sheffield, S. Yorks.
*Wide range of wood preservatives, stains
and varnishes.*

WOLF ELECTRIC TOOLS LTD
P.O. Box 379, Hangar Lane, London
W.5.
Power tools.

EARNEST WRIGHT AND SON LTD
Kutrite Works, Smithfield, Sheffield,
S. Yorks.
*Specialist tools, including scissors, knives
and cabinet-maker's tools.*

WOOD

THE ART VENEERS CO LTD
Industrial Estate, Mildenhall, Suffolk.
*Mail order specialist with huge range of
cabinet and marquetry veneers, plus inlay
bandings and motifs and marquetry tools.*

LEONARD BALL
44 Market Street, Lutterworth, Leics.
*Wooden frets and mouldings, cabinet
fittings and restoration materials.*

JOHN BODDY AND SON LTD
Riverside Sawmills, Boroughbridge,
N. Yorks.
Wide range of unusual British hardwoods.

J.W. BOLLOM AND CO LTD
P.O. Box 78, Beckenham, Kent.
*Wide range of wax polishes, sealers and
varnishes.*

BOWDEN WOODCRAFT
Viables Centre, Harrow Way,
Basingstoke, Hants.
Wood veneers and veneering supplies.

JAMES BRIGGS AND SONS LTD
Lion Works, Old Market Street,
Manchester, Gt. Manchester.
Antiquax wood treatment products.

**CONSTRUCTION AND
ENGINEERING CO LTD**
Faraway House, Pygons Hill Lane,
Lydiate, Merseyside.
*Manufacturers of Patinex non-caustic
wood-stripping system.*

CUPRINOL LTD
Adderwell, Frome, Somerset.
*Cuprinol wood preservatives and
woodworm killer.*

D. FARMILOE
15 Kent Close, Bexhill-on-Sea, Sussex.
*Manufacturers of Touch and Go furniture
refinishing kit.*

HENRY FLACK LTD
Borough Works, Croydon Road,
Beckenham, Kent.
*Numerous refinishing products, including
lacquers, waxes, varnishes and gold size.*

HOROLOGICAL SOLVENTS LTD
Proctor Street, Bury Lancs.
Products for restorers and cabinet-makers.

NORTH HEIGHAM SAWMILLS
Paddock Street, Norwich, Norfolk.
*Unusual air- and kiln-dried hard-woods,
including ebony, kingwood, lime, etc.*

PICREATOR ENTERPRISES LTD
44 Park View Gardens, London NW4.
*Manufacturers of Renaissance acid-free
wax polish, approved by the British
Museum for use on many types of surface.*

TURNBRIDGES LTD
72 Longley Road, London SW17
*Products include French polish, gold size,
knotting compound, scratch dressing and
linseed oils.*

WEAVES AND WAXES
53 Church Street, Bloxham, Banbury,
Oxon.
*Shop and mail order service with wide
range: polishes and waxes, veneers, inlay
bandings and stringings.*

WOODFIT LTD
Whittle Low Mill, Chorley, Lancs.
Comprehensive mail order catalogue of cabinet and furniture fittings.

DECORATIVE FINISHES

See also TOOLS AND SUPPLIES and WOOD.

COLOURWAYS
70 Alderman's Hill, London N13.
Various paints, including flat paint, signwriters' colours, transparent oil glaze, metal leaf.

GEDGE AND CO LTD
88 St John Street, London EC1.
Wood stains, pumice powder.

A.S. HANDOVER LTD
Angel Yard, Highgate High Street, London N6.
Brush manufacturers with unusual selection: lacquer brushes, gilder's tips and sable artist's brushes.

F.A. HEFFER AND CO LTD
24 The Pavement, London SW4.
Wide range of specialist brushes.

E. PLOTON LTD
273 Archway Road, London N6.
Range of artists' materials, including pigments and brushes, metal leaf and metal powders.

J.H. RATCLIFFE AND CO LTD
135A Linaker Street, Southport, Lancs.
Transparent oil glaze and special undercoat, specialist brushes and graining combs.

GEORGE ROWNEY AND CO LTD
12 Percy Street, London W1.
Comprehensive range of artists' materials; mail order service.

SIMPSONS PAINTS LTD
122-124 Broadley Street, London NW8.
Signwriters colours, flat paint, transparent oil glaze, metal leaf.

GLASS AND STAINED GLASS

See also TOOLS AND SUPPLIES.

JAMES BRIGGS AND SONS LTD
Lion Works, Old Market Street, Manchester, Gt. Manchester.
Manufacturers of specialist glass and mirror cleaner.

JAMES HETLEY AND CO
Beresford Avenue, Wembley, Middx.
Glass, leads, solder, tools and glass paints.

KASHA CRAFT
37 Armroyd Lane, Elsecar, Barnsley, S. Yorks.
Cathedral and opalescent glass, bevels and glass-working tools.

LEAD AND LIGHT
15 Camden Lock, Commercial Place, London NW1.
Tools, fittings, fluxes, lead canes and six types of opal, cathedral and semi-antique tint glass.

STAINED GLASS SUPPLIES
Unit 5, Brunel Way, Thornbury Industrial Estate, Thornbury, Avon.
Glass, leads, solder, tools and glass paints.

BAMBOO, CANE, RUSH, RAFFIA AND WILLOW

ARMITAGE
West Hall Farm, Sedgeford, Hunstanton, Norfolk.
Straw suppliers.

TOM ARNOLD
Wildcroft, Holywell, Huntingdon, Cambs.
Supplier of rush; personal collection preferred.

THE BAMBOO PEOPLE
Godmanstone, Dorchester, Dorset.
Bamboo and cane supplied by mail order.

GEOFF BERRY
Acadia, Swansbrook Lane, Horam, Heathfield, E. Sussex.
Chair caning materials and tools, rush and seagrass.

I. AND J. BROWN
58 Commercial Road, Hereford, Heref & Worcs.
Suppliers of rushes.

THE CANE STORE
377 Seven Sisters Road, London N15.
Suppliers of bamboo, rush, seagrass, willow, cane and tools.

COUNTRY CHAIRMEN
Home Farm, School Road, Ardington, Nr Wantage, Oxon.
Rush suppliers; will send quantities over two bolts.

MAURICE DERHAM
Rose Farm, Lower Knapp, Somerset.
Supplier of willow.

THE EATON BAG CO LTD
16 Manette Street, London W1
Whole and split canes, natural grass, raffia, palm, woven cane matting and bamboo in various diameters.

NIGEL HECTOR
The Willows, Stoke St Gregory, Somerset.
Supplier of willow.

JACOBS, YOUNG AND WESTBURY
Bridge Road, Haywards Heath, Sussex.
Chair cane, rush, seagrass, imported willow and tools.

THE ROPE SHOP
26 High Street, Emsworth, Hants.
Suppliers of natural ropes, cords and threads in sisal, hemp, jute, manila, coir, cotton and flax.

SMIT AND CO. LTD
99 Walnut Tree Close, Guildford, Surrey.
Centre cane, chair cane, tools, seagrass and bases.

GEORGE SNEED
Bacons Barn, St Michael, Bungay, Suffolk.
Supplier of imported rush.

K.J. TRAYLER
Fir Close, Frostenden, Wangford,
Suffolk.
Supplies canes, seagrass and rushes.

LEATHER

J.T. BATCHELOR
146 Fleet Road, London NW3.
*Leatherworking tools such as stamps,
cutters and gouges, plus leather stainers,
finishers and restoratives; range of hides
and aniline dyes.*

ECOTECH
Crocodile Crafts, Lodge Road,
Westport, Co. Mayo, Eire.
*Leather matching service on receipt of
sample; upholstery leather and table top
inlays; specialist embossing tools and
waxes.*

PICREATOR ENTERPRISES
44 Park View Gardens, London NW4.
*Manufacturer of a leather reviver and other
restoration supplies.*

TAYLOR AND CO LTD
54 Old Street, London EC1.
*Manufacturer of rolls and stamps for gold
leaf leather tooling and special finishing
tools.*

**VANDERVILLES LEATHER
LINING**
47 High Street, Nantwich, Cheshire.
*Suppliers of goatskin skivers or liners for
desk and table tops in wide choice of
colours with optional gold tooling.*

STONE

See also TOOLS AND
SUPPLIES.

A. BELL AND CO LTD
Kingsthorpe, Northampton,
Northants.
*Manufacturers of a cleaner, polish and
sealer for marble and stone.*

ALEC TIRANTI LTD
21 Goodge Place, London W1.
Stone-carving tools.

TEXTILES AND
UPHOLSTERY

**ART NEEDLEWORK INDUSTRIES
LTD**
7 St Michael's Mansions, Ship Street,
Oxford, Oxon.
*Authentic shades in crewel wool for
tapestry restoration plus range of cotton and
linen threads and fabrics.*

**DISTINCTIVE TRIMMINGS CO
LTD**
17 Kensington Church Street,
London W8 *and* Marylebone Lane,
London, W1.
*Specialist suppliers of furnishing
trimmings, including fringes, tassels,
gimps, braids and ruches. Will send
samples on receipt of fabric cuttings.*

D.L. FORSTER LTD
17 Tramway Avenue, London E15.
*Varied range of mail order upholstery
sundries, including stretchers, webbing,
tacks, needles, calico, etc.*

HEIRLOOM EMBROIDERY
9 Burnley Road, London NW10.
*Pure cotton thread dyed to match vegetable
shades, linen threads and lace yarns.*

HOLYWELL TEXTILE MILLS
Holywell, Clwyd, Wales.
*Yarns for knitting and weaving in natural
colours and fibres without dyes, chemicals
or detergents.*

**ROYAL SCHOOL OF
NEEDLEWORK**
25 Princes Gate, London SW7.
*Threads, canvas and embroidery wools;
mail order catalogue.*

SILKEN STRANDS
33 Linksway, Gatley, Cheadle, Cheshire.
*Rayon threads and cords in hundreds of
colours, linen and cotton yarns, metallic
threads, feathers, beads and sequins.*

WEAVES AND WAXES
53 Church Street, Bloxham, Banbury,
Oxon.
Upholstery supplies.

G.T. YOUNG AND CO LTD
Ogilvie Road, High Wycombe, Bucks.
*Upholstery sundries such as twines,
needles, baize, webbing and hessian.*

CARPETS AND RUGS
See TEXTILES.

POTTERY AND
PORCELAIN

See also TOOLS AND
SUPPLIES.

ARDENBRITE PRODUCTS LTD
57 Farringdon Road, London EC1.
*Manufacturers of Ardenbrite metallic
paints in various shiny or matt shades.*

JAMES BRIGGS AND SONS LTD
Lion Works, Old Market Street,
Manchester, Gtr. Manchester.
*Manufacturers of specialist porcelain
cleaner.*

R.J. EDGE
158/160 Star & Garter Road,
Lightwood, Longton, Stoke on Trent,
Staffs.
Specialists in china painting requisites.

POTTERYCRAFTS LTD
105 Minet Road, London SW9 *and* 75
Silver Street, London N18.
*Comprehensive range intended mainly for
potters, but including china paints.*

METAL

ARDENBRITE PRODUCTS LTD
57 Farringdon Road, London EC1.
*Manufacturers of Ardenbrite metallic
paints.*

DIVERTIMENTI
68-72 Marylebone Lane, London W1.
*Re-tinning service for copper kitchen
utensils.*

LONDON BULLION LTD
73 Farringdon Road, London EC1.
*Suppliers of jewellery requisites including
gemstones, gold and silver in all forms; gem
testing assaying and plating.*

E. PARSONS AND SON LTD
Blackfriars Road, Nailsea, Bristol,
Avon.
*Manufacturers of metal primers and black
spirit enamel for grates and stoves.*

PLATING AND TINNING SERVICE
125 Broadley Street, London NW8.
*Re-tinning of copper utensils, as well as
plating.*

STERLING RONCRAFT
Chapeltown, Sheffield, S. Yorks.
*Manufacturers of Kurust metal treatments:
Double-Action which kills rust and primes
for painting, and Kurust jelly which
dissolves rust on chrome and bare metal.*

TURNBRIDGES LTD
72 Longley Road, London SW17.
*Manufacturers of Joy paint products,
including heatproof stove black, flat black
for wrought iron and fillers such as
"Plastic Metal".*

PAPER

ATLANTIS PAPER
105 Wapping Road, London E1.
*Suppliers of specialist papers, including
Japanese paper and silicone release paper.*

GEDGE AND CO LTD
88 St John Street, London EC1.
Suppliers of pumice powder.

GEORGE ROWNEY AND CO LTD
12 Percy Street, London W1.
Suppliers of artists' materials.

Index